# YOU CAN'T
# F*CK UP
# YOUR KIDS

# YOU CAN'T F*CK UP YOUR KIDS

A Judgment-Free Guide
to Stress-Free Parenting

# LINDSAY POWERS

**ATRIA** PAPERBACK

New York   London   Toronto   Sydney   New Delhi

This publication contains the opinions and ideas of its author. It is intended to provide helpful and informative material on the subjects addressed in the publication. It is sold with the understanding that the author and publisher are not engaged in rendering medical, health, or any other kind of personal professional services in the book. The reader should consult his or her medical, health, or other competent professional before adopting any of the suggestions in this book or drawing inferences from it.

The author and publisher specifically disclaim all responsibility for any liability, loss, or risk, personal or otherwise, which is incurred as a consequence, directly or indirectly, of the use and application of any of the contents of this book.

Names with asterisks have been changed, for privacy.

**ATRIA** PAPERBACK

An Imprint of Simon & Schuster, Inc.
1230 Avenue of the Americas
New York, NY 10020

First Atria Paperback edition March 2020

**ATRIA** PAPERBACK and colophon are trademarks of Simon & Schuster, Inc.

For information about special discounts for bulk purchases, please contact Simon & Schuster Special Sales at 1-866-506-1949 or business@simonandschuster.com.

The Simon & Schuster Speakers Bureau can bring authors to your live event. For more information or to book an event, contact the Simon & Schuster Speakers Bureau at 1-866-248-3049 or visit our website at www.simonspeakers.com.

Interior design by Jill Putorti

Manufactured in the United States of America

1  3  5  7  9  10  8  6  4  2

Library of Congress Cataloging-in-Publication Data is available.

ISBN 978-1-9821-1013-0
ISBN 978-1-9821-1015-4 (ebook)

*For Brad,*
*I am the luckiest*

*And Everett and Otto,*
*who made me a mom*

# CONTENTS

# CONTENTS

# INTRODUCTION

# It's Time for #NoShameParenting

I'll never forget the time a woman marched over to me in a crowded restaurant, took one look at me openly breastfeeding Everett, who was then ten months old, and whipped out her phone. She snapped a photo of me and then murmured "disgusting" under her breath before storming out. I was stunned. I wasn't exposing myself. My son wasn't crying. I was just eating a cheese and pepperoni pizza with my family.

But that wasn't the first time I'd felt judged as a parent. Before I'd even given birth to my son, my doctor, a thirty-six-year-old woman with dark hair and a condescending voice, nitpicked at my pregnancy weight. A stranger sat next to me on the subway and asked if I was planning on staying home to raise my kids "because that is best." My grandmother told her hairdresser, a virtual stranger to me, that she never thought I'd be a mom because "she loves her career too much."

When Everett was born, the shame and blame only got louder. Within my New York neighborhood, I witnessed moms one-up each other with humblebrags about their private tutors and fancy strollers. I was excluded from certain playgroups because I had a job ("No nannies allowed, only real moms"), lectured about childcare by strangers at Target ("Why are you out of the house with such a small baby?"), shamed for breastfeeding in public ("You shouldn't breastfeed here"),

1

and couldn't go online without finding viral blog post after blog post that started out with "Well, I know I shouldn't cast judgment, but . . ."

After enduring endless criticism during the first year of Everett's life, I decided to do something about it. I gathered my small but mighty team around a big square table at Yahoo!, where I worked at the time, and rallied them around a simple concept: Let's use our massive platform to lead people to think twice before making snide comments about other parents. We need to shine a light on the fact that we're all doing our best. Instead of nitpicking one another about pointless things, we should instead funnel that energy into supporting one another. The movement started with a simple tweet: "Ever felt judged as a parent? No more shaming! #NoShameParenting." I was fed up with how parents were criticizing one another, the way we all made ourselves feel terrible for not living up to unreasonable ideals of perfect parenthood that didn't match the reality I knew. Parenting was hard; parenting was messy. I wasn't perfect, but I was doing okay. I wrote a blog post decrying the judgment I'd faced (and how I was okay, for example, with my son occasionally eating crackers for dinner), and the idea caught like wildfire. The hashtag began to trend on Twitter. It turns out that I wasn't alone.

If you're a parent today, you're damned if you do and damned if you don't. But as a longtime journalist, I know only part of the story is being told. As the founding editor in chief of Yahoo! Parenting and the creator of the #NoShameParenting movement (which to date has reached more than 170 million people on social media), I am determined to set the record straight.

I've examined the research. I've spoken to doctors, psychologists, sleep gurus, pediatricians, and more than fifty families around the country from big cities to small towns. I've read a bunch of the books (so you will never have to).

And here's what I learned: There are a couple of general guidelines parents should follow. A trusted doctor is a great partner. Don't send your kids into obviously dangerous situations involving weaponry. Not all experts suck. Your kids obviously need love, food, a place to sleep, and healthy boundaries. But overall: We as parents are stressing ourselves out way too much. You can't fuck up your kids by getting them the wrong stroller. You can't fuck up your kids by feeding them formula rather than breast milk. You can't fuck up your kids by putting them in a reputable daycare rather than leaving your job and staying home with them. And you certainly can't fuck up your kids if they cry for a couple of nights during sleep training.

"But the studies! The studies!" frazzled, exhausted parents would fret to me as I explained these realities over coffee while they juggled an inconsolable newborn and a giant stroller full of wooden toys. "Didn't you hear that sleep training ruins babies' lives? What if they never form a secure attachment?"

You're being way too hard on yourself. The research that everyone cites ad nauseam as proof that sleep training ruins lives involves rats licking each other and Romanian orphans who were chained to a crib for twenty-four hours a day for the first three years of their lives. Surely even the most sleep-deprived parent can see these extreme conditions are hardly relatable to their child's experience.

Why do experts scare parents so much? Several reasons:

* *Money*. Baby products are cash cows. Formula alone is an $11.5 billion business. Most of the top baby experts are selling something, including products, services, and/or their personal belief system (and the organizations behind them). Which brings us to . . .

* *Power and Hidden Agendas*. So many things we're shamed about (or shame one another about) have roots in religion, patriarchy, sexism, racism, or class wars. La Leche League, which

so many of us rely on for breastfeeding advice, was founded by Catholic housewives who were totally against women working out of the home. The Baby Wise sleep book that's touted in Facebook mommy groups actually started as a religious manual called *Preparation for Parenting: Bringing God's Order to Your Baby's Day and Restful Sleep to Your Baby's Night.* Dr. Sears, called the father of attachment parenting, and his wife, Martha, are evangelical Christians who believe in "God's plan for raising children in a family where the husband is the head and the wife is subservient." Formula was at one point preferred by the upper classes until the backlash over more women in the workplace was expressed through pro-breast-feeding campaigns.

❋ *Thin Science.* You can't ethically experiment on babies, families, or pregnant women, so many studies are based on correlation (A and B happen, so they might be related) vs. causation (A causes B to happen). Research that is only tangentially related to children—or not even conducted on actual humans—is given more weight than it probably should.

Meanwhile, the fetishization of parenthood—and childhood—is growing. Ask your own parents how many times they pureed baby food for you, paid $35 for a baby-caregiver yoga class, or if they mastered infant massage. In today's hyper-connected world, parents' worst fears and neuroses are manipulated by a promise of perfection that's unreal and unattainable. We're guilted into raising our children as very special little objects who get every opportunity in the world. Meanwhile, we are constantly trying to keep up with millions of people on social media, whether it's the Kardashians or somebody we haven't seen since junior high.

It's no wonder that parents today—especially millennials who get more advice from social media like Snapchat, Instagram, Twitter, and Facebook than from their own mom or dad—are so confused, bewildered, and overwhelmed.

But it doesn't have to be this way. What if you could do more for your kids by doing a lot less? Less stress. Less drama. Less work. More sleep. More fun.

Reading this book will tell you how to do precisely that. The title says it all: *You Can't F*ck Up Your Kids*. It's the bible of the viral #NoShameParenting movement and a comforting companion for stressed-out parents.

In this book, I will give you the tools to shut down judgment, ease your fears and anxieties, and help you focus on what makes you—and your family—happy. I'll give you permission to stop doing something that feels unnatural to you just because some expert tells you it will somehow benefit your kid.

Struggling to breastfeed? All that effort may equal . . . one fewer tummy bug, studies show when stacked up against each other. "You and your child will have slightly better health outcomes in the long run if you breastfeed, but the effect of breastfeeding is less than you getting a good night's sleep, less than you eating healthfully, less than you having a place to live, less than you exercising regularly. I don't want to downplay it either, but it's less than many other things that will affect the long-term health of a woman and her child," Dr. Aaron Caughey, professor and chair of the Department of Obstetrics and Gynecology at Oregon Health & Science University, has said.[1] Feeling guilty about formula? It's an actual lifesaver. "If every 3-month-old baby could have a sufficient amount of formula, they'd all live," Dana Raphael, an anthropologist at the Human Lactation Center, once said.[2]

Stressing out about daycare? High-quality childcare may actually make your kid smarter in the long run, according to the National Institute of Child Health and Human Development.[3] Feeling guilty about quitting your job to stay home? Well, I've got another study that proves your kids might be smarter in the long run, too. I also have proof it's okay to drink a little while pregnant, to let your kids interact with screens, and to discipline your kids. (In fact, more parents spank than you might imagine, according to an exclusive Yahoo! Parenting poll of more than 1,000 moms.)

In other words: You can't fuck up your kids.*

There are a couple of truths in parenting that underlie sound advice: Put the newborn to sleep on his or her back. Don't microwave the breast milk. Read early and often to them. Love and feed them. The organic baby wipes, $250 electronic swings that simulate the womb, and infant flash cards are just extras. Unless you genuinely enjoy looking at flash cards with your three-month-old, in which case: Carry on! Your enthusiasm is what will translate to your baby—not whatever is printed on the cards.

This book will speak to the Modern Family. Gone are the days when families *only* consisted of a man, wife, 2.5 kids, a dog, and a white picket fence. Today, up to nine million kids have gay parents.[4] Forty percent of all babies born in America in 2013—1.6 million—are being raised by single mothers.[5] Children and parents are living farther away from extended families and creating unique arrangements with friends, neighbors, and exes to raise their children. I'll examine the "birdnesting" phenomenon, when divorced parents switch weekends while their kids remain in their family home; the very specific ways families with unique setups are shamed; and even how much sex parents are really having.

Too many parenting books focus exclusively on moms, leaving out half the population. My husband, Brad, wants to be just as good of

---

* There is a caveat. It's true that not every parent who envisions himself or herself as a great parent is in fact an amazing one. Kids face devastating neglect and abuse and hardships across the country and world every day, and I don't want to ignore or gloss over these realities. But this is the fact of the matter: Most parents are not abusive or neglectful or drug addicts. And some parents are, and their kids still turn out okay. I know this from personal experience, and I'll share my story later.

a parent to our two sons, Everett and Otto, as I do. This book will speak to moms *and* dads. And aunts, uncles, grandparents, and anyone who was raised in a family, or who thinks they might want to raise one at some point in the future.

This is a unique time in our culture. More than 91 percent of moms admit to judging another parent.[6] Yet, people are embracing their so-called "flaws," whether it's stretch marks or being a nontraditional parent. On Instagram, there are more than 2.9 million results for "body positive" photos. #NoShameParenting is a part of this empowering movement.

There's also a lot of attention on millennials who grew up with participation trophies and as victims of "failed parenting," as Simon Sinek explained in a lecture on YouTube viewed more than eleven million times.[7] As a millennial myself, I will explore all the ways not to raise entitled children against the backdrop of my own complicated childhood.

I'll also explain my theory of being an "airplane parent" rather than a "helicopter" one—the benefit of guiding what our children do from 30,000 feet above the ground instead of meddling in every single move they make.

So here's your permission to shed the guilt. Quit questioning every decision you make. Let go of the fear. Stop spending thousands on baby junk, wasting time researching sustainable wood high chairs, beating yourself up over deciding to pump (or not pump). Return to work, stay home from work, get divorced, roll your eyes at some mythical idea of "having it all." After reading this book, you'll be equipped to diffuse any judgment, whether that voice is on the playground, at daycare drop-off, or even coming from your own head (which is perhaps the harshest voice of all).

✻

Before my DMs explode on Twitter, let me explain five things you shouldn't do as a parent:

1. *Smoke While Pregnant.* If you're pregnant and you walked by somebody on the street who was smoking, relax! Your baby will be fine. Very limited, occasional exposure to smoke will not have lasting effects. But if you're pregnant and smoking, or live with a smoker, your unborn baby is at risk of negative side effects. Smoking restricts oxygen to the fetus, which could cause a host of developmental issues or miscarriage. Nicotine can also damage the placenta, which delivers nutrients and oxygen to the fetus. The good news, though: As soon as you stop, the negative side effects do too.[8] One study showed that babies born to moms who used products such as the patch or nicotine gum were bigger than babies born to cigarette smokers.[9] So it's never too late to quit, even if you need a little help.

2. *Skip Vaccinations.* There is no sound science proving vaccines are linked to autism, despite what a former Playboy bunny once told Oprah. This myth stemmed from a study of twelve children that has since been retracted after follow-up studies of more than a million children could not replicate the results.[10] The doctor who did the study was found guilty of falsifying his records and is banned from practicing medicine. Yes, autism rates have gone up—but this has more to do with how we now diagnose autism. Children who would have been diagnosed as "intellectually challenged" a generation ago now receive an autism diagnosis. We also have a correlation vs. causation issue here. Many symptoms of autism present themselves around two or three years old, which is when many children receive their vaccinations. There's a town in Japan where no children have received their MMR vaccination since 1993. If the MMR vaccine were connected to autism, you would think the autism rate in this town would have fallen. It has remained steady. Many vaccinations require "herd immunity" to be effective, meaning

8

95 percent or more of the population must be immunized. Kids who are sick or have certain allergies are unable to be vaccinated, and therefore are incredibly vulnerable when herd immunity is broken. I understand an emotional parent struggling with their child's diagnosis and grasping at straws for answers. But vaccines are not it.

3. *Neglect.* It's one thing to occasionally ignore your kid when they're being especially annoying and you just need five minutes of silence. But neglecting your kid 24/7 has the potential to fuck them up.

4. *Abuse of Any Kind.* Don't beat your child. Don't sexually abuse them. Don't yell at them all day, every day. Abusive behaviors can fuck up your kid.

5. *Starvation.* You should offer your child food regularly, ideally three meals a day and a snack or two. A starving child cannot function, learn, or survive.

Okay, now let's move on to all the things that won't fuck up your kids.

# 1

## Drink a Little Wine!
## Why It's Okay to Break Most of
## the Pregnancy "Rules"

I was only seven months pregnant, but felt as if I looked a hundred months pregnant, with a bulging belly that was even more pronounced on my petite 5-foot, 2-inch frame. Wearing a navy blue tunic, maternity stretch pants, and rubber Crocs (the only shoes my swollen feet would fit into at the time), I inelegantly plopped down at a tiny wood table on the front patio of a sushi restaurant on a busy thoroughfare near my Brooklyn neighborhood.

"I'll have the spicy tuna roll," I told the Japanese waitress, "*and* a glass of rosé."

She didn't bat an eye, despite my ordering not one but two forbidden-to-pregnant-lady items: raw fish and alcohol. I felt defiant. *I dare one of these people to judge me*, I thought, making eye contact with everyone who passed by. Any person who saw me locked eyes and then quickly looked away. (In hindsight, it was less that anyone was judging me and more that New Yorkers really just don't care how you live your life.)

The Japanese waitress probably didn't feel the need to shame me because in Japan, pregnant women eat plenty of sushi. Japanese doctors recommend it as part of good neonatal nutrition.[1] The dietary restrictions Americans put on pregnant women are largely excessive, which I'll explain in more detail in this chapter.

11

It feels like there is so much conflicting advice out there: Eat balanced meals, but don't eat soft cheeses, lunch meat, sushi, or anything, really! Indulge in some wine, but you might be damaging your kid. (The actual guidelines, just for reference, recommend avoiding high-mercury fish, raw or undercooked meat and fish, unpasteurized dairy, more than one cup of coffee a day or too much caffeine overall, any and all alcohol, and deli meats and other food that *may* be vulnerable to a bacteria called listeria, which can cause late miscarriage and stillbirth.)[2] You're eating for two, but don't gain too much weight! Luckily, you don't have to be too hard on yourself because you really can't fuck up your kid if you do all of the above—as long as it's in moderation.

## Bottoms Up! It's Okay to Drink a Little

Doctors tell pregnant women not to drink because there is a dearth of studies on the effects of light to moderate alcohol consumption while pregnant. Not that I blame science; it would be unethical to tell one pregnant woman to remain sober, another to try one drink a night, a third to consume a couple of glasses nightly, and a fourth to try a bottle a night . . . and then measure the IQs of all their kids years later.

But as a result of this "careful" science, the few studies that exist are flawed. For example, a frequently cited study of 2,000 women published in 2001 in the journal *Pediatrics* found that even one drink a day could cause behavioral problems in their unborn children later.[3] However, when you delve into the results, you see that 18 percent didn't drink at all and a whopping 45 percent of women who had one drink a day also reported using cocaine while expecting. Perhaps it was the kind of behavior that would lead a pregnant woman to do illicit drugs—and not the occasional beer—that led to childhood behavioral issues. Yet the cocaine angle is rarely, if ever, mentioned when this study is brought up by the media, doctors, or well-meaning parents on the playground.

However, abroad, where it's more culturally acceptable to drink while pregnant, large-scale studies have shown statistically insignificant differences in children's behaviors and IQs between nondrinking mothers and mothers who classified themselves as light drinkers (depending on the country, that's two to six drinks per week) while pregnant.

I was particularly drawn to a study that got a lot of press attention when it was published in 2016. Some headlines declared that the study proved it was okay to drink while pregnant. Others were more cautious, with a variation of, "Health risks of light drinking in pregnancy confirms that abstention is the safest approach."[4] When I dug into the study itself, the results seemed to confirm the former: Up to four drinks a week of either beer or wine, which is the limit recommended by the U.K. Department of Health, is totally fine.[5]

I called up one of the study's senior researchers, Dr. Luisa Zuccolo, to break it down. She was friendly but guarded, speaking to me from her home base at the University of Bristol. She explained that her team looked at 5,000 prior papers studying the effects of drinking alcohol while pregnant and examined the results of twenty-six relevant studies.

"I think the devil is in the details to be honest with you," she explained, adding that "communication in this case is really tricky.

"For example, when we talk about limiting eating tuna because of mercury, it's okay to say, 'Limit yourself to two portions of tuna a week,' because people aren't going to become addicted to tuna." But booze "is very different. For some people, it's harder to stop. They feel more relaxed with their friends, and they've had three drinks and maybe they'll have a fourth.

"Some argue this is paternalistic," she admits. Indeed: It seems that doctors think pregnant adult women can't control themselves enough to stop after one glass of wine, so they just tell us not to drink at all, like we're toddlers who need reprimanding. Still, "some people are better at stopping themselves than others," Dr. Zuccolo concedes. So you should know this about yourself: If you are the kind of person who lets go of all your inhibitions the minute you have a drink and don't think you'll be able to stop, then just don't drink while pregnant. If a glass of wine with dinner or after a hard day helps you relax, well, that's fine then. The stress relief has major health benefits too.

"Anxiety raises cortisol in pregnancies," Dr. Zuccolo says. A chronically increased rate of cortisol, otherwise known as the "stress hormone," has been linked to an increased risk of anxiety, depression, digestive issues, headaches, weight gain, memory impairment, heart disease, trouble sleeping, and more, according to the Mayo Clinic.[6] This is why, she says, that doctors tend to downplay situations such as a woman finding out she's pregnant a couple days after going on a bender. (I downed two bourbon cocktails the week before I found out I was expecting my firstborn, Everett.) "We do not want to cause alarm unnecessarily such as that the mom gets really stressed out about alcohol in pregnancy before she realizes she's pregnant. Demonizing that definitely doesn't help. A burden or sense of guilt doesn't help." (Another friend's doctor advised her to continue using pot while pregnant to avoid stress. But you should check with your doctor before doing this.)

So why all the caution with Dr. Zuccolo's research? The study found that up to four beers or glasses of wine a week may very slightly increase your chance of having a smaller baby *if* he or she is born prematurely—but drinking won't make you more likely to deliver prematurely. And it's pretty obvious that your baby may be slightly smaller if delivered earlier regardless of whether you occasionally have a beer with dinner.

This study caused blaring headlines about how alcohol equals smaller babies, but it never said how much smaller the babies could be. A baby born at four pounds faces the potential for many more health issues and longer hospital stays than a baby born at eight pounds. When I asked Dr. Zuccolo about this, she said that the weight difference is so small, it's negligible, "so you would not be likely to say this baby really suffered from their mom drinking half a glass of wine every month."

Some research shows that babies born to mothers who have an occasional drink actually have better outcomes than mothers who completely abstain. A 2010 study of 3,000 pregnant women in Australia, another place it's more culturally acceptable to drink, looked at behavior issues at age two, and then followed the kids until they turned fourteen. It showed that kids of light drinkers (classified as two to six drinks per week) are "significantly less likely" to have behavior issues than children of moms who didn't drink at all.[7] Another Australian study found no difference in IQs between children born to moms who had one drink a day compared to those who completely abstained. (That study of 7,200 women also tested the kids again at age eight and found, you guessed it, no difference in IQs.)

As statistician Emily Oster explains in her excellent book, *Expecting Better*, "researchers tend to find that women who drink moderately in pregnancy have children with higher IQ scores." This is due to the fact that women who drink moderately tend to be better educated—which plays a much more important role in how kids grow up than the occasional glass of sauvignon blanc. As Dr. Zuccolo says, many studies don't take into account the life situations of their subjects. Data is only taken on whether the parent drinks or doesn't drink, but other factors—such as their education, income, marital status, and age—are not considered. And all of these things can skew the research. Then, sweeping generalizations are made for large groups of people based on a small number of people studied who may have exceptional life circumstances.

## *It's Okay to Get Your Caffeine Fix*

Another controversial drink while expecting: coffee. Some doctors say to avoid it altogether because it can increase your chance of miscarriage. Many of my friends didn't have any and instead suffered through caffeine-withdrawal headaches. I settled on half-caf for my second pregnancy, with Otto. Oster, the statistician and author, explains this tenuous link to miscarriage: Many pregnant women are too nauseous in the beginning of their pregnancies to drink very much coffee. Those who aren't nauseous continue drinking it as usual. But women who aren't as nauseous are more likely to have a miscarriage.

So perhaps it wasn't the coffee that caused the miscarriage, but the lack of nausea that was a telltale sign of an impending miscarriage. After all, women who drink other caffeinated beverages such as Coke or tea aren't more likely to miscarry. As with drinking alcohol during pregnancy, we're looking at flawed research because it would be unethical to conduct an experiment where one group of pregnant women drank an entire carafe of coffee a day, another consumed a couple mugs, and others abstained, and then measure all three groups for miscarriages later. Oster also found no statistical likelihood that women who drink coffee while pregnant give birth to smaller babies, so she decided up to four cups a day was okay during her own pregnancy.

My doctor had me ditch green tea when I was pregnant, which was harder for me than coffee at the time. I dug into the research and determined that she was probably overreacting. Tea contains an antioxidant called catechin, which has been linked to a bunch of health benefits, such as lowering your risk of heart disease, stroke, and cancer. Unfermented green tea has the highest amount of catechin, followed by oolong, and then black tea. Some studies have found that consuming more than three cups of tea with a lot of catechin per day can inhibit your absorption of folic acid. A folic acid deficiency may increase your risk of delivering a baby with a condition called spina bifida (SB), where an infant's spinal cord doesn't form properly. So if you want to drink a little tea, go for it—but just don't drink gallons per day. Using data from nearly 7,000 moms,researchers found the following: "Our data do not support the hypothesis that tea consumption overall increases the risk of SB."[8]

## Why You Should Indulge Those Cravings

The pee stick had hardly turned pink when the cravings for lox set in. Morning, day, and night, I dreamed about smoked salmon. But advice on the Internet was mixed: Was I supposed to eat it or not? It all seemed to depend on whom I asked. My doctor at the time, who was overly cautious in most of her advice, told me with a wink and a half smile that it was okay to consume it. So, on a trip to London, I dug in. And when I got home, I continued to pile it tall atop Brooklyn bagels. And I munched on it as a snack. (To this day, Everett loves to eat lox, and I joke that this probably explains it. He gets all kinds of funny looks when he noshes down on "fishies" as a five-year-old.)

But the idea that I couldn't find a place that definitively told me whether it's okay to eat lox points to an issue. Pregnant women are told to avoid a laundry list of foods, ranging from soft cheeses to deli meats to raw fish. There are a number of government agencies in the United States that have released guidelines regarding which foods pregnant women should avoid. One goal of the Food and Drug Administration's endless list[9] is to lower the chances women would eat anything that could possibly have been infected with the harmful bacteria listeria.

When you dig into the statistics, as Oster did in *Expecting Better*, you see that two foods were responsible for 30 percent of listeria outbreaks during the ten-year period between 1998 to 2008: *queso fresco*, a Mexican soft cheese, and turkey deli meat. Let's say you're craving a sandwich, so you choose ham over turkey. As Oster found, eating ham would lower your risk of listeria from 1 in 8,333 to 1 in 8,255. (Meanwhile, your risk of getting in a car accident during the course of your lifetime is 1 in 114—and pregnant women still drive every single day.)[10]

The rest of the listeria outbreaks are random, such as pine nuts found in hummus, celery, or cantaloupe. Even ice cream experienced a huge listeria outbreak in 2015. So how can you prevent yourself from getting listeria? Keep your refrigerator below 40 degrees Fahrenheit, don't eat things that have been sitting in your refrigerator a long time or at room temperature for longer than two hours, do eat pasteurized foods, and wash your hands well and often, says the American College of Obstetricians and Gynecologists.[11]

In the meantime, why are pregnant women spending so much time anxiously tracking every single ingredient they put in their mouths when they'd lower their chance of miscarrying if they'd avoid just two foods: *queso fresco* and turkey deli meat? Here's yet another instance of sexism, as government officials and doctors apparently couldn't believe that women were capable of taking our own precautions to avoid a smaller list of foods. Easier to just ban everything! Pregnant or not, I'm not going to eat sushi sold at a gas station. But while pregnant, it's important to just make sure that sushi is consumed in moderation (like all foods), mostly avoid high-mercury varietals like tuna, and only eat in clean restaurants.[12] In the United States, it's a law that all sushi must be flash frozen before served, anyway, which kills most bacteria and parasites.[13]

### *Fighting Depression? Don't Ditch Your Antidepressants Cold Turkey*

Millions of women are taking antidepressants,[14] and it's normal to be concerned about how the medicine will affect your unborn baby—

and your own mood if you stop. Most antidepressants are totally fine, especially when compared to the alternative: A depressed mom may not take care of herself, including getting good prenatal care. The Mayo Clinic also reports that depression during pregnancy is associated with an increased risk of premature birth, low birth weight, decreased fetal growth, and postpartum depression.[15] So if you're on antidepressants, you should definitely talk to your doctor.

The FDA recommends that pregnant moms on Paxil switch due to a small increase of fetal heart defects. But if that's the only medicine that stabilizes your mood, the benefits may outweigh the very small risks. Pregnant women on average have a 1 percent chance of delivering a baby with a heart defect, a doctor writes on *MedicineNet.*[16] The risk of heart defect only jumps to 1.5 or 2 percent for a pregnant woman who takes Paxil.

And please don't quit taking your antidepressants cold turkey once you find out you're pregnant! Stopping antidepressants abruptly may lead to a depressive episode, digestive issues, and dizziness, among other potential side effects.[17] Call your doctor, and he or she will help you find the best solution so you can stay mentally healthy while pregnant and after. Remember: Mom's mental health is just as important as your unborn baby's. How can you take care of your baby if you don't take care of yourself?

## Why You're Not Weird If Your Baby Arrives "Late" or "Early"

I had no idea when I got pregnant with Everett. I'd been on the pill for a decade and my period hadn't returned in the months Brad and I were "trying" for him. One day, I was drinking bourbon with my girlfriends and complaining about how I was *never* getting pregnant; the next day, my boobs were throbbing in an exercise class, and then I got a positive pregnancy test.

When I called my doctor to make an appointment, the receptionist's first question was, "How far along are you?" I had no idea. Two weeks? Four weeks? Five minutes? Using a sonogram to measure, my doctor determined I was six weeks along. But the sizing kept bouncing around the due date. First I was due on November 11. Then it changed to November 4. Then October 31. Everett arrived on October 21.

It took eleven months of "trying" for me to get pregnant with Otto. I know the exact *day* we conceived him, thanks to the $250 Clearblue Easy Fertility Monitor I splurged on. (Other weird things I used to determine fertility: a little white tube I could spit on and examine for "ferns"; a book with photos of vaginal mucus during different phases of a woman's cycle; and many, many apps.) When I finally got that positive pregnancy test, I was the one who told my doctor my due date. Still, Otto arrived during week thirty-eight, just like his big brother.

How do doctors determine your due date? They add 280 days to the first day of your last period, which equals the "average" forty-week-long pregnancy. But some research shows that pregnancy length can vary by as much as five weeks. Only 70 percent of women deliver within ten days of their estimated due date, according to an Oxford University Press study.[18]

So don't feel like you're weird if your baby comes "early" or "late."

## Why Gaining Extra "Baby Weight" Is Not So Bad

For both of my pregnancies, I gained and then lost fifty-two pounds. One of my ob-gyns shamed me endlessly about my weight gain. In my third trimester, I inexplicably gained seven pounds in two days, despite doing my weekly prenatal yoga, continuing to walk around NYC as well as I could, and not eating any differently. My doctor was aghast and told me I needed to start getting on a treadmill on an incline and speed walking. My next appointment was with another doctor in the practice. He examined my blood pressure and it turned out I had a life-threatening pregnancy complication called preeclampsia. Speed walking on a treadmill could have put me into premature labor at best or caused me to have a stroke and killed me (and probably the baby) at worst. He immediately put me on modified bed rest. The pounds I'd packed on could be attributed to water weight; swelling is one of the telltale signs of preeclampsia, and he suspected it as soon as he saw how swollen my feet were.

Why do some doctors freak out if you gain more or less than the recommended twenty-five to thirty-five pounds while pregnant? This comes from an effort to assure your baby is normal size, as the more weight mom gains, the bigger baby tends to be. Babies who are small for gestational age (SGA), or born smaller than average, may have more negative side effects, such as breathing issues and neurological complications. Babies who are SGA and also born prematurely are at higher risk for these complications. Babies who are bigger in utero, or large for gestational age (LGA), have lower risks for health complications but can be tougher for mom to deliver due to their size. (Although I've known plenty of women who delivered babies bigger than nine pounds vaginally, I delivered my nine-and-a-half pounder via C-section.)[19]

If by chance a baby is born prematurely, he has fewer risks of developing health complications if he's also larger in utero (LGA). This is why I find it so incongruous that doctors today shame women for gaining an ounce over the recommended thirty-five pounds. I'm of course not recommending that pregnant women eat ice cream for breakfast, lunch, and dinner, as moderation is the key message of this book—but some bodies just gain more weight. Don't be too hard on yourself if you put on a couple extra pounds. Gaining twenty extra pounds shouldn't merit shaming, which in itself can be harmful to a mother's mental health. I know I would have been way less stressed if my doctor hadn't pressured me to be unreasonably thin.

Not once has a doctor brought up my weight in an annual physical, yet my weight was front and center in every single one of my prenatal appointments. Strangers on the street used to regularly say things like, "Whoa mama! You're huge!" and, "You look like you're going to pop!" (Um, yeah thanks. I was only six months pregnant when I heard the second one.)

Just sixty years ago, doctors recommended women only gain ten to twenty pounds during pregnancy. "They realized that moms didn't do that well and babies didn't do that well," Dr. Sanford Lederman, chair of ob-gyn at New York–Presbyterian Brooklyn Methodist Hospital, tells me. Then the pendulum swung far in the other direction, and "women would gain fifty to one hundred pounds during pregnancy," which wasn't healthy either. Eventually the recommendation fell into the middle of a twenty-five to thirty-five pound weight gain, but even that isn't one-size-fits-all. "Everyone has a different body. You have tall women, short women. . . . You may tell a woman who is extremely overweight during the pregnancy [that she] should only gain ten to twenty pounds, and a woman who is too thin to gain more." The twenty-five to thirty-five pound weight gain recommendation is just the average weight gain "so that babies won't be restricted as far as growth is concerned and women hopefully won't develop high blood pressure [which can turn into preeclampsia]," Dr. Lederman explains.

So here we've got a bit of sexism with a side of one-size-fits-all pregnancy advice. If a woman has blood pressure in a healthy range, why shame her for gaining a few extra pounds? Yes, it'll be harder to lose. But no woman needs a "perfect post-baby body" three minutes after giving birth. Nine months on, nine months off—or longer. You shouldn't feel pressure to look a certain way or hit a number on a scale after giving birth. Our bodies are all different.

## Timing Your Pregnancy

There's a memorable scene in *My Cousin Vinny* where Marisa To-mei's character, clad in a full-body flowered spandex jumpsuit that bares her back, stomps her foot, and screams, "My *bio-log-ical* clock is ticking!" Many women can relate to Tomei, even though she was only twenty-eight years old when the film was released. Any woman older than thirty-five is given the dreadful title "geriatric pregnancy" in America, thanks largely to a study that says a woman's fertility plummets in her mid-thirties. True, there are biological pitfalls to bearing children the older you get, but a door doesn't slam shut on your thirty-fifth birthday.

Shockingly, the oft-cited study that says women older than age thirty-five will have trouble conceiving was based on church birth re-cords of French women in the 1700s, when life expectancy was con-siderably shorter than today's seventy-nine years. (Not to mention, these women had "no access to modern healthcare, nutrition or even electricity," the BBC notes.[20] They may not have even been trying to get pregnant—or having sex at all—when the data was gathered.)

Newer research does show that fertility dips as women age, but not as drastically as we're led to believe. Women aged twenty-seven to thirty-four, in the so-called golden window of fertility, have an 86 percent chance of getting knocked up within a year of trying. Women who are between thirty-five and thirty-nine have an 82 per-cent chance of getting pregnant within a year, according to a 2002 study published in *Human Reproduction*.[21] A 4 percent drop is not exactly falling off a cliff.

"Nowadays, we take care of women well into their 50s who are pregnant, some of them [pregnant] spontaneous, some of them via IVF or assistive reproductive techniques," Dr. Lederman says. A recent *New York* magazine cover story proclaimed that tens of thousands of women up to age fifty were wrongly told they couldn't get pregnant with IVF. You do have a higher chance of chromosomal abnormalities with age, but "59 out of 60 women aged 40 and above will have no chromosomal problems in their baby at all," David James, of the United Kingdom's National Institute for Health and Care Excellence fertility guideline development group, told the BBC.[22]

This doesn't mean you should put off having children indefinitely. If you're waiting for a perfect time to have kids, I'm here to tell you that it doesn't exist—unless you're the rare unicorn who believes you've finally got enough money, the most flexible job, tons of time and energy, and the ideal partner! The rest of us do the best we can with what we've got. We make it work.

Younger parents have more energy and probably aren't as far along in their careers yet, so it might be easier to take a pause for children. Older parents have more work experience and thus probably more money and savings. With extra work experience comes more seniority, and the chance you may be able to demand more flexibility in your career. As with anything in life, there are pros and cons to every situation.

Don't freak out on your thirty-fifth birthday if you don't have a child yet. But don't rely on technology to work for you when you get around to having kids. Today, many companies offer egg freezing as a perk, alongside free frozen yogurt and ping-pong tables, as if to assuage women that they can work twenty-hour days and just get pregnant later.

As soon as I turned thirty-five, my Instagram feed filled up with ads promoting what seemed like a breezy egg freezing procedure. But freezing your eggs is like going through IVF—think daily hormone injections, mood swings, and then surgery to retrieve eggs. The good news is the frozen eggs can be stored for ten years or more. The bad news is that most research is done on women younger than thirty-eight, which is the cutoff age for freezing eggs recommended by the American Society for Reproductive Medicine.[23] Some centers will harvest eggs from women older than that age; the University of Southern California Fertility center, for example, says on its website that it has achieved pregnancies from frozen eggs taken from women older than forty, but it doesn't name a specific success rate.[24] Another study found that women who freeze their eggs after age thirty-six have less than a 30 percent chance of giving birth.[25] (The American Society for Reproductive Medicine has an even lower estimate, saying that each frozen egg yields only a 2 to 12 percent chance of becoming a baby later.)[26]

The first baby from egg freezing was born in 2005,[27] but the technology was still considered experimental until 2012. It doesn't come cheap. Expect to pay $10,000 to undergo an egg freezing cycle (including doctor's appointments and medicines), $5,000 to have them retrieved, and more for storage fees until you're ready to have them fertilized and reinjected. The more eggs you retrieve and store increases your chance of success, but it also costs more.

I'm not against egg freezing technology. But you shouldn't assume that egg freezing is guaranteed to work. The good news is that reproductive technology is constantly improving. In 1978, only one baby had been born via IVF. In the forty years that followed, eight million more were born using the same method.[28]

## Time to End the Stigma About Pregnancy Loss

Christene is one of those women you love to follow on Instagram for her chic Brooklyn apartment, stylish #OOTDs, and enviable job as founder and global editor in chief of *Refinery29*. Despite the perfect social media appearance, she's been very open about the wide range of emotions she's experienced following seven miscarriages: embarrassment, shame, guilt, shock, sadness, fear that if only her husband were "married to someone younger and presumably more fertile, he could be a father right this very moment," as she wrote in an emotional essay on her site.[29]

She writes of being "haunted" by images. "Picture this (because I do all the time): My tall, athletic, seemingly ageless husband, walking down the sidewalk in our quiet Brooklyn neighborhood, with a child. They stroll along, smiling, my husband often glancing down at this mini-person; the mini-person, continuously gazing up at my doting husband, in attachment, wonder, and love. And then, I literally want to crush a wine glass in my hand to punish myself for having robbed my husband of this reality—an idyllic scene that, in a parallel universe, with said younger, prettier, more fertile wife, is actually happening."

When Christene first found out she was pregnant, she giddily shared the good news. Then, she had to untell people when it ended in miscarriage. She recalls awkwardly blurting it out to a longtime business contact at a work function. Despite their warm relationship over the years, the woman "very faintly stiffened and gradually angled her body and drew her eyes away. And then, she did something possibly even worse than recoiling in her not-so-secret horror—she just ignored it. That was it.

"I was immediately embarrassed. What the fuck was I thinking?" Christene laments. "How could I share such personal information with someone I really didn't know as well as I probably wanted to? Stunned by her reaction, I quickly attempted to move on to another topic, but the space between us, whatever mutual kindness we shared, was suddenly gone."

Instead of two women sharing a moment about something that happens to many of us, Christene had another takeaway: "It honestly had never occurred to me before—up until that moment, I had no clue that I might or should be ashamed of my miscarriage. How could I not see it? That it exposed my broken-ness, my regret, possibly every mistake I'd made throughout the course of my life. It was the failure of everything."

For some reason, miscarriage, stillbirth, and fertility struggles are still rarely spoken about in polite company, or even among good friends. This is shocking to me, given that studies say up to 30 percent of all pregnancies result in miscarriage.[30] That's right: Look to your left and your right. If you haven't experienced a miscarriage, likely a woman sitting next to you has. I remember reading one book where the narrator, a medical student, lamented how shocked he was that babies are born at all given the complicated physiological processes that must occur during fertilization, pregnancy, and labor and delivery. And yet UNICEF says nearly 386,000 babies are born every single day around the world.[31]

Of course, that is cold comfort for the people dealing with pregnancy loss or struggling to get pregnant at all. Instead of the facts—that pregnancy loss is incredibly common—Christene and so many other women internalize that anything wrong with the baby is their fault. And that is so fucked up. Again, the research doesn't make it any easier when you're reeling from pregnancy loss, whether you've been pregnant for nine minutes or nine months.

Christene announced in 2018 that she had finally gotten pregnant.[32] And she noted an unintentional side effect of her brutally honest essay about her fertility struggles. "There's much more openness and maybe even warmth when it comes to discussing anything having to do with fertility or the lack thereof. Something that was immediately clear from the unexpected outpouring of emails and comments I received in the days and months following—less shame and desperation, more support and encouragement that things could work out the way you want them to."

If you experience pregnancy loss, just know you're not alone. It's important that we share our stories to erase the stigma that some of us feel.

Jaime is a gregarious brunette with a New Jersey accent who loves to shake things up in her conservative Alabama town. I first met her through mutual friends when I worked at a big magazine, and I've stayed in touch with her during the years. She's a true hustler: She launched her own public relations company, then her own vlog *Coffee Talk* that eventually drew more than two million viewers an episode, which she spun off into a reality show called *Jersey Belle,* and now she's developing scripts at a major movie production company. The girl doesn't quit. She's also a mom to three with a handsome Southern husband (thus her move from Jersey to Alabama).

When I was editor in chief of Yahoo! Parenting, Jaime wrote about a heartbreaking ectopic pregnancy she'd experienced. At that point, she was mom to two kids: Olivia and Max. She had found out she was expecting Max when Olivia was just ten weeks old, which she recalls "provided plenty of laughs for everyone but me."[33]

When Max was nine months old, Jaime experienced what she thought was a crazy-heavy period and was shocked when doctors told her an eight-week-old fetus was growing on the outside of one of her fallopian tubes. She sobbed as she told her husband. Then the guilt set in. She felt guilty that she couldn't carry this baby to term. She also felt guilty about her mixed emotions when she found out she was pregnant with Max just ten weeks after giving birth to her first daughter.

Guilt is a common feeling following miscarriage. A doctor who studied guilt after pregnancy loss explains that a woman tends to think she caused the miscarriage to happen by doing something like lifting a heavy object once or eating something weird. "The truth is that in the vast majority of cases, there is nothing that the woman did that caused the miscarriage," Dr. Zev Williams told *New York* magazine, adding that a genetic abnormality is usually to blame.[34] But this doesn't mean it's easy to rationalize what happened. And we shouldn't do that anyway. We should feel free to take time to process what happened. We are entitled to feel every emotion, especially because suppressing them will do more damage in the long run. But you should not beat yourself up for the rest of your life because something went wrong with a pregnancy. In parenting, we should always be kinder to ourselves. Pregnancy loss is not our fault.

Knowing that doesn't make the ridiculous things people say easier though. "I had surgery to remove the baby and repair my tube. After it was over, I found myself alone in my hospital room, staring out the window into the darkness and wondering how the sun would ever shine again. I felt so empty. It was a sadness that reached every fiber of my being. A nurse came in and offered me food. When I refused, she smiled and said, 'Think of the two healthy babies you have at home,' before she closed the door behind her. Tears welled in my eyes. My throat burned. I felt outraged, out of control. I wanted to scream at her that the loss of one child is not redeemed by others at home—that the way a mother's heart works is like having individual hearts for each child, and when one is broken, it cannot be made whole by another," writes Jaime. "It must heal on its own. But I said nothing. I just cried."

After losing a pregnancy or baby, it's normal to feel forever changed. "I sobbed because I knew that my life would forever be 'before loss' and 'after,'" Jaime writes. Eight months later, she was pregnant again. "Often, well-intentioned people would say, 'See? You're getting that third baby,'" Jaime recalls. "But Charlie was not my third child—she was my fourth. I will always mourn that baby. I will always remember the sound of her soothing heart beating, and my heart will forever ache knowing she tried so hard to make it work, even when I couldn't."

Pregnancy loss is a terribly sad event. "The pain of losing a baby is a pain so heavy and unique, it's hard for others to understand if they themselves have not experienced it—much like the love for a baby that can't fully be understood until someone experiences that, too,"

Jaime writes. But we shouldn't feel shame. Talking openly about our experiences is a good coping mechanism. Don't be afraid to reach out to friends, family, or a support group—whether it's online or in person. We are not alone.

That's the whole point of #NoShameParenting: Sharing our stories disables the feeling of shame.

**#NoShameParenting Takeaway:** It's a good idea for expectant mothers to listen to their bodies and be aware of the definite no-no's of pregnancy, but we don't need to stress as much as we do. Generally speaking, it's okay to enjoy a glass of wine or gain a few extra pounds during pregnancy, and we shouldn't be afraid to try to conceive in our thirties—or forties, or even fifties. That's just *not* going to fuck up your kid. As for pregnancy loss, we didn't fuck up our embryos. It just happens. That doesn't make it easier to handle, but you shouldn't blame yourself.

# 2

## C-Section vs. "Natural":
## Why the Way We Give Birth
## Shouldn't Be a Competition

Before even getting pregnant, most women have seen a birth scene on TV or in a movie. Usually this involves a brief moment of a sweaty woman screaming, followed quickly by her contentment as a tiny baby is placed on her chest. "See, that wasn't so hard!" the media seems to reassure us.

Yet, it's tough to shake that nagging feeling that giving birth might be a *little* messier than how it's depicted in popular culture. Which is probably why thousands of "birth plans"—checklists of what you hope happens (and doesn't happen) while in labor—are available to download on Pinterest. Taking the time to plan out a "perfect" labor and delivery gives us the illusion of control in a situation where we usually don't have a lot of it.

I'm glad women's voices are being honored more during labor and delivery—we've come a long way since women were drugged and babies delivered in what was called "twilight birth." I just wish that the pendulum hadn't swung *so* far; that there wasn't so much pressure to deliver a certain way, and so much shame if we don't follow those carefully laid plans. The reality is that labor and delivery cannot be perfectly controlled and, in order to bring our baby into the world, we need to trust our medical providers and their calls in the heat of the moment.

That's why it's so important to find a doctor you trust *before* you give birth. Don't second-guess that inner voice if it's saying that you're not on the same page with your doctor or medical professional. If you trust your medical provider, you will trust her when she says you need a C-section or another method to deliver your baby healthfully, despite whatever pressure you might be feeling from friends, mommy blogs, or Facebook parenting groups to bring a child into the world a certain way. You should be empowered to give birth in whatever way is best for you and your future child—without shame, stress, or judgment.

It's a lesson that Tessa learned the hard way, unfortunately. Despite having access to world-class medical services as a resident of New York City, she was essentially shamed by her mom, midwife, and doula into giving birth as one would in the Guatemalan desert. (An interesting analogy she used the first time we met in person—which I never forgot, despite the fact that this was more than two years ago!)

I got to know Tessa via email first, when we were both in the same online baby group (my second kid, her first). When our babies were both about six weeks old, she came to a weekly brunch I organized for new parents. Tessa seemed more than thrilled to be making small talk with near strangers while juggling a newborn. "I haven't left my house since Oliver was born," she told me. I was stunned that she was housebound for six whole weeks! Even I hobbled to my street corner and back a week or so after both my C-sections.

Tall and thin, with pale skin and light brown hair, Tessa described a harrowing birth story that started out with the best of intentions. She partnered with a doula and midwife, determined to give birth at home. She had a careful plan that fit in with her healthy lifestyle of regular ballet and yoga. Her pregnancy was uneventful, so she figured her delivery would be as well. When her baby turned breech at 38.5 weeks, she tried acupuncture and meditation and it appeared the baby flipped.

Everything was going to plan—until her labor stalled after more than thirty hours. Her midwife and doula encouraged her to keep pushing, keep waiting, to listen to her body because it knows what it's doing. She'd already invested so much time and energy into her birth plan. She couldn't give up now. She was determined to keep trying to give birth at home.

She eventually began to hit an emotional wall and was taken to the hospital by her midwife and doula, where she checked into the birthing center and continued to labor. She tried the hot tub, which didn't work. She considered an epidural, but decided against it. Tessa had grown up with a mom who worked as a doula and remembered her calling women who used epidurals "weak." She was determined not to be one of those "weak" women.

"I was ripping my teeth out. I felt invisible, angry, and afraid," Tessa says. Her labor reached thirty-six hours, when she learned that her indescribable pain was caused by her baby resting on her sciatic nerve. Her midwife grabbed a surgeon, figuring that talking about the possibility of a C-section might motivate during those final pushes to get her son out. Her midwife also found a nurse who agreed to do a manual delivery.

When Tessa pushed next, the nurse stuck her arm up Tessa's vagina and literally pulled her son out—causing a fourth-degree tear from her vagina to her asshole. "I should have been a C-section," Tessa says.

Oliver weighed in at nine pounds, two ounces and was perfectly healthy. Tessa, meanwhile, had to go to physiotherapy after her stitches healed. She was at risk of suffering incontinence for the rest of her life. Her painful recovery kept her housebound for the first bewildering weeks of her baby's birth.

"I couldn't walk for a month. I couldn't carry my baby for the first six weeks of his life. I literally felt like I was losing my mind. I thought I was never going to speak to another human being again. It was total isolation," Tessa told me recently as we sipped white wine in my backyard. The calm breeze and our easy conversation was a far cry from our first meeting. Now, Tessa sat up straighter and was quick to smile and make jokes. Two years ago, during our first conversation, she often stared into the distance and felt small to me, even though she's nearly six feet tall.

"It was traumatic. I mean, nobody died, but it was traumatic," Tessa says. "I am livid and angry on behalf of women all the time." She pressured herself to give birth a certain way because she told herself that there was a right and wrong way to do it, and she didn't want to let down her mom, midwife, and doula in the process. (Even though she says that they never directly told her she had to deliver at home or not use an epidural.) She thinks she might have PTSD and would seek professional help if she and her husband decide to have another child. "I had too much pride. I internalized everything: the epidural, my birth plan." Tessa is also frustrated by the lack of support she received after she gave birth and as she struggled to recover. She's now focusing on building a career as a postpartum health specialist, helping new moms overcome pelvic floor issues and diastasis recti, which is a common condition in which a woman's abdomen muscles separate.[1] (I fixed mine via physical therapy.)

When I asked her if she wishes she'd just gotten that C-section, she says: "Holy God, I would have operated."

＊

When I think back to my first pregnancy, the idea that I'd deliver my firstborn via C-section made me quiver with anxiety. It didn't matter that I planned to give birth to him in one of the most technologically advanced hospitals in the middle of Manhattan, so I probably didn't need to worry about an inexperienced surgeon slicing open my abdomen. Or that it seemed a C-section was my destiny, seeing how my grandmother, mother, and aunt all delivered their giant kids that way.

During the hospital tour, while cradling my bulging baby bump, I tried to mentally prepare myself for all possibilities. *This is the room where births go all wrong,* I told myself as I peeked my head into the hallway containing the operating theater, noticing the stark metal instruments and chilly temperature. *I wish I was brave enough to deliver here*, I said inside my head as I examined the birthing center, filled with slightly outdated but warm, wooden furniture, not unlike a Holiday Inn, and a bathtub in the corner. Women who opted to deliver in these rooms were not allowed to have an epidural, instead laboring without medical interventions as doctors stayed in the background in case they needed to step in and assist. The best of both worlds. *It's not such a bad thing to cave and get an epidural,* I thought as my group crowded inside the standard issue room with those giant stirrups you hoist your splayed-open legs on to push out your screaming newborn.

Looking back at that time period, there were so many ways I could have softened the dialogue in my own head and been easier on my self. But I know I'm not the only one who told myself there was a "right" and a "wrong" way to give birth, as evidenced by countless conversations with friends and parents across the United States. I also read plenty of blogs featuring eye-catching headlines and so-called experts promoting "natural" birth or criticizing C-sections. So many women are told "it's not about the outcome, it's about the process," Harvard-trained ob-gyn Amy Tuteur tells me. "It seems to me that a lot of people who promote these processes believe you can't be a good mother unless you suffer."

\*

Nabiha is athletic, with muscled legs that easily allow her to chase her two kids around the playground. But that didn't make delivering her firstborn any easier. After twenty hours of labor and a couple hours of pushing, doctors wheeled her into surgery. "It was never made clear why I had a C-section. Neither of us were in any danger," she says, referring to her daughter, Ameera, now four.

A couple years later, a colleague told her about having a VBAC, or vaginal birth after C-section. "We were sitting at lunch and I was almost in tears listening to this woman's story," says Nabiha. "I always kind of felt cheated [with my first birth]. There's a lot of layers of guilt there. It just never sat right with me for some reason."

So when Nabiha got pregnant the second time, she used the same medical practice as her colleague, where certified nurse midwives worked alongside doctors. One of those midwives recommended she and her husband take a VBAC class. "I was like, sure, okay, whatever. But it was pretty transformative," Nabiha says. In four hours, the couple learned different positions to labor in, and ways to ease the pain, and left feeling completely empowered. "Erik walked out of there feeling like he was the king of the world: 'Oh, I have a role here, I have a voice here, I know what to ask for [at the hospital],'" Nabiha says. "We had a whole new set of knowledge that we just didn't the first time around."

Despite her very normal second pregnancy, Nabiha was skeptical about her ability to have a VBAC, but she was determined to try. When she went into labor with her son Aiyaan, it was an entirely different experience. Her midwife coached her through different positions, including bouncing on a ball. She accidentally missed her window to get an epidural. (She admits she was secretly relieved: "I was nervous that if I had an epidural again, I wouldn't know how to push. I didn't know during my first delivery that you can adjust the meds you get, or that you can shut off the epidural or turn it down when it's time to push. How come I didn't know that?")

Nabiha says she would have been okay if doctors or her midwife told her she needed a second C-section. "I would have known I tried, and that I understood my options, and what was going on in my body." But when Aiyaan was born vaginally, Nabiha was ecstatic. "I was just so scared with Ameera for a lot of reasons. I was exhausted, I didn't know what I was doing." With Aiyaan, "I had never felt so much elation in my life, I was on cloud nine for days . . . I felt vindicated. It was proof to me that my body could do that."

*

If you're feeling overwhelmed about giving birth, take a deep breath. It's going to be okay. As long as you receive sound medical advice from a doctor or certified nurse midwife you trust and together choose an option that feels safest and most comfortable for you (while keeping an open mind that plans sometimes need to be abandoned in labor), you're not going to fuck up your kid.

## The Business of Giving Birth

Giving birth has become big business, driven up in price by an industry of bloated healthcare costs, midwives, doulas, organic products, and parents with the best of intentions who are willing to spend any amount of money or endure any kind of pain to give their kid a step up in life. It costs more to have a baby in the United States than any other country in the world—starting at $10,000 for a complication-free vaginal birth. Double that for a C-section. Factor in prenatal care, and you're looking at a hospital bill starting at $30,000 and going up from there. To put it in perspective, that's more expensive than Kate Middleton's royal baby birth in the fancy Lindo Wing of a London hospital, which cost about $9,000.[2] Of course in England, they have single-payer healthcare.

The way most American women give birth today has changed dramatically. Just before the turn of the twentieth century, most women gave birth at home without any medical interventions.[3] Back then, it was safer to give birth at home—women who entered hospitals were likely to die from sepsis because doctors didn't understand they needed to wash their hands. Hospitals at the time were also seen as only for poor women without support systems, while affluent women always birthed at home.[4] Moms and babies died at staggering rates. In some U.S. cities, 30 percent of infants died before their first birthday, the CDC reports.[5]

In 1910, a report on the sad state of medical care in the United States decried obstetrics as "the very worst" of all practices. Shortly after, the first maternity hospital opened and the business of childbirth begin to shift from female midwives to male doctors—who performed more medical interventions, ranging from forceps to "twilight sleep," where mom was totally knocked out with a mix of scopolamine and morphine during delivery.[6] American society was also changing at this time. Families were moving farther apart, leaving many new mothers without a natural support network of mothers, sisters, and extended family, and America was becoming more urban. As doctors started to learn more about pathogens and sterilization, delivering in hospitals became safer than delivering at home. Still, in the 1920s, a baby (and its mother) had about the same chance of surviving if delivered at home by a midwife or in a hospital by a general practitioner or obstetrician.[7]

In the 1930s and 1940s, mom and baby were more likely to live if delivered in a hospital. This is thanks to medical advancements both big (penicillin and blood transfusions) and small (doctors learned they needed to wash their hands). This time period was arguably the start of the chasm between midwives and doctors that we still see today. We'll talk more about this later in this chapter. Team midwife dissed male obstetricians as behaving paternalistically toward women and accused them of convincing women that childbirth was "unnatural and dangerous" so that they'd deliver in hospitals. The doctors' side says this narrative falsely created the belief that birth was "safe and routine," and that there was a "natural"—and thus "unnatural"—way to give birth. Doctors also pointed out that women were demanding the latest medical advances. In the not-too-distant past, before giving birth, women routinely prepared themselves, their spouses, and their children for the reality that they could very easily die.

In the 1950s, twilight sleep began falling out of favor thanks to scary photos of women tied to beds and covered in feces (lovely!). Some 90 percent of women delivered in hospitals during this decade. Doctors and nurses began to approach childbirth as "normal and healthy" instead of the "pathological" thinking of recent decades. Ultrasounds were invented, but the machines produced blurry images and were nicknamed "dinosaurograph" due to their giant size.[8]

In the 1960s, 99 percent of women delivered in a hospital. Fetal heart monitoring was invented (and birth control was also approved by the FDA, giving women the option to space out their children for the first time in history).

In the 1970s, twilight sleep was finally replaced with Lamaze, hypnosis, water immersion, and other relaxation techniques. The modern epidural also became popular.

In the 1980s, half of all women opted for an epidural. Many women still gave birth in hospitals, but the American Association of Childbearing Centers was established in 1983,[9] which helped to popularize birthing centers and midwives (again). Thanks to the invention of Doppler ultrasound technology (the first 3-D image of a baby in utero was taken in 1986), parents were able to hear and see their baby's heartbeat in utero.[10] It wasn't until the 1990s that fetal ultrasounds became routine to find out the gender and check development.

It's crazy to think how much technological growth in pregnancy monitoring has occurred in one generation. I was born in 1982, four years before the first 3-D ultrasounds were taken in utero. By the time I was pregnant with Everett in 2013, I could have gone to a mall and done a full photo session in 4-D of my baby in utero.

From 1900 through 1997, the maternal mortality rate declined nearly 99 percent, according to the CDC. In the 2000s, the majority of women still gave birth in hospitals, but the percent of women who gave birth outside of hospitals began to slightly rise to about 2 percent.[11] Maternal death rates also increased for the first time in decades, even though the risk was still extremely low (13 deaths per 100,000 white women). Researchers blamed the higher rate on more C-sections being performed and the rising obesity rate—although the motherhood maternal rate was so low that an accounting error could be to blame. Several states changed the way they documented death certificates, which was enough to show that the maternal death rate was on the rise.[12]

It's important to note the disparity of motherhood mortality rates between white and black women; the latter are three times as likely to die from pregnancy or childbirth-related causes, which is a staggering tragedy.[13] NPR points to several reasons: Black women are less likely to have health insurance, they are more likely to give birth in lower quality hospitals than white mothers due to historical segregation, and they are more likely to be discriminated against in hospitals.[14] It doesn't matter if they're educated and affluent or even a celebrity. Serena Williams nearly died from a pulmonary embolism a couple days after giving birth to her daughter. She tells *Vogue* that she had to demand the medical care she needed.[15] "I was like, listen to Dr. Williams!" she says.

## What Does Natural Childbirth Even Mean?

In short: Nothing. *Natural* is a made-up word that sounds healthy, but it is not regulated and could mean whatever you want it to mean. Nobody chooses "natural dentistry" and refuses Novocain for a root canal. So when people ask, "Did you give birth naturally or via C-section?" you should reply, "Do you mean vaginally or via C-section?" I think people are just too squeamish to say *vaginally,* which is kind of silly. #ReclaimVaginally. No? You don't want to start that hashtag? Fair enough. But just know: There is no unnatural way to give birth. If you had a baby, you gave birth.

## Why It's Okay to Get an Epidural

Not surprisingly, epidurals have changed over the years. In the late 1800s, a German surgeon injected cocaine into spinal cords.[16] By

1909, doctors used Novocain, which made the procedure safer. (Surprise!) In the 1980s, patients were given the option to administer their own doses. In 2018, women were given a quarter of the dose they received even thirty years ago, Dr. Stephen Halpern, an obstetric anesthesiologist in Toronto, told LiveScience.[17]

Today, about 60 percent of women use epidurals during childbirth, but some still feel guilty. We shouldn't, though. Getting an epidural does not affect baby's health, according to multiple studies. They won't be more lethargic, thus score lower on the test administered right after birth, which most people know as the Apgar test (the letters stand for Appearance, Pulse, Grimace, Activity, and Respiration). Another controlled trial found no impact on breastfeeding, either.[18] Epidurals won't directly increase your chance of needing a C-section, according to multiple studies.[19]

Epidurals can slow down labor among first-time mothers, who took on average 5.5 hours to deliver vs. 3.5 hours without an epidural during the second stage of labor, when we're pushing the baby out.[20] One study of 6,000 women found that epidurals may increase your risk of having a vacuum or forcep delivery by 38 percent.[21] But your chance of having an instrumental delivery is dependent on lots of random things, such as where you live. In the South, up to 25 percent of women's babies are delivered with a vacuum or forceps. In the Northeast, it's less than 5 percent.[22]

Epidurals may lower mom's blood pressure, which can affect the baby's heart rate[23]—or could help if mom has preeclampsia (like I did), a disorder that causes mom's blood pressure to spike.

If the epidural needle punctures the wrong spot on your spine, you can get a spinal headache, which has been compared to "the worst hangover in the world."[24] Doctors were nervous this could have happened to me after I delivered Otto, as it took them multiple tries to get my epidural in. To prevent it, I got a "blood patch" in the recovery room, where blood was drawn from my arm and literally injected into my back, where the epidural catheter was still inserted. It didn't hurt; it felt kind of warm and weird.

If you need an emergency C-section and have an epidural inserted, you already have anesthesia, so you're less likely to go under general anesthesia.

You will likely need a catheter though, which means you may not be as mobile. (I loved not worrying about getting to the bathroom after giving birth as I recovered from my C-sections. Comic Ali Wong jokes about how much more she could achieve in her life if only she always had a catheter.)

If you search Dr. Google long enough (admit it, we're all guilty— even though I don't recommend it!), you'll find the occasional horrifying story of a mom who was paralyzed by an epidural. Usually it's one side of her body. It's so uncommon that doctors have trouble even finding a large enough sample size to measure. Risks of getting a spinal hematoma are 1 in 150,000 after epidural and 1 in 220,000 after a spinal block.[25] In other words, you're more likely to get struck by lightning over the course of your lifetime.[26] "Obviously any procedure could have a complication, but it's a safe procedure that's widely utilized," Dr. Sanford Lederman, chair of ob-gyn at New York–Presbyterian Brooklyn Methodist Hospital, tells me.

There's also the fear that epidurals hurt. I can tell you from experience that they're not too bad, especially if you're in the midst of a long labor. I was in screaming labor with Everett, got an epidural, and then took a nap. My friend Renee got an epidural, read a book, and then pushed out her daughter in a couple of minutes. My friend Laura arrived at the hospital too late to get an epidural when delivering her second child, but the experience taught her that she preferred to labor without one. She intentionally skipped an epidural for her third birth.

If you don't want an epidural, don't get one, and don't look back! You don't have to explain your decisions to anyone. If you want an epidural, go for it. There's no wrong decision regarding epidurals when it comes to your—or your baby's—health.

## Why C-Sections Are Demonized

Some 32 percent of births in the United States are via C-section.[27] There's a lot of hand-wringing over this statistic and attempts to lower it because of a World Health Organization recommendation that only 10 to 15 percent of births should be C-sections.[28] "But that's fake news," says Harvard's Dr. Tuteur. "A bunch of old white men decided that childbirth is 'better' when women experience it without pain relief, that vaginal birth is superior to Cesarean section, and that foolish women should be taught that the pain of childbirth is all in their heads."[29] Tuteur explains that a pediatrician named Dr. Marsden Wagner, who was the director of Women's and Children's Health for the WHO, convened a conference in 1985, where attendees declared the 10 to 15 percent was optimal with no evidence. (Wagner also wrote in a journal article criticizing the "global witch-hunt" against home birth.[30])

In 2015, Harvard and Stanford teamed up to study the 10 to 15 percent recommendation and found "C-section rates below 19 percent lead to preventable maternal and neonatal deaths." In other words, they show that the WHO's "'optimal' rate . . . is actually deadly," Tuteur writes.[31] "They also show that C-section rates above 19 percent are *not* harmful. There appears to be *no* increased risk of either maternal or neonatal mortality for rates as high as 55 percent."[32]

I certainly don't want to make it sound like a C-section is a walk in the park. I had two, and they were a tough recovery. I was so jealous of my little sister, who gave birth vaginally and easily walked up stairs just two days after giving birth, when it took me at least a couple of weeks to do the same without pain. In America, we demonize C-sections and then downplay the fact that they're major surgeries.

I'm guilty of doing it myself; when doctors ask me if I've ever had surgeries, I always say, "Just two C-sections," and they typically raise their eyebrows at me as if to say, "*Just* two major abdominal surgeries in two years?"

If you choose to have a C-section, you're opening yourself up to the possibility of surgical complications, but C-sections are generally very safe in America today. Tania* is petite with dark black wavy hair. She opted to have a C-section due to trauma she experienced in college during an abortion, when she felt powerless and overheard a doctor say, "Oh shit, we ripped her cervix."

"My OB is amazing. I never explained this to her in detail, but she knew I was getting increasingly more terrified by the day and she sensed there was a reason. At the end of the pregnancy, she tried to do an internal exam and I was so tensed up, she couldn't do it. So she offered a C-section as an option, with no pressure," Tania tells me. "In my opinion, her offer means she is a good doctor—able to look at the patient and pregnancy holistically and offer a solution tailored to *my* needs, not her personal opinion or what she 'should' do as a doctor. She knew labor and childbirth terrified me, which means it wasn't the best choice for me, period."

Tania—who, along with her husband, is now raising a three-year-old daughter who inherited her curls—has given a lot of thought to her decision, and doesn't regret it. "There are many reasons one might consider an elective C-section. Yes, all surgery comes with risk, but C-sections are also completely routine, not a new procedure, and surgery OBs can do it in their sleep," she says. "*Elective* projects the idea that it's a frivolous, shallow decision, but it also means *choice*. You're choosing it that way because it's your body. And the most important thing I learned from childbirth class is that women should be

---

* Any time you see a name with an asterisk, it has been changed to protect the privacy of the person sharing their story with me.

in charge of their birth experience—as long as they're not jeopardizing the health of themselves or their baby."

There are a lot of myths about C-sections. Let's break some of them down.

1. You won't be able to breastfeed if you deliver via C-section. *False*. The American Academy of Pediatrics[33] confirms the method of delivery has "little effect on your ability to nurse." Once the placenta is removed from a woman's body, whether it's squeezed out from her vagina or taken out by doctors in a C-section, the hormone that stimulates breast milk production spikes.[34] Stress can inhibit breast milk production, though, and the AAP says moms who are disappointed by giving birth via C-section may be more stressed, which in turn could affect their supply. The AAP also says doctors may be less likely to push breastfeeding on an exhausted mom who just labored for a long time and then had major surgery. I had two C-sections, and I successfully breastfed Everett for nearly sixteen months and Otto for nearly fifteen months. I even gave them formula the first few days of their lives (C-section recovery is no joke!), and then went on to exclusively breastfeed later. More on this later in the breastfeeding chapter.

2. C-sections deprive your baby of helpful bacteria. *It's too soon to tell.* Some experts believe that a full-term baby has a sterile gut and is then "seeded" with mom's bacteria via her vaginal canal on delivery. That bacteria supposedly helps develop the baby's immune system and gastrointestinal tract and may reduce inflammation later on. I examined research on this, and it seems that not much is known definitively.[35] Scientists are starting to debunk the "sterile gut" theory, speculating that fetuses may be exposed to mom's bacterial DNA by drinking

45

amniotic fluid in utero. Doctors examined a bunch of babies who had varying bacterial flora right after they were born, but their bacteria was pretty much the same by the time they turned one. The study also says it's "naïve" to think that babies are only exposed to mom's bacteria in her vaginal canal. Babies have "constant exposure to vaginal flora" after mom's water breaks, which often happens during labor before a C-section. Some parents are "seeding" their own babies born via C-section. A piece of saline-soaked gauze is put into a woman's vagina an hour before her surgery. After the baby is delivered, her partner (or I guess a really good friend?) removes it and swabs it all over the newborn's face, eyes, and inside his mouth. "My doctor had never heard of it, but thought it sounded like a great idea," says Charlotte,* who felt guilty that her firstborn suffered from a dry skin condition called eczema—which some friends told her might have been caused by C-section birth.[36] (Science debunks this.) So she was determined to "seed" her second baby to try to prevent eczema. The process "seems to disturb the nurses quite a bit," Dr. Philippe Girerd, an ob-gyn with the Virginia Commonwealth University Medical Center and a member of the Vaginal Microbiome Consortium, noted with a laugh to Yahoo! Parenting. "If it's happening passively [in the birth canal], nobody really thinks about it. But when you do it with forceps and gauze, it makes some people very uncomfortable." Doctors advised against seeding in 2017,[37] saying there was just one rigorous study of the process that involved only four babies, and that risks were high of passing on STDs and streptococcus. "If someone tries to deliver vaginally and is allowed to labor long enough for the membranes to rupture [meaning the water has broken], then that's better than seeding," says Dr. Girerd.

3. C-sections raise your baby's risk of asthma and allergies. *Well, it depends on your definition of risk.* One study found that having a C-section may increase your child's risk of having asthma from 1.1 to 1.3 percent.[38] Which is incredibly small, let's be honest. The same study also said that breastfeeding for six months could negate the increased risk. Two other major studies found no correlation between C-sections and asthma.[39] Some say the risk may be *slightly* higher (we're talking 1.18 percent vs. 1.33 percent) for children born via planned C-section vs. unplanned C-section because the baby may have had more access to mom's vaginal bacteria if she went into labor first. (But, as we saw in myth No. 2, more research is still needed to determine exactly how vaginal bacteria affects autoimmune disorders and gut growth.) There's also a report that women who have asthma are more likely to deliver babies via C-section, leading to some speculation that asthma could cause moms to be predisposed to C-sections. There's also the "hygiene hypothesis,"[40] which speculates that kids today grow up in an "overly clean environment," which can raise a kid's risk for autoimmune issues like asthma and allergy—regardless of how they were born. So, this is the answer: The risk is low and the connection unproven. If you need a C-section, it's not going to hurt your kid.

4. C-sections make your kid obese. *False.* A study of more than 16,000 siblings,[41] one born via C-section and the other born vaginally, showed no difference in weight at age five. The study results "suggest that unmeasured variables—lifestyle or sociocultural factors—might account for the observed associations that were seen in other studies," lead author Sheryl L. Rifas-Shiman, a research analyst at Harvard Medical School, told the *New York Times*.[42] "Reducing C-section delivery rates will not have a big effect on the ongoing obesity epidemic."

5. Once a C-section, Always a C-section. *False*. Research shows that women who attempt a vaginal birth after Cesarean, known as a VBAC, have a 60 to 80 percent success rate.[43] Talk to your doctor, and also find out if the hospital where he or she delivers allows them. When I asked my doctor if I should attempt a VBAC for Otto, she asked me a critical question: If I were in labor for twenty-four hours and *then* had surgery, which was how I gave birth to Everett, how would I feel about that? I told her I'd be so angry at myself for not scheduling a C-section. That's when I decided to schedule my second birth. (Even though I went into labor anyway before my C-section.) If the answer to my doctor's question was, "I'd be happy I at least tried to deliver vaginally," then an attempted VBAC would have been right for me. As long as your doctor identifies no other risk factors, then it's your personal preference!

## Is It Okay to Deliver at Home?

Perhaps you've seen the headlines screaming that births outside of hospitals are *on the rise*. Technically this is true, but they've gone from 1 percent to about 1.5 percent of all births in the United States from 2004 to 2014.[44]

Beth has short red hair and a kind inquisitiveness that makes her easy to befriend. She knew she wanted to give birth at home ever since she briefly dated a woman in her twenties who was training to be a midwife. "She showed me all these birth videos she had from school, and she said something to me I never forgot: The majority of us grow up having seen videos of somebody being killed, but never witness a birth. She was the first one who really made me think about how this culture views birth. It's not integrated into normal life, and it's fucking life!" Beth told me over the phone from her downtown Manhattan office, where she's a senior editor at a big website. "We sat there and watched these home birth videos, and I was overwhelmed. It was the most beautiful thing I've ever seen. When I gave birth, I wanted it to be homey and intense like that. So I filed that away."

Fast forward a decade, and Beth, now married, attended her sister-in-law's home birth. "She had a pool in her beautiful house, and it was the most amazing, peaceful thing I've ever witnessed. That was right about the same time as Ricki Lake's *The Business of Being Born* was released, and it was all coming together for me. Before that movie, I thought, *How am I going to have a home birth in a tiny apartment?* I thought I needed a big house with flowing curtains!" Beth laughs. "But then I watched the movie, and thought, *How much room do you really need? How big is a hospital room?*"

When Beth got pregnant at thirty-eight, she and her wife began interviewing midwives and fell in love with a certified nurse midwife named Miriam, who had more than twenty years of experience delivering babies. "She would come do prenatal checkups at our apartment. She didn't have an office," Beth recalls, adding that she did go to the hospital for the anatomy scan, which is typically done around twenty weeks. The hospital she chose, located in Manhattan's Greenwich Village neighborhood, was known for being "midwife friendly."

Beth and Kiki's daughter, Lula, came eleven days early. "It was really late at night. I got up to pee and my water broke. I remember my midwife said not to panic when my water breaks, but I was texting her," Beth says. The next morning, Beth and Kiki went out to breakfast and took a walk around Central Park, ending up in a playground. "I was having contractions pretty far apart still. I remember sitting in that playground thinking, *Oh my God, we're going to be coming here soon.* It was so foreign to be sitting in a playground."

Later in the afternoon, as the contractions got more intense, Beth and Kiki called Miriam the midwife and their good friend George, who had attended birthing classes with them and wanted to be present. "I got in the shower. It was the only place that felt good. I was standing under hot water and freaking out and starting to lose it. George and Kiki were trying to inflate the tub, and I could hear them cursing and freaking out. They were having all this trouble. And then I look up and Miriam was there. Once Miriam was there, it all chilled out and it all came together.

"I think I was in labor for eighteen hours, and three were really fucking hard and then forty minutes were hell," Beth says. It never crossed her mind to go to a hospital or ask for pain meds. "There was no epidural in the house, first of all. I was too late," she jokes. "I was very psychologically prepared for having pain and going through it. It wasn't fun, that pain, but I knew there was a purpose to it, that there would be a really amazing ending, and I felt really powerful. And I am someone who does not have a high tolerance for pain. I go get my lip waxed and want to kill myself! But this was just different. Giving birth to a human is gonna hurt, sorry, there's a head coming out of your vagina. I was okay. I didn't like it, but I knew it was going to be over soon, and I handled it. I was surprised at how awesome I handled it."

Beth remembers her birth as "this odd party with Me and Kiki and George, and our midwife, who we loved. The sun was going down, and I was sitting in the pool, and just kind of chatting between contractions. It was right before the presidential election, so we were talking about politics. We'd be having a really good conversation and then all of the sudden I'd have a painful contraction and Miriam would talk me through it and George would stick an ice pop in my mouth. It was so beautiful. Everyone was taking care of me, and it was exactly what I wanted. I know I'm lucky because you can plan until you're blue in the face, and it doesn't always work out that way."

If the birth was not going smoothly, Beth says she would have accepted Miriam sending her to a hospital. "She was my Sherpa! She was guiding me. She knew, and I trusted her implicitly. I think that's really important: To trust your caregiver. Sometimes I feel angry with friends or people I know who tell stories about being mistreated about caregivers and shrugging about it. Maybe call it a judgment or not, but it makes me angry when women—when people—don't think that they deserve to be treated well. When someone tells me their doctor is being borderline abusive, then you need to leave that doctor! Treat yourself better, you deserve it!"

After the baby arrived, they were all completely in awe and quiet. Beth and Kiki sang a song they'd been singing throughout Beth's pregnancy, "Good Morning Starshine" from *Hair*. And then they suddenly remembered to check out the baby's gender; they'd had a girl, whom they named Lula. "We kept her attached to her umbilical cord, then Kiki cut the umbilical cord, and I rinsed off in the shower while Miriam did all the tests you do on a baby." Kiki, Beth, and Lula all climbed into bed together, and George made pasta. "It was the best bowl of pasta I've ever eaten. We all just sat together and snuggled. Lula found my nipple right away and started nursing. It was amazing." The next day, George and Kiki cleaned and drained the giant bathtub that consumed the entire living room of their Upper West Side apartment, and then returned it to the Hasidic Jewish woman who rents them from her Brooklyn home.

Beth's decision to give birth at home was met with resistance by her mother's "sheer terror" over the prospect. Beth remembers questioning women who told her they would be too afraid to give birth at home. "The judgment really comes out of you," she says astutely. "I've become so much less judgmental as Lula has grown. I think a lot of that [judgment] must come from an insecurity because, when you're a new parent, you're obviously going to be more insecure. You're going to want to see people reflecting what you believe because then it strengthens your position. Now I'm just like, 'Whatever.'"

Today, Lula is a thoughtful ten-year-old—who still lives in the same New York City apartment where she was born. ("She's so sick of her birth story, it's ridiculous," Beth laughs.) Beth often writes stories about birth, including profiling women who had home births in Alabama, where it was illegal until 2017.[45]

The chasm between doctors and midwives, who view each other with suspicion, "is stupid," Beth says. "You both have different sets of skills and knowledge, and they're all worthy. Why not combine them all and give women the best outcome, in the manner she desires? OBs aren't going anywhere, they're not going to be put out of business by the small percentage of the population that wants to [home birth]. I don't understand the anger and bullying and pushback that goes on."

Giving birth at home is riskier. The chance of infant mortality is very low regardless of where you give birth, but it does slightly increase for home births: 2 in 1,000 vs. 0.9 in 1,000 for hospital births. But when things go wrong, they can go very wrong: Babies and moms can die if they can't get to the hospital in time.[46]

It's also interesting to note one demographic that is seeing a much higher spike in home births: non-Hispanic white women. In 2014, one in every forty-four births of a non-Hispanic white woman was at home.[47] Women who give birth at home are also more likely to be affluent, have higher college graduation rates, and are less likely to smoke. And 66 percent of the moms who delivered at home paid out of pocket, as many insurance companies will not pay for it due to risks.[48] (Beth's insurance covered her home birth.)

If you decide to give birth outside of the hospital, the most important thing is that you have a low-risk pregnancy. In fact, after the British National Health Service recommended that low-risk mothers might be better off giving birth outside of hospitals, an editorial in the *New England Journal of Medicine* agreed.[49]

"We're taking excellent care of high-risk women," Harvard Medical School's Dr. Neel Shah, who wrote the *New England Journal of Medicine* editorial, told NPR, "and leaving low-risk, normal women behind. We're the only country on Earth with a rising maternal mortality rate."[50]

The American College of Obstetricians and Gynecologists supports laboring with a midwife instead of a doctor but does not recommend home birth. It argues that women get better and earlier prenatal care in the United Kingdom thanks to their universal healthcare system, while many women in the United States don't have access to doctors. (The rates vary greatly depending on your race; just 4 percent of white women don't receive prenatal care, while 10 percent of black women don't.[51]) And in the United Kingdom, doctors and midwives work closely together, and women who need more specialized care are seamlessly handed off to an OB.

Whereas in the United States, "it seems there are midwives on one side and obstetricians on the other—and there's this opposition," Yinka Sokunbi, who worked as a midwife in London before her husband was transferred to Dallas, tells NPR.[52] Indeed, in the United States, only 9 percent of births are attended to by a midwife, whether it's in a hospital or not.[53] (Beth wrote a story about the documentary *The Mama Sherpas*, which explores "the middle ground between the two extremes [of home birth and doctor-led hospital birth]," as Brigid Maher, the film's director, explained to her.[54] "Not only does it show the diversity of how midwifery is practiced within the hospital system, but [it shows] the diversity of births you can have, which is incredibly important and empowering for women to see. It can help normalize our views about the birthing process, which we often think of as terrifying—and it doesn't have to be that way.")

When you dig into the data, you see that low-risk pregnancies have pretty good outcomes at home. So if you have a low-risk pregnancy and you want to give birth at home and your medical providers agree, then go for it! But don't convince yourself to give birth at home because some headline told you to.

"Women who plan to have their babies at home aren't really like women who plan to give birth in a hospital. Home-birth women tend to be rich, highly educated, and white. Babies born to women in this group are less likely to die regardless of where they are born, so it's misleading to compare them to a random sample of babies born in the hospital," Oster writes in *Expecting Better*.[55] "The women who actually *end up* giving birth at home are those who have such an easy birth that they don't end up as part of the 30 percent who go to the hospital. So of course if you compare women who have their babies at home to other women, they will almost always look like their babies do better, but that's *very* misleading."

＊

There's a movement called "free birthing," where women give birth without any medical professionals present whatsoever—including midwives, doulas, doctors, and nurses. Sometimes the laboring moms are completely alone. Lifetime even created a reality TV show to document this, called *Born in the Wild*, which they described as "what happens when the craziest experience of a woman's life becomes truly wild." The Free Birth Society Facebook page had more than 13,000 followers—but, as I was writing this book, the group moved off Facebook after its founder faced criticism for Facebook messaging with a laboring mom who delivered a stillborn baby.

Medical professionals do not recommend free birth. In 1983, the CDC partnered with the Indiana State Department of Health to study members of the Faith Assembly congregation, a religious group that refused medical treatment. Babies born to members of this congregation were ninety-seven times more likely to die, and laboring mothers were three times more likely to die than the state's general population.[56]

Giving birth was once very dangerous. While it's now much safer, it's not completely without risk. That's why it's important to trust whichever caregiver you choose, whether that's a doctor or a certified nurse midwife, who is a registered nurse who gets further training in delivering babies. And you should keep an open mind. If you trust your medical provider, you will trust her when she says you need to change course in the middle of laboring.

"I just feel lucky, and really grateful that I had the birth that I did. When I tell the story, sometimes it's so magical and perfect that it could be annoying to someone," Beth says. "I totally understood that it could have not gone that way. I'm so lucky about that. I want every woman to have the birth that they want."

\*

My second birth was completely different than my first one. When I was pregnant with Everett, I had doubts about my doctor but I didn't listen to that inner voice. After all, I'd been seeing her for my annual pap smear for eight years. But that once yearly visit is very different than the frequent prenatal appointments. We soon clashed over everything. She was overbearing and kept testing me again and again—apparently refusing to believe that a woman who was 5-foot 2-inches could birth a baby who was measuring big. (Even though I was nine pounds, six ounces at birth, and my husband was more than eight pounds.) She wrote off my weight gain as laziness; I was diagnosed with the life-threatening disorder preeclampsia (which causes swelling) by another doctor in her practice. When my blood pressure spiked, she admitted me to the hospital and induced me, but she wouldn't let me have a say in any part of my labor. I remember fighting with her over the phone at 11 p.m. one night, as I lay in bed with contractions. She wanted to give me something called magnesium sulfate, which I did not want, because it meant I could not move around throughout my entire labor.

"You can't turn this down. Unless of course you want a stillborn baby," she told me—which is arguably the worst thing you can tell a laboring woman, and terrible bedside manner. After twenty-four hours of labor and three hours of pushing, I got a C-section. My veins were collapsing because my blood was drawn every two hours due to the magnesium sulfate, all throughout the night, so I got no sleep and was in a ton of pain. I had to be taken off that medicine because it was making my blood "toxic." I felt completely belittled, ignored, and afraid my entire labor.

When I brought Everett to my postnatal checkup six weeks after giving birth, I was chastised for "making patients uncomfortable" by breastfeeding in the waiting room, written a prescription for birth control, and sent on my way fuming. I later ordered my surgical report from the hospital and discovered I was actually diagnosed with HELLP syndrome, which is a rare disorder that can lead to seizures and increases the risk of death in childbirth.[57] Would have been nice for my doctor to discuss this with me instead of just yelling at me about how I need to give birth.

For my second pregnancy and birth, I made a conscious decision to join a practice that was known for being more laid-back. OBs and certified nurse midwives work side by side and deliver in the local hospital. I decided I still wanted another C-section, with their help, and they completely supported me. I trusted all the doctors in the practice, and my second delivery could not have been any more different. I scheduled my surgery for a Tuesday morning. I planned to spend the weekend before doing laundry and getting my home ready for a new baby. On Friday night, my water broke as I stepped out of the shower at 11 p.m., but it was a trickle, not a gush, and I was in denial. "Well, I guess we'll know in a couple hours!" I nervously laughed to myself as I climbed into bed. At 3 a.m., I woke up in intense labor. I decided I was going to walk around my house until 6 a.m., when it would be easier to get childcare for Everett, and then we could all head to the hospital. My body clearly had other ideas, and I had to wake up Brad by 3:30 a.m. because I knew the baby was coming. At 4 a.m., Brad convinced our downstairs neighbors to come upstairs and sleep on our couch to care for Everett when he woke up, and then we headed to the hospital.

By the time I got to the hospital, I was seven centimeters dilated. (You typically give birth at ten centimeters dilated.) I was fully dilated by the time my doctor showed up (thanks for coming at 6 a.m. on a Saturday morning, Dr. G!). He asked me one last time if I wanted to try to VBAC, I said no, and off we went to the OR. The mood was so much lighter the second time. Even though I was having so many contractions that it was hard for the epidural to be inserted, the doctor was making jokes and before we knew it, Otto was born at a whopping nine pounds, six ounces!

What's the difference between Tessa's, Beth's, and my stories? Empowerment and the trust we had for our caregivers. When we trust and respect our caregivers and believe they have our best interest in mind, then we feel more in control of how we give birth. "No one should have to feel sad about" the way they give birth, Beth says. But we set up language and parameters for ourselves, such as "caving" to an epidural when that wasn't in our original "birth plan."

**#NoShameParenting Takeaway:** Let go of all the judgment and shame that surrounds childbirth in American culture. Speak up when you feel unnerved or scared. Make an informed decision that feels comfortable for you. Feel free to make a birth plan, but be flexible in the moment. As long as you have a licensed medical provider whom you trust, and you both have an open mind about how you give birth—you're not going to fuck up your kid. Doesn't matter if you have an epidural or not, a C-section or not, or even if you swab vaginal bacteria all over your newborn.

## Protein Is Protein:
## Breastfeeding, Formula, and Why It Doesn't
## Really Matter Which One You Choose

One of the biggest battle lines in the so-called mommy wars is between formula and breastfeeding. Mothers who give their children formula are shamed for supposedly depriving their children and not fulfilling their "roles as women." Some women become martyrs to the idea of breast milk as "liquid gold," and they pump and breastfeed no matter the cost, both monetary and physical. Women who embrace breastfeeding and choose to continue it past a year are then judged again for being freakish or having attachment issues. I've personally been the martyr (screaming at a TSA agent who ruined my pumped milk while traveling on a business trip) and judged (starting with a lecture in a shopping mall bathroom when my baby was three weeks old). By my second kid, I had a much more relaxed attitude toward breastfeeding and had no problem making it to fifteen months, when Otto weaned himself.

My friend Donna, who interviews celebrities for a living, struggled with breastfeeding before finally giving her son formula. "I made myself crazy. Actually, I owe an apology to the word crazy. I, in fact, became deranged with guilt," she wrote in an essay on Today.com.[1] "Every time someone asked if I was breastfeeding, I launched into my harangue: 'I tried so hard, but he was tongue-tied and never latched and I had no milk and I pumped and pumped but nothing came out or at least maybe just an ounce and he's such a big baby and so I finally had to resort to formula.'

"To overcompensate for being a working mom who excelled at interviews with Meryl Streep and Brad Pitt but who was a flop at feeding her son, I spent hours at farmers markets buying certified organic produce, which I would then meticulously steam and turn into baby food—saved only in glass containers, due to BPA fears. His sheets were fair-trade organic cotton. As were his clothes. I fixated on everything but what mattered—spending intimate time with my husband, who was undergoing chemotherapy for brain cancer, and our son."

Donna says her obsession with balancing out what she perceived to be negative effects of formula would have gone on indefinitely if her ob-gyn had not called her out on it. "She commented on what a big, healthy baby Alex was, and asked how feedings were going. I immediately kicked into my prepared remarks, not even catching my breath as I ranted apologetically about why I was such a failure as a mother, despite the breasts that should be performing their milk-producing function. She told me to please take a breath and calm down. 'Donna, do you have access to clean drinking water? Do you have access to quality formula? Is your son thriving? You'll be fine. Stop beating yourself up and enjoy your time with your baby.'"

Donna is one of the many, many parents obsessed with the idea of breastfeeding their child. Endless headlines quote the benefits of breast milk. Government health organizations tout it—even through they're often citing questionable studies or making up recommendations out of thin air or based on people who live in very different societies than the modern American. (A recommendation for a mom who lives in rural Africa without access to clean water should be different than one for a mom in a first-world country like the United States. Yet, it's not.) The world seems to be screaming: Breastfeeding is easy, it's natural, it's not a big deal, it'll make your kid smarter, slimmer, less asthmatic, and overall a better human! But this message is at odds with one of the biggest myths in early parenting: That breastfeeding is easy.

*

In popular art and television and on social media, you see beautiful women simply lifting their baby to their breast with little to no hassle. Take Gisele Bündchen's infamous photo on Instagram that showed her seamlessly breastfeeding her one-year-old daughter while simultaneously getting her hair blown out, makeup applied, and nails manicured. So glamorous! So effortless! It was liked more than 166K times and received more than 6,340 comments.[2] (Later even she admitted she "had all this horrible, self imposed guilt" about her parenting choices, perfect Instagram photos be damned.[3])

The reality is that breastfeeding is painful at first. It takes practice to figure out how to latch your baby to your breast, and it's hard to focus when said baby is screaming of hunger and you're too tired to think straight or you have other kids to care for. Moms who master the latch then get one curveball after another thrown at them: If they work outside the home, they may have to return to work relatively quickly, depending on their company's leave policy (and the majority of working moms return to work before the AAP's recommendation of exclusive breastfeeding for six months).[4] It's really hard to breastfeed when you're not around your baby all day. Breast milk is based on supply and demand, so your supply dwindles fast when there's no demand. A lot of companies don't have comfortable designated areas for women to pump, even though the Affordable Care Act requires businesses with more than fifty employees to provide space.[5] You might think twice about giving your baby milk that you pumped while balancing on a toilet in a bathroom stall. And not many women have the kinds of jobs that allow them to take an hour out of their workday every single day to pump. Moms are also shamed for daring to show a breast in public while feeding their baby, so some do not leave their homes for the first months of their children's lives. Cue loneliness and depression mixed with guilt and shame.

But breastfeeding is worth it, we tell ourselves, because the studies say our kids will have higher IQs, they're less likely to be obese or have asthma, less likely to get sick, and on and on. So we feel terrible about giving our kids formula, as if we're depriving them of all those benefits. We suck it up and pump even if it jeopardizes our job security or sanity. We clean all those little pump parts multiple times a day, even if we're stressed and exhausted.

*

It doesn't have to be this way. I've dug into many of the studies and spoken to some of the researchers behind them, and I can tell you this: The benefits of breastfeeding may not be as vast as experts would lead you to believe.

A researcher named Michael Kramer came up with a smart idea to study breastfeeding on a large scale. He found a group of mothers in Belarus who already breastfed and strongly encouraged half of them to continue breastfeeding exclusively. He didn't intervene at all with the second group, the control group. The group that was encouraged to breastfeed longer did in fact breastfeed longer than the control group.

The study found statistically insignificant differences in weight, ear infections, allergies, or blood pressure in the babies who were breastfed longer versus those who were not.

Kramer did discover that the babies who were breastfed longer were 40 percent less likely to have a gastrointestinal infection.[6] Yes, you read that right: Breastfeeding could lead to one less tummy bug. Maybe!

Kramer summed up his findings this way: "Studies about the benefits of breastfeeding are extremely difficult and complex because of who breastfeeds and who doesn't," referring to the socioeconomic and educational differences between who tends to breastfeed or not.

The CDC reported in 2013 that 92 percent of mothers with a college degree have tried breastfeeding, compared to less than 70 percent of mothers with less than a high school degree. At the six-month mark, 70 percent of women who earned 600 percent of the federal poverty level income—a salary of about $117,000 or above for a family of three[7]—were still breastfeeding. Only 38 percent of women living at the poverty level, which is less than $20,000 for a family of three, were still breastfeeding at six months.[8] Knowing that only a certain privileged population has access to breastfeeding, Kramer has said: "There have been claims that it prevents everything—cancer, diabetes. A reasonable person would be cautious about every new amazing discovery."

The reason it's so hard to study breastfeeding is because of ethics issues, as is the case with most research related to parenting. It's unethical for researchers to tell parents what to feed their newborns—so most science focuses on just comparing the differences between giant groups of breastfed vs. non-breastfed kids. And then you've got the ever-present correlation vs. causation issue. Just because 100 kids wear blue shirts and glasses does not mean wearing blue shirts makes your eyesight worse.

Okay, you might argue, the kids in the study above got *some* breast milk, so maybe that's why there was no difference. What about kids who got no breast milk? Economists Eirik Evenhouse and Siobhan Reilly wanted to find out. They studied 523 biological siblings with one major difference: One was breastfed and one wasn't. These siblings had the same parents with the same education level, environment, parenting styles, and socioeconomic situation. The caveat: You couldn't rule out *why* the parents stopped breastfeeding between siblings. The mom could have had breast cancer or some other traumatic experience—but, even if the family did undergo a hypothetical rough period, it didn't seem to affect the kids in any way. Researchers found no difference in levels of intelligence, diabetes, asthma, allergies, childhood obesity, or mother-child bonding between the siblings who had been breastfed vs. the ones who had not. They declared in their 2005 paper that the "long-term effects of breast-feeding have been overstated."[9]

Still don't believe me? I get it: There are so many voices telling you to breastfeed, and the idea that the benefits have more to do with your life than the liquid that comes out of mom's boobs seems unbelievable.

Let's take a closer look at the kind of woman who is most likely to breastfeed in America these days. She tends to have enough money to take an unpaid leave from work to focus on her new baby. This means she probably has a partner who contributes cash to their household, making her more affluent. Having a partner means she also has somebody to support her emotionally and split childcare with, making for a less stressed mom. If she works, she tends to be employed in a white-collar job, meaning she probably has a higher salary and relatively stable hours and the kind of freedom to step away from her desk multiple times a day to pump for twenty to thirty minutes a pop. Because she likely doesn't work multiple shift jobs with unpredictable hours, she probably has more time to spend engaging with her newborn, reading books, and creating routines. She can afford higher-quality childcare with engaged caregivers, or she can stay home to care for her child herself. As Corinne Purtill and Dan Kopf put it in *Quartz,* "Well-off parents have access to the infrastructure that supports breastfeeding . . . and—perhaps most importantly—immersion in a culture that unconsciously views breastfeeding as a desirable status symbol and pressures them to continue to that hallowed six-month mark and well beyond."[10]

To put it bluntly: Our society gives rich, educated, married moms more opportunities to have smarter, healthier babies no matter what they feed them.

But wait, you might say, "There's no way I'd consider myself affluent. I can't afford a nanny or the nicest Montessori daycare in my neighborhood. My kid plays with plastic toys instead of wood ones. I work a lot of hours and always feel stressed out." Yes, I hear you and empathize. But let's put this in perspective. Parents who are juggling multiple jobs to pay the bills are more likely to use formula because they don't have the time to breastfeed. And when you look at their kids as a giant group—not individually—they may have some health or educational setbacks anyway. It has nothing to do with the lack of breast milk, and everything to do with how busy their parents are just trying to survive the day-to-day of a chaotic life. And honestly, most of these kids will be okay too. I grew up in a home where the electricity bill often got paid late, with no food on the table and sometimes uninvolved parents, and I turned out fine. If you are struggling to make ends meet, as so many families are, that doesn't mean your kid will grow up to be dumb and unhealthy. It just means that society is set up to make raising kids harder for you. (The best way to solve this issue is to vote.)

"Although it is true that children who were breastfed as babies have higher intelligence than bottle-fed children, the reason for the correlation is in the mother's brain, not her breast," two neuroscientists wrote in *Bloomberg View*. "A U.S. mother whose IQ is fifteen points higher than her neighbor's is more than twice as likely to breastfeed. Women who breastfeed are also more educated and less likely to smoke. Intelligent parents pass along their genes and also create a more stimulating environment, two advantages for the baby's development. In short, smart mothers have smart babies."[11]

Knowing all this, it seems like a lot of stress, pumping, bloody nipples, and expense with only marginally improved health outcomes for your kid, huh?

\*

The point of my telling you this is not to convince you to buy formula. It's to play devil's advocate the next time somebody tries to make you feel bad about the way you feed your baby.

I actually loved breastfeeding my two sons. I breastfed Everett for sixteen months, and Otto for fifteen months. I think it was a great way for us to cuddle after we'd been apart all day while I was at work. (Although we could just as easily have cuddled while I held a bottle.) It helped me lose the baby weight because it can burn up to 700 extra calories a day, according to a doctor on the board of the American Pregnancy Association.[12] This also helped me continue to eat the chocolate croissants I had gobbled with abandon while pregnant. (Um . . . and led to me gaining ten pounds within a couple weeks of weaning my firstborn!) I liked having a couple quiet moments to myself to pump and think about my kids over the course of the workday, which made the separation less painful, especially when I first returned to my job after maternity leave. My friend Alex occasionally FaceTimed with her son and his nanny as she pumped at work. Also, taking time for myself was rare, even if it had to occur while I was naked from the waist up at my office, with vacuum tubes attached to my breasts. (A rookie mistake is wearing a dress while pumping, as then you are literally sitting in only your underwear at work. Only do this if you have a very secure lock on your pumping room or office!) When I was breastfeeding my kids, it was often the only time they stopped moving around, especially when they were a little older.

There are plenty of considerations to keep in mind if you decide to breastfeed. We tend to only think about how it affects our children. We don't think about how it affects our relationships. I'm not talking about breast behavior during sex (yes, orgasm can trigger a "let down," which is the term for when breast milk flows). I'm talking about the power shift that can occur when mom breastfeeds—even if you have a very modern relationship and split household duties down the middle. Both parents, regardless of sex, can do laundry. Both can wash dishes. But usually only the woman who gave birth can breastfeed children.

So suddenly there is one very important task that only mom can do:

Feed the child. In those blurry, early months, breastfeeding is one of the ways to calm down a crying baby. A baby doesn't realize what time it is, or that mom just sat down to eat dinner. A baby is hungry, and so mom is at the baby's beck and call 24/7. So the thinking goes—Why should dad wake up at 3 a.m. for that overnight feeding when you'll *both* just be exhausted the next day? It makes sense, but it can be infuriating in the moment, tipping the workload more heavily on mom's shoulders.

A solution that I adapted: I started pumping as soon as I brought Everett home from the hospital. My goal was enough milk for one bottle. (When they're newborns, that's hardly even two ounces.) My husband, Brad, then took over the 2 a.m. feeding using the pumped bottle, which gave me a longer stretch of sleep and made me a lot less resentful. A couple of months in, we sleep trained (more on that later!) so that nobody had to wake up overnight—and the extra milk from my daily pump went straight into the freezer, which gave me a small stash (and peace of mind) before going back to work.

That routine worked for my family. It takes a little bit of time to get a good routine if you decide to breastfeed, too. You have to figure out how to hold the kid in a way that feels comfortable and get past the first week or two of sensitive nipples. (Don't worry, they harden up, ha! And until then, slather on olive oil or Lansinoh cream.)

Some other benefits I found from breastfeeding:

It's easier to cart around just your boobs than formula and bottles. Because I'm raising my kids in the people's republic of Brooklyn, I rarely felt the need to bring one of those giant tit tents to cover up my breasts while feeding my kids. (My sister in Iowa, meanwhile, had some very cute patterned cover-ups because it made her feel more comfortable for baby No. 1. By baby No. 2, she ditched the scarves too.)

Breastfeeding also meant that there was one less thing I had to buy for my kid. One website calculated the cost of a year of "average" formula to be more than $1,700. Yet, many of the well-to-do parents I've encountered over the years special-ordered formula from Switzerland or Germany. I imagined their internal dialogue to be something like, "If I'm not going to breastfeed, I am going to buy the *fanciest, hardest-to-find* formula in existence." It wasn't available on Amazon or the local grocery store; instead, they'd order it in bulk and then sell off the extra on my local parent LISTSERV.

And let's be honest, few things calm a fussy baby faster than shoving a boob in his mouth. I can't tell you how many adult conversations I've had, and how many conference calls I've attended (laptop camera strategically facing up), while breastfeeding one of my kids. Breastfeeding is fast, it's always available, the milk comes out warm.

Breastfeeding was also a great way to get my infant sons to nap. When I was still on maternity leave, I'd let them nap with a boob in their mouth while I'd online shop on my phone or watch TV. And I often breastfed them to sleep when they were really little too.

So, there you go: There are plenty of benefits to breastfeeding. They're just not ones that will affect your kid's life for the better or worse.

*

There is another option that a doctor never brought up with me: Why not combine breastfeeding and formula feeding? You could breastfeed in the morning and night and formula feed during the day so you don't have to pump at work. Your supply will adjust. After Otto turned one year old, I started pumping just twice a day instead of three times. A couple months after that, I stopped pumping altogether at work. I breastfed in the morning and evening, and Otto drank my freezer stash during the day. On the weekends, I picked up breastfeeding again when we were together all day, and my supply adjusted in real time.

There was one period when I gave both my kids formula: The days after they were born. Which seems sacrilegious, seeing how everyone will scream at you that that's when you establish your milk supply. (I know parents who won't even give their kids pacifiers until they're a couple weeks old because they don't want to supposedly screw up their supplies by giving their kids something else to suck on other than a breast.)

After Otto was born, I asked my nurse, a thin brunette originally from Israel, if my son could sleep overnight with her in the nursery while I recovered from my C-section. "Should I bring Otto to you to breastfeed overnight?" Chaya* asked. "No, just give him formula," I said, not even knowing if I had enough energy to get out of bed to use the bathroom, let alone feed my newborn all night long.

Record screech. "I'll need a prescription for that," she told me. "I'll get a doctor to sign off."

Hold up. Since when is formula illegal? I mean, its hefty price should be against the law, but why was this nurse shaming me hours after a doctor cut through seven layers of skin and muscle to remove a nine-pound, six-ounce baby from my abdomen?

Luckily, I was a second-time mom by this point. I swiftly informed the nurse that I'd given my first son formula overnight in the hospital and then went on to breastfeed exclusively for sixteen more months. She acquiesced, Otto had formula for two nights, and I got two nights of sleep while recovering from major surgery before returning home to care for both my newborn and 2.5-year-old.

Why is formula so villainized, after all? It's not like an alternative to mom's milk is a sudden, new need; wet nurses have been around since the dawn of time for women who were unable to breastfeed. (Even the Bible notes that Moses was fed via a wet nurse.[13]) Primitive bottles have been found in the graves of newborn infants as far back as 2000 BC.

Breastfeeding has fallen in and out of fashion throughout time, usually depending on the preferences of wealthy women. In 2000 BC, breastfeeding was considered a "religious obligation" so rates were high. By AD 950, women of status hired wet nurses. In the Middle

Ages, "breast milk was deemed to possess magical qualities," and use of wet nurses declined as "a mother nursing her own child was valued as a saintly duty." During the Renaissance, breastfeeding was once again out of vogue. "It was unusual for aristocratic women to breast-feed because the practice was considered unfashionable and because the women worried it would ruin their figures. Breastfeeding also prevented many women from wearing the socially acceptable cloth-ing of the time, and it interfered with social activities such as playing cards and attending theater performances. The wives of merchants, lawyers, and doctors also did not breastfeed because it was less ex-pensive to employ a wet nurse than it was to hire a woman to run their husband's business or take care of the household in their place," one medical journal explains.[14]

As the Industrial Revolution kicked off, families moved from rural to urban locations. Due to higher living costs, poor women started working to support their families—and it was impossible for them to breastfeed, so they started hiring wet nurses. Rich women then started breastfeeding again as a status symbol, and rumors were spread about wet nurses being distrustful. (To be fair, one of their favored home remedies, nicknamed "quietness," actually included opiates. But I doubt this was used only by wet nurses.)

Animal milk has always been used to feed newborns as well. The thinking that "breast is best" may have even stemmed from the knowledge that breast was *better* than the milk of cows, donkeys, or whatever other animal was around. This knowledge was determined in 1760. (Note to self: Medical advice has changed *a little* in the last couple centuries.)

Formula was invented in 1865. Less than twenty years later, there were more than twenty-seven brands. As doctors started to under-stand how germs spread, parents started refrigerating it and cleaning bottles, making formula-feeding safer. Companies started fortifying formula with vitamins and minerals. Doctors routinely recommended formula (and even sometimes just condensed milk) from the 1930s until the 1950s, when it was determined to be a more scientifically precise way to feed children. The breastfeeding rate plummeted to about 20 percent. (This is the same time hospitals knocked out women for twilight births and then bound their breasts to make their milk dry up.)

Also in the 1950s, a group of Catholic housewives who were members of the Christian Family Movement gathered in a suburban Chicago living room to fight for the right for women to stand up against formula, twilight births, and routine episiotomies. They called themselves La Leche League, *leche* meaning "milk" in Spanish. "You didn't mention *breast* in print unless you were talking about Jean Harlow," cofounder Edwina Froehlich has said.[15] They modeled themselves on Eve from the Bible (as they wrote in their first pamphlet called *The Womanly Art of Breastfeeding*, published in 1958: "Her baby came. The milk came. She nursed her baby.") and called breastfeeding "God's plan for mothers and babies." Pediatricians were usually "condescending, paternalistic, judgmental and non-informative" men who took away a mother's autonomy to make the best decisions for her body and baby, they said. "Everything we did was radical," says another cofounder, Mary Ann Cahill.

The group has evolved during the years in its recommendations. In the 1981 edition of their book, they implored women not to work: "Our plea to any mother who is thinking about taking an outside job is, 'if at all possible, don't.'" By 2004, the book ballooned to more than 400 pages, and the tone became more critical: "The experience of reading the 1958 edition is like talking with your bossy but charming neighbor, who has some motherly advice to share. Reading the latest edition is like being trapped in the office of a doctor who's haranguing you about the choices you make," writes Hanna Rosin in *The Atlantic*. Subsequent editions of the book also tout breast milk as an "arsenal against illness" without much proof.

I don't mean to hate on La Leche League, as I think they can be a great support group and help women who want to breastfeed. So many women have called on the group for help with breastfeeding or read their online resources for advice. Plus, if you live in a town that hosts in-person La Leche League meetings, they're a good place to meet other exhausted new parents. But I think it's important to know the group's religious roots, which can be a major source of judgment, especially for women. And that the tone of the group's literature has become increasingly judgy as more women enter the workforce and gain access to birth control, two factors that have earned women plenty of backlash from the patriarchy.

*

The point of this chapter is not to put formula on a pedestal. The baby food industry is a massive business worth $70 billion worldwide.[16] The CEO of the company that makes Enfamil formula gleefully informed shareholders in 2016 that breastfeeding rates have stopped growing as quickly as the "strengthening labor market and workforce participation rates."[17] In other words, more women going to work equals fewer women breastfeeding and more formula purchasing.

Formula has also been involved in a number of marketing practices that have killed babies around the world, most notably in third-world countries. In the 1970s, journalists exposed how Nestlé sent female salespeople dressed up as nurses into rural Africa to promote formula as cleaner and more desirable by sophisticated Western women. Without access to clean water and instruction on how to properly mix the formula, babies were malnourished and died.[18] (And still today it's estimated a million babies a year die due to reliance on formula in third-world countries. Parents either don't use enough powder because formula is so expensive and they're trying to conserve, or they mix the formula with contaminated water. "A baby who does not suckle loses the immunological protection that mother's milk provides against the bacterial assault of polluted water and primitive sanitation," The *New York Times* reports. "In Western countries, where contamination is seldom a problem, the loss of these antibodies is not disastrous.")

Formula companies have also targeted hospitals. In 1975, Similac's parent company wrote in a selling manual: "When one considers that for every 100 infants discharged from the hospital on a particular formula brand, approximately 93 infants remain on that brand, the importance of hospital selling becomes obvious." The company signed a contract in 1974 guaranteeing every new family leaving a city hospital a free one-day supply of Similac.[19]

In the late 1980s, census data showed for the first time in America's history that more women were working outside the home instead of staying home to raise children.[20] I like to call this the Murphy Brown effect, because that's when the show featuring the iconic working woman premiered (drawing up to seventy million weekly viewers).[21] Around this time, studies began to emerge showing the health benefits of breastfeeding: slightly lower incidences of SIDS and asthma, higher IQs, more fortifying antibodies passing from mother to child—which was kind of surprising, given that breastfeeding wasn't exactly a popular activity in the 1980s. One medical journal later connected this surge in breastfeeding studies to the backlash of women returning to work, and gaining a lot of power in the process. "Until recent years, the health benefits of breastfeeding were not emphasized, and synthetic formulations were popular. Only of late have health professionals become involved in the promotion of breastfeeding as a return to traditional values and the 'natural' vs. the 'artificial' way to feed infants," the *Journal of Nutrition* noted in 2001.[22] "The same century also witnessed unprecedented cultural, social and technological changes, involving the roles of women, their income and education, and their childbirth practices." (As one anthropologist I interviewed for this book notes: "There's a lot of culture that infiltrates our data.")

Today, breastfeeding is yet again a status marker among affluent women. As reported by Quartz Media, the *Atlantic*'s global news network, a middle-class person may be able to splurge on an $800 Pottery Barn crib, but she may not have the luxury of time to pump and maintain her supply for the six to twelve months doctors recommend breastfeeding.[23] "The most socially desirable form of infant nutrition has been whichever is harder for poor parents to access," *Quartz* explains. Indeed, the states with the lowest median income tend to have the lowest breastfeeding rates.

And yet, so many studies proclaim that breastfeeding is free—or at least a lot cheaper than the average yearly cost of $1,700 for formula.[24] But that's not the whole story when you factor in the value of the time a woman spends breastfeeding. *Quartz* estimates the cost at $14,000 per woman who earns $60,000 a year and works fifty hours a week. (If only women could put in a timesheet somewhere to get our $14,000 back!)

Another study found that women who breastfeed for longer than the recommended six months earn a lower salary five years later.[25] I called up the researcher behind this study, an associate professor of sociological and anthropological studies at the University of Ottawa named Phyllis L. F. Rippey. She was extremely personable over the phone and got right to the point: "Women who breastfeed for longer than the six months, who do what they're supposed to do . . . those are the women who are more likely to exit the labor force, which leads them to have lower earnings over time. They take a much bigger hit." Rippey clarified this study didn't include only women who exclusively breastfed; it included women who breastfed *at all*.

"People say, it's free, it's free, but is it really?!" she said. "So much of the policy [around breastfeeding] is just about convincing women and not being honest about what the reality is. It's like this fear that if we're honest, then women won't do it. It's convincing women through fear that their kids will be low IQ and chronically ill and *die* if they don't. That doesn't happen."

Breastfeeding is then promoted as aspirational. "I was in a low-income clinic and there was a poster that said, 'Breastfeeding makes your child smarter and less obese,'" Katja Rowell, a family physician who focuses on feeding, tells me. "The message is 'if you don't, you're a bad mom and your baby will be fat and stupid.' The shaming, and also the lack of acknowledging inequality and privilege around the different realities and the lack of choices so many moms face, is breathtaking. If you're back at work two weeks after giving birth, as are a quarter of moms in America . . . someone will have to bottle-feed your child."

\*

Rest assured, if you decide to use formula, you are certainly not alone. Seventy-five percent of women in the United States do not exclusively breastfeed for the first six months.[26] Some don't produce enough milk. And some just don't want to. And that's all okay.

Marianne is a strawberry blonde who's not afraid to talk to anyone, including Howard Stern, whom she credits for launching her career (she worked for him as an intern and has remained close with his orbit over the years). When she got pregnant, she knew from the get-go that she didn't want to breastfeed. "It's weird, I never felt that breastfeeding would be the way to bond with my child, and since I had my baby late, at forty-two, I *knew* I would need to take care of myself," she tells me. "I need proper sleep, and am prone to depression. . . . I don't need to be a martyr and I don't need to experience pain and sleep deprivation. Again, in order to take care of her, I need to be functioning and happy. Me depressed is not a good me."

Before giving birth, she read about bottle-feeding and spoke to doctors about her decision. "I was formula-fed, my siblings were, many friends were. We are all smart, functioning members of society. In the end, I honestly didn't think it was a big deal."

In the hospital, Marianne got lucky: "I had no one in my room for my four-night stay and I had a river view." Her daughter? Not so lucky. "My baby had to go to the NICU right away for jaundice, but it turned out to be a blessing because I had a C-section and I never would have been able to breastfeed her on demand [while] in so much pain."

Marianne and her husband were more focused on surviving those intense early days of childbirth instead of what their daughter was eating. "My mom passed away and we didn't have really any help around, so I relied on my husband to also feed her, which helped me sleep and recover."

Months later, Marianne says she still "100 percent" stands by her decision to formula feed her daughter. "She's a smart, beautiful, funny baby. And Mommy is well rested much of the time!"

She doesn't let the pressure to breastfeed get to her. "People judged, but I did not feel judged. I'm forty-three. I know what I want and why I chose bottle," Marianne says. "Many, *many* people had an opinion, and honestly I never asked anyone outside of doctors what they thought of my decision. They simply felt the need to weigh in. 'You really should just *try* it' was a popular one. I just said I'm not and that was that. No one knows what's best for you but you."

The pressure to force women to breastfeed does not sit well with some doctors, either. "I really have a problem with vilifying formula when it leads to health problems. I think it's dangerous to say that formula is dangerous when babies' lives are at risk," Dr. Rowell says. Adds Dr. Tuteur: "Breastfeeding is based on the fundamental lie that all breastfed babies survived. But the mortality rate in societies that have access only to breastfeeding is astronomical."

For example, babies are more likely to get jaundice if they're dehydrated, which can happen if they're not getting enough breast milk. Jaundice left untreated can turn into an extremely rare disorder called kernicterus, which can lead to brain damage and death. Again, extremely rare. But don't let an aversion to formula lead to ignoring a health problem in a baby.

If you do decide to breastfeed, this doesn't mean you shouldn't be proud of yourself, by the way. Shit, I feel like I deserve the Nobel Prize of Breastfeeding for keeping it going for a combined thirty-one months while working and traveling and living. Just as we celebrate life milestones like birthdays, we should celebrate accomplishing breastfeeding—just not at the expense of those who can't or don't.

*

Parents deluged with pressure to breastfeed newborns start getting very mixed messages after their babies turn one year old. Suddenly, they're participating in "extended breastfeeding" and stigmatized, as if society is saying, "Okay ladies, it's time for your boobs to go back to being just for sex again!" Paradoxically, they're also celebrated and held up as saints for dedicating their bodies to their children for so long. Case in point: The 2012 cover of *Time* magazine featuring a young blonde mom with her three-year-old son standing on a stool to nurse. The headline taunted, "Are You Mom Enough?" Yet, "this image sparked a kind of outrage and judgment I still haven't managed to wrap my mind around," that mom, Jamie Lynne Grumet, wrote on Mom.com in 2016.[27] "I wasn't even the subject of the story my image was promoting. . . . I never, ever expected the reaction, the anger, the sarcasm and distortion from perfect strangers, including professional journalists, after that issue of *Time* came out."

The battle lines over breastfeeding have been drawn depending on age, wealth, and across state and even country lines, with the decision to nurse becoming not just personal—but political. Nursing mothers gather in Walmarts to protest after a mom is kicked out for feeding her baby in a dressing room. Young women are shamed for breastfeeding in public by older women and men who find the act vulgar. (Even Facebook banned breastfeeding images at one point, while allowing beheading videos to remain.) Many women (especially millennials and celebrities) post #humblebrag hashtag photos of themselves breastfeeding on social media, further perpetuating the act as a status symbol. Why not mobilize to fight the government for things like paid family leave instead of spending all our energy fighting one another about whether we're better parents for breastfeeding or not?

If families buckle to the pressure to feed our children a certain way—or pressure one another to feed their babies a certain way— we're just feeding into a culture that continues to shame parents. And for what? One less tummy bug for our babies?

Whatever you decide, let go of the guilt and move on because you're not hurting your baby. As my aunt, a high school teacher in a bucolic Midwestern suburb for nearly three decades, says, "I have no idea which of my students were breastfed or not."

**#NoShameParenting Takeaway:** In a world where we have access to clean water and instructions on how to mix formula, should parents feel shamed about going that route? In a word: No. Breastfeed because it fits into your life. Breastfeed because you want to. Don't breastfeed because you're terrified your kid will be obese, asthmatic, and dumb if you don't. We should not feel guilty for a second for using formula, whether it's from birth or because our supply fluctuates. Whether it's from breast milk, formula, or a combination of both—all that matters is that our children are being fed.

## 4

# Knock Yourself Out:
# Letting Your Kid Cry Himself to Sleep
# Won't Ruin His Life (And It May Save Yours)

One of the most stressful and frustrating challenges we parents face is getting our precious bundle of joy to sleep. The bad news? There's no one-size-fits-all solution. The good news? You *do* have several methods to choose from, and whichever one you pick, you're still not going to fuck up your kid. Cheer emoji!

I know what it's like to stumble into a coffee shop with dirty hair, a screaming baby in tow, and order the biggest latte on the menu—extra sugar. Attempting to have a conversation? Ha. Don't even make eye contact with me. I literally hate everyone.

I also know what it's like to put a baby down at 7 p.m., pour myself a beer, grab a seat on the back porch with my husband, Brad, and blissfully watch the sunset. And then not speak or look at my sleeping baby until the next morning. I feel like I've totally mastered parenting. For that day anyway.

Luckily, the second scenario is more typical in my household these days. It can be your reality too.

In this chapter, I will explore the most popular sleep philosophies, ranging from *The No-Cry Sleep Solution* to the infamous "extinction" sleep training (aka *all* the cries). I will expose little-known stories behind each one. (Shocker: Many of the leading experts on this topic are super religious, have a product to sell you, or both!) I'll introduce you to multiple families who have tried these various methods, and I'll share how I got my kids to sleep through the night so I could drink that aforementioned beer. My neighbors are so jealous.

There's a myth that you have to pick one sleep philosophy and stick with it forever to the detriment of your sanity and the sanity of the rest of your family—even if it's not working. The myth's premise is that you'll irretrievably confuse your kid if you experiment with different methods. After all, attachment parenting believers scare the shit out of us with warnings of "shut down syndrome," where kids "freeze in order to preserve life" if you make them cry a couple of minutes in their crib. Your mother-in-law probably warns you against "spoiling" your baby by being too cuddly. Just google it: The top two results are how you "cannot spoil your child," followed by a link declaring, "looks like you can spoil your kid." There is a chorus of people telling you what to do, and you're probably too exhausted to know what's right or even hear your trusted inner voice.

Here's the truth: There are a lot of different experts touting different theories, but there's no one-size-fits-all. (If there was one technique that *guaranteed* every single baby would sleep at least eight uninterrupted hours, the person who invented it would be a billionaire.) You shouldn't feel obligated to take up one philosophy or the other, but there's definitely a method that will work—and you're *not* going to fuck up your kid, even if it takes you a while to find the right one.

✻

Because you don't have time, I read a bunch of the prerequisite books and websites, and here I'll break down some of the methods. They're ranked below from most tears to least tears:

* *Extinction (Cry It Out) Method:* The extinction method suggests you close the door at 7 p.m. and come back at 7 a.m. the next day, despite cries. The pros? Within days, your kid will

magically sleep, and you will feel human again after getting some sleep yourself. The cons? Even the pediatrician who touts this technique, Dr. Michel Cohen, warns: "Be prepared for three or four brutally hard nights."[1] Opponents of this method argue that leaving an eight-month-old baby alone to cry can create "toxic stress"—but those so-called experts often base their assertions on thin science and irrelevant studies (like those poor orphans in Romania) that I'll expose later in this chapter.[2] Even so, cry it out isn't always the answer, especially if it induces "toxic stress" in parents. (Self-care is a thing!) This is my favored method of getting my kids to sleep through the night, even if I think it requires a giant bottle of wine and a lot of willpower not to storm into their room and rescue them from their cries. Emma, a blonde mom from Chicago, says, "We just closed the door and let our son just figure it out. Took a few weeks, but now he sleeps like a champ, and we have some alone time at night! We'd do it a million times over." Adds Emma, whose girls are known to sleep until 9 a.m.: "We did extinction with both kids after failing miserably at Ferber. I remain nearly incapable of walking in the room without picking them up for a snuggle. We've had to do lots of remedial CIO when they get sick or teethe or we travel and I screw them up."

✳ *Baby Wise Method:* If you're the kind of person who wears a business suit and uses phrases like "think outside the box" nonironically, you may find some takeaways from this popular but hugely controversial method put forth in Gary Ezzo and Robert Bucknam's book *On Becoming Baby Wise.* This book brings a little clarity to the chaotic early days of infanthood by naming a baby's three basic cycles: feeding time, wake time, and nap time. (So you can ask yourself: "Did I just feed baby? Yes. Has he been awake for a little bit? Yes. Okay, maybe he's tired. I'll try to put him down for a nap.") The book's promises of sleep are alluring: Up to eight hours by seven to nine weeks, and eleven hours by three months old. But then it goes off the rails with an "infant management" concept that centers around a rigid "parent-directed feeding" schedule—unrealistic for a newborn at best and leading to malnourished babies at worst. *Baby Wise* originated as a Christian parenting guide called *Preparation for Parenting: Bringing God's Order to Your Baby's Day and Restful Sleep to Your Baby's Night.* (This is Ezzo's personal philosophy: "Raising good children is not a matter of chance but a matter of rightly applying God's principles in parenting.") Religion is one way some experts try to scare parents. Surely, if something is God's way, then it must be right. It may also conveniently be lucrative to the expert prescribing it. Still, Julie, a Missouri mom of two kids aged three and five, swears by this method. "People acted like we were neglecting our kids or something, but I would 100 percent do it again and have recommended it to many friends," she says. "I knew I was going back to work and there's no way I could function on little sleep and waking up in the middle of the night. I had heard what I considered to be horror stories of coworkers, family, friends who were still getting up multiple times a night, sometimes even with toddlers! Some days weren't easy but for the most part it went well and I still have good sleepers to this day."

❊ *Ferber Method:* Dr. Richard Ferber's advice has become so popular, his name has been turned into a verb. "We Ferberized our kids," parents will whisper at daycare drop-off. (For the record, the Harvard pediatrician has said he hates that his name is a verb.[3]) Basically, Ferber advises gradual weaning of night wakings and night feedings. To start, you do your bedtime routine, then put your baby into his crib sleepy but awake before leaving. If he goes to sleep, you're done! If he cries, come back in five minutes and reassure him, but don't pick him up. Leave again. If he cries again, come back in ten minutes. Then fifteen minutes, and twenty minutes, and so on. With your continued reassurance, the kid will eventually go to sleep and learn how to soothe himself, the book says. Ferber has hefty credentials and offers straightforward, sensible advice. "Children are very flexible. They can sleep well in many different settings and do terrifically," he has said. I wanted this method to work for my kids so badly. It seemed like the perfect mix of tough love and support. But when we tried it on Everett at fourteen weeks old, it had the opposite effect: Instead of hearing my calming voice and settling down to sleep, he freaked out, and I imagined him screaming at me: "Why are you in here when I'm crying but not picking me up!?" Ten minutes would pass, I'd reappear. "Pick me up, lady!" Fifteen minutes would pass. "I'm still effing crying and I know you're out there!" After a couple of nights of that, my husband and I were so sleep deprived and anxious, we finally gave up and did Extinction cry it out. Everett actually slept through the night after that. But that's not to say Ferber doesn't work for others. Anne, a mom of two who lives in Brooklyn and freelances, remembers sleep training "as a blur. It took us three nights. She cried for an hour, then forty-five minutes, then ten minutes. [We did it] around five months, I think. The problem is she kept regressing, then she had night terrors, nighttime anxiety (she still gets really bad dreams)—so nothing really stuck until she grew out of it."

* *12 Hours by 12 Weeks Method:* This method is based on a book that's also sometimes called *The Baby Sleep Solution*. It was written by Lisa Abidin and sleep coach Suzy Giordano, who fell into the career after she helped her friend's triplets get on a

daytime and nighttime schedule. Giordano, a mom of five, believes parents should keep logs of their normal eat-sleep-wake schedule for the first eight weeks of their babies' lives, and then keep their kid on that schedule. For example, if he wants to eat earlier than his usual time, try to distract him for a little until you get closer to the designated eating time. Once the daytime feeding is established, she believes you should focus on the nighttime schedule. "Parents are too scared of crying. Crying is just a way of communicating. And the parents rush in and try to fix it, when sometimes they need to stand back and watch," she has said.[4] "Of course, with my method, which is a limited-cry solution, I always tell them, 'Don't let them cry it out.' Because I believe babies can get to a hysterical stage where they feel lost, like they don't know how to get out, and it's the parents' job to step in. So when they're hysterical, go in, calm them down, and it's like, let's try again, and again, and again, until he gives in and is like, 'Oh, okay, now I know what I'm supposed to do.'" Christy, who grew up in Kansas, swears by this method for helping her chill son to sleep. "We followed 12 hours by 12 weeks to the T and he was sleeping through the night by ten weeks. I remember because the first night he slept straight through was the best Valentine's Day gift ever!" she says.

❋ *Elizabeth Pantley's The No-Cry Sleep Solution:* Pantley's method involves multiple phases, starting with comforting your baby until she is almost asleep with your arms around her and whispering "key words" of support, and then gradually cuddling less as she settles in her crib, and eventually comforting her from outside her bedroom door. This method might be for you if you're Type A and the idea of keeping tons of logs chronicling everything, ranging from naps to bedtime routines to night wakes, is appealing to you. It can also serve as a "temperate alternative" to cry it out if you do things like flipping light switches on and off to teach your baby the difference between light and dark and whispering reassuring words to your baby as he/she cries. Her method is "not a quick-fix plan," Pantley warns, and indeed it seems like it could take years. I call her method "attachment parenting light," which is no surprise since she is closely aligned with the father of attachment parenting, Dr. Sears. Calvin, a dad of two who grew up in Iowa, says that this method failed him: "I call *The No-Cry Sleep Solution* 'the book of three lies': There's lots of crying, nobody sleeps, and it solves nothing," he jokes. "Ferber all the way."

* *Attachment Parenting Method:* If you subscribe to this method, you co-sleep with your baby and quite possibly your other kids in a giant family bed. The doctor behind attachment parenting, Dr. William Sears, skyrocketed to fame alongside his wife, Martha, after they coauthored *The Baby Book* in 1992, which has sold more than 1.5 million copies translated into eighteen languages. Three of their sons are also doctors—perhaps you'd recognize Jim Sears from *Dr. Phil* or his spinoff, *The Doctors*. The Searses don't skirt around their distaste for cry it out. Martha told *Time* magazine that crying it out can induce mental illness, and Dr. Bill says prolonged crying damages a child's brain.[5] Let's just say that the Sears method focuses on "nighttime parenting" instead of "how to get your baby to sleep." Attachment parenting also believes that your baby should essentially never cry, which I'll get into more later in this chapter. A baby who never cries sounds great to me, but this means that baby is usually attached to mom 24/7, so she doesn't have a lot of independence. For some people, it works great. Like Beth, who says cry it out "went against every instinct in my body. And though it caused great exhaus-

tion and had me up every two hours to breastfeed for the full first year, I would not have done it any differently." Her daughter, now ten, still wakes her up if she has a nightmare. "I go and lay with her—which annoys me in the moment, but which I try to cherish still, because I know I'll miss that when it's over, too," Beth says. To be clear, co-sleeping is officially not recommended by pediatrician groups as it has resulted in infant death. Certain behaviors drive up the risk of co-sleeping, like if you're impaired by drinking. But many parents still choose to do it out of sheer exhaustion (they fall asleep with the baby in bed) or because it feels more natural to them. So if you decide to do it, be cautious. Make sure there are no blankets for the baby to get tangled in. Make sure you have a firm bed, not a couch or anywhere a baby could roll into a wall and suffocate. Again, make sure you're completely sober. And you may want to consider a co-sleeper, which is the same height of your bed and can roll up next to it, and which is considered a safer co-sleeping option. Michelle, a mom of two and an elementary school teacher in Missouri, says, "I couldn't bear the tears and crying for mama when my daughter outgrew the bassinet, so I opted to co-sleep . . . with my husband's support. It worked really well for us because we did extended breastfeeding. She slept with us until the age of three (I did not breastfeed until three. . . . That's just when we decided it was time to move her into her own space.) We felt like she was able to better understand what was happening and that we were still there if she needed us. We did a short reward system until she was sleeping through the night without waking or stalling at bedtime. She is now four and a half. Our three-month-old is in a bassinet in our room until he grows out of it. We will try the crib, but I have a feeling he will be a co-sleeper, too. Co-sleeping helped me bond with my daughter and I am so happy we did it."

This is just the start. There are plenty of other methods to soothe a baby. Dr. Harvey Karp's *The Happiest Baby on the Block* is a personal favorite, and it is also available on DVD or VOD—which is handy for a sleep-deprived parent. (And, if you're feeling particularly flush and/or exhausted, he also sells a $1,160 bassinet called a SNOO that supposedly rocks and shushes babies overnight.) The "2-3-4 Method" started springing up on blogs around the time Otto was born, offering a straightforward way to organize your day: Put your newborn down for a nap two hours after she wakes for the day, for another nap three hours after that, and then to bed four hours after that.

Don't feel like you have to spend any money at all on products that purport to help baby sleep. They often just confuse us or add to our anxiety, which is a dangerous combo when we're so sleep deprived following the birth of a baby. Luckily, life gets easier once we figure out the whole sleep thing a little bit better.

## The Truth About Attachment Parenting

So many parents drag themselves around exhaustedly—or feel guilty when they try sleep training methods like cry it out—because they've read about Dr. William Sears's theory of "attachment parenting," which he explained first in 1982 in his book *Creative Parenting*. Attachment parenting has also been called "intensive mothering," as Sears, a pediatrician, and his wife, Martha, a registered nurse and La Leche League leader, advised that women carry their babies in slings instead of strollers, share their bed (co-sleeping), quit their jobs, and breastfeed on demand for years.

While Sears does have some interesting ideas, especially when taken in moderation with what works with your family, there's this feeling that we're not good parents if we don't follow every single tenet of his philosophy. And given that breastfeeding, co-sleeping, and quitting work is not feasible for a large population, that creates an expectation that only a privileged few can live up to.

Religious and women's studies professor Cynthia Eller details her misery at attempting attachment parenting in an essay for *Brain, Child* magazine.[6] "In my opinion, it is a cruel thing to tell a new mother that babies who are mothered 'naturally' (read: correctly) never cry. It turns your baby's every whimper into an indictment of your naturalness and adequacy as a mother," she writes.

Religion is at the core of the Searses' advice. In *The Complete Book of Christian Parenting and Child Care*, they write: "The type of parenting we believe is God's design for the father-mother-child relationship is a style we call 'attachment parenting.' . . . We have a deep personal conviction that this is the way God wants His children parented."

The Searses rely more on their beliefs than sound science to back up their advice. For example, Dr. Sears points to observations of African tribes as justification as to why this is the right way to parent children, a conclusion that doesn't easily translate to the way American families live today. He had an epiphany about the benefits of baby wearing after he and Martha interviewed two women from Zambia during an international parenting conference.

By idolizing a population with vastly different lives than those of typical American women, Sears has set unrealistic expectations of a mother, one of his critics, Harvard trained ob-gyn Dr. Amy Tuteur tells me. "There's an attachment parenting idea that women just sat around all day and mothered their children. That's the last thing that they did.

"They had to contribute to the survival of the tribe. Mothering is something that they did in the spaces between all the other things that they did. Now the pressure is that mothering should be your occupation, which is fine if that's what you want," Tuteur adds. "But if you don't want that, there's no reason to think that it's going to harm your children, because from time immemorial, mothers always worked. They went out and they searched for nuts and berries. These things took hours and hours. And the children played in the dirt next to them or were stuck on their back or whatever." Tuteur says the ideal of a bygone era where women spent all their time with their children, even sharing a bed with them, "literally never existed."

Attachment parenting is a "philosophy of privilege," writes Tuteur in her book *Push Back: Guilt in the Age of Natural Parenting*.[7] Indeed, a mother cannot wear her baby in a sling to a job at McDonald's. A mother cannot quit her job unless she has enough money to do so. And, according to "natural" attachment parenting, this mother is judged as less than. "I decided a long time ago that any rule that automatically makes a Latina woman that works at Walmart to feed her children a bad mother has got to be wrong," Tuteur tells me. "It reminds me of when poor people were thin, being fat was a desired characteristic. Being thin is for rich people now. When poor people had to work out in the field and they got a tan, being perfectly white and wandering around with a parasol and gloves on your hands, that was a sign of being rich. Now that you have to go away to a tropical place to get a tan, a tan is a sign of being rich. There's so much sociological stuff going on on every level. Like the Paleo Diet. Well, the ultimate Paleolithic individual was the Neanderthal and they're extinct. So why are we copying them?"

Some experts link attachment parenting's rise to resentment over feminism. "In the twentieth century, some women in some places were finally emancipated and got more political rights and economic rights. Nothing that momentous happens without backlash," Tuteur says. "I think the backlash from the right has been expressed as religious fundamentalism in which women are forced back into the home. But that's not an option on the left. You can't frame it that way. So it's been framed as, 'what children need is these natural mothers' who have a vaginal birth without pain relief, who breastfeed regardless of the cost to themselves, who carry their babies around all the time with attachment parenting, which means they never go back to work. . . ."

I wouldn't go so far as to say that attachment parenting is anti-feminist. Feminism should open a woman up to more choices, and if our choice is to attachment parent, then that is great. But it should be just that: A choice. Women should not feel shamed or like we're worse or less dedicated mothers because we don't believe in attachment parenting.

This is not meant to be a takedown of attachment parenting, but rather a call for finding balance. I myself breastfed for thirty-one months. I gave both my sons formula in the hospital in the days after their birth. I co-slept with my older son for a couple of months. I made both my boys cry it out in their cribs. I loved carrying my boys around in the Ergo because I thought it was easier to navigate small neighborhood stores and the subway stairs. But I also regularly used a stroller.

"It's not all or nothing," *Big Bang Theory* actress Mayim Bialik, who calls herself an attachment parent to her two boys, points out in *Time* magazine.[8] Bialik has her PhD in neuroscience and is the author of *Beyond the Sling: A Real-Life Guide to Raising Confident, Loving Children the Attachment Parenting Way.* "Some people sleep with their kids, some people breastfeed their kids until they're five and some people don't. The core principle is that a child's voice matters." (You can still show your child that his or her voice matters without breastfeeding until they're five years old, just to note.)

If this is something you want to do and you have the resources to do it, great! I'm glad it works for your family. If you feel pressure to be an attachment parent but it doesn't work for you, then stop! You won't fuck up your kid if you don't share a giant family bed and breastfeed until they're four years old.

## *Why Cry It Out Is So Controversial*

There are few things that rile up a Facebook parenting group more than "Cry It Out," aka leaving your baby to cry alone in his or her room to teach them to sleep through the night. I completely get both sides, and I've been there. It's heartbreaking to hear your kid cry. They're so little and helpless! I'm just sitting outside the door! It's a literal biological urge to stop your baby from crying!

"Your body is telling you one thing and science is telling you another. If your body is telling you, 'My baby needs me,' it feels absolutely wrong not to respond to that," Dr. Janet K. Kennedy, a clinical psychologist and author of *The Good Sleeper: The Essential Guide to Sleep for Your Baby (and You)*, tells me. "But what I tell my clients is that it's not even been one hundred years since the infant mortality rate dropped. One hundred years ago, kids didn't make it. This alarm system we have isn't so out of date, historically speaking. Now we have vaccines, we have knowledge about safe sleep practices: Simply putting the baby to sleep on his back with no soft bedding cuts the infant mortality rate exponentially. We have [pediatrician] checkups, all of these things that we've established to keep babies healthy and give them a strong start so they make it through infancy. These things all mean that when your baby is fussing in the night, chances are he doesn't need you. Once they reach that point of being able to self soothe, typically somewhere around twelve weeks, the meaning of those calls you get in the night change."

I am admittedly a cry it out devotee. It's how I got both my kids to sleep through the night. For my family, it worked wonders. That's not to say we picked one method and stuck with it, and it worked immediately.

For Everett we tried Ferber (fail), then extinction (success!). Then I went back to work, and Everett started waking up again at night. So we co-slept from month four to six (success!). Then Everett started kicking us in the head too much and moving around too much, so we did CIO again—and it only took one night to get him back in the crib routine.

My younger son, Otto, gave us a run for his money. Instead of a couple of nights of tears, he cried for hours. He barfed in his crib, he was so upset. So we quit sleep training and invested in one of those $40 Baby Merlin Magic Sleepsuits. (Well, actually, my friend Alex overnighted me one after taking pity on my depressed texts at all hours of the night.) They're a cross between a swaddle and the Stay Puft Marshmallow Man. A couple of months later, when Otto was six-ish months old, we tried sleep training again and it worked.

"Ultimately the vast majority of people need to learn how to tolerate their child's distress," Kennedy says. "This isn't something that's a one-time deal. You're going to have to let your baby fuss and cry from time to time. This is a skill they need to acquire." You could look at it as the first lesson in resilience, from a very young age.

Let's talk a little bit about the science behind why experts love and hate sleep training. There are a couple of studies cited by Dr. Sears and countless others as to why sleep training is bad, and why forcing a baby to cry alone in a crib will lead to "insecure attachment." They freaked me out until I delved into them for more details.

"Haven't you ever heard of the Romanian orphans? They were left to cry in their cribs and never formed a 'secure attachment.' That's why I won't sleep train," wrote one parent on a Facebook group I'm in. The Romanian orphan story is truly devastating. The former dictator of Romania, Nicolae Ceauçescu, banned abortions, birth control, and divorce to keep the population from shrinking after the end of World War II.

It's a real *Handmaid's Tale* type of craziness: Women were forced to undergo gynecological exams at work to ensure pregnancies were caught early before they could be aborted. Women weren't allowed to get abortions unless they had five children at home under the age of eighteen or were older than forty-five years of age. Childless couples were taxed monthly. While wealthy couples were usually able to skirt the laws, single moms, troubled families, factory workers, and other lower-class families were not so lucky. The rate of unwanted children grew exponentially. Many were abandoned by desperate parents in a country with a destroyed economy.[9] By the fall of communism in 1989, there were an estimated 100,000 children in Romanian orphanages (but some reports say up to 500,000 children survived the bleak institutions).[10]

The institutions were devastating places described as "slaughterhouses of souls" by orphan Daniel Rucareanu, who at age thirty-eight still has trouble making eye contact with other people as a result of his horrific upbringing.

The *Washington Post* described the scene in 1990: "On the second floor of the state-run institution here, dazed toddlers lie or sit in iron cribs in closed, stuffy rooms. . . . Some cry, but most are silent and appear bewildered behind their bars, with the doomed air of laboratory animals. Down the hall, other cribs hold smaller children, pale skeletons suffering from malnutrition and disease. Despite the heat of the day, several of the children are wrapped in dirty blankets. From one still bundle, only a bluish patch of scalp is visible. Asked if the child inside is alive, an orderly says, 'Of course,' and pulls back the covers. The tiny skeleton stirs, turns onto its side and groans."[11]

A doctor from a relief organization told Human Rights Watch that 40 percent of the children in one home died in one year due to infectious diseases and neglect. "They die of hunger, of very dirty environment, of nobody touching them, and of never getting out of their beds." The kids were fed gruel out of rusty buckets, many of them had no clothes or only the "filthiest rags," and many kids had untreated hepatitis B or HIV due to needles being rationed and used again and again. (Antibiotics were routinely administered via shots.) Staffers didn't know their names. "Children are handcuffed to beds so tightly that their cuffs eat into their wrists, according to doctors. Those too small or unable to feed themselves often waste away because their milk bottles, propped on piles of rags, slip away and there is no one to right them," the *Washington Post* continues. Some older children were tied together to prevent them from running away, with 10 to 15 children sharing a single mattress.[12]

Daniel, who grew up in one of these orphanages, told Public Radio International: "We were wiped out as human beings—silenced, humiliated. Our personalities were dissolved." One nurse says many three- to four-year-olds were incorrectly labeled mentally disabled: "Because they were not stimulated, they couldn't walk, they couldn't talk. You had to feed them," she said. Children were routinely beaten. "Even I had to slap the older ones who would have crises sometimes," the nurse said. "They couldn't calm down otherwise. Those kids didn't know any other way to be instructed."[13]

Why am I telling you the heartbreaking story of these Romanian orphans? Because I want to illustrate the vast differences between the way these children were raised and the way many children in modern America are raised. Most children will never experience being abandoned by their parents, ignored by caregivers, starved, and tethered to a crib for three *years* of their lives. Yet, parents who allow their child to cry for an hour or two (or less) in their cribs are told they'll have similar outcomes as the tragic orphans. There is literally no way you can put them in the same category.

The other study that is often used to illustrate how terrible it is to let your kid cry involves rats and licking. Baby rats are called pups. Pups that had moms that spent a lot of time licking and grooming them grew up to be calmer adults. Pups that didn't get as many licks from mom were more anxious. To make sure this was more nurture than nature, scientists switched pups so that some were "adopted" by mom rats who licked more, and some were adopted by mom rats who didn't groom as much. The pups raised by rats who licked less turned out more anxious, even if they were biologically born to lick-loving mom rats. This was studied over the course of a week, which is the time baby rats typically spend in the nest before heading out into the rat race. (Couldn't resist.)

From this study, the researchers deduced that stress could be "epigenetic," or passed down through genes. Stressed pups become stressed mom rats who are less likely to lick their own pups, and that pup grows up more stressed and less likely to lick her own pup, and so forth.[14]

This rat study then became the basis of an alarming headline in *Psychology Today,* "Parents Misled by Cry-It-Out Sleep Training Reports."[15] In it, Darcia Narvaez, a professor of psychology at the University of Notre Dame, writes, "Infants can experience PTSD, toxic distress, depression and dissociation in response to crying-it-out." But she links to the rat study, which equates mom rats who don't lick their babies over the course of a week (which is neglecting them completely, as they can't even poop unless they're licked) with human moms who allow their kids to cry for a very short period of time. Child psychiatrist David Rettew, the author of *Child Tempera-ment: New Thinking About the Boundary Between Traits and Illness,* writes his own rebuttal to the rat research: "Certainly, animal data is not irrelevant to humans, but to make such specific and pro-vocative claims such as those made here and then cite rat licking as the primary source is needlessly alarming and heavily misleading."[16]

I called up Dr. Narvaez to get her point of view, and many things she said made a lot of sense: Babies who don't grow up with a lot of support can be more stressed out. That agrees with the core tenet of this book: Loving, feeding, and housing your child will lead them to become a happy and healthy person. "You need to take into ac-count the age of the child," she says. "I've emailed with parents who sleep train a six-week-old, leaving him alone all night crying, which is hugely damaging." No disagreement there. You shouldn't leave a brand-new baby to cry all night long. "If you've got a three-year-old and you've been very affectionate all along, it's a very different matter. They can understand you're not going to disappear from their life. A baby can't think ahead."

Sleep training, like so many aspects of parenthood, has shades of gray. This is why you can't take every headline you read as a hard and fast rule. If you want to sleep train, don't let some alarmist headline discourage you. Make the decision with your gut—and with a trusted physician, if it makes you feel better. My pediatrician recommends sleep training as long as the baby is eight weeks old and ten pounds. That felt too little to me, so we sleep trained both our kids around fourteen weeks, when they were both at least fifteen pounds. I felt confident about that decision—which led to me becoming a happier parent.

Any rational adult knows they're not completely neglecting their child by letting him or her cry a little overnight. In fact, you could argue that you're helping them to self soothe, which is a very important skill later in life. Pam, who runs her own business between juggling her three children, explains her family's decision to sleep train this way: "We felt like it was one of the first things we'd ever teach our kids. I remember having a conversation and us agreeing that, when helping our kids with their future math homework, we didn't want to be the kind of parents who did it for them. We wanted to be able to adapt and try different methods and work with our kids to figure out how best they learn the math. We paralleled that with how we approached the sleep training. . . . We have always said you do what works for your family and do it until it doesn't work anymore."

If the whole idea of sleep training makes you wince, don't do it. If you don't mind waking up overnight, then carry on. "I didn't do CIO . . . however in the long term, he sleeps great (he's almost three). We still co-sleep every once in a while and I really enjoy it. Once the demanding baby stage ended, it dawned on me that he'd be off to college before I know it and I'd better get all the cuddles while I still can," Amanda, a mom of one who lives in Brooklyn, told me.

If you change your mind about sleep training, my pediatrician warned me that it's harder at eighteen months. Yes, this is true in the sense that your kid can now ask for you by name, and it's pretty heartbreaking to hear "Mommy! Daddy!" again and again. (Been there, done that, multiple times.) But, at the same time, there isn't a point of no return. Even if you sleep train at fourteen weeks, it's more of a philosophy than a one and done—you're going to have to reinforce sleep training every time you get back from vacation or overcome a big sickness. It gets easier with age (my five-year-old can fall back into his routine pretty easily, but my two-year-old is extra teary at bedtime for a couple days after traveling). So don't let anyone tell you that you can only sleep train by a certain age and then you're shit out of luck if your kid won't sleep. You need to do what works for you and your family. There is no hard and fast rule.

✳

Speaking of hard and fast rules—remember how I said there's no magic bullet to ensure a kid sleeps through the night, but if there was, the person who invented it would be rich? Okay, I kind of found one. Well, at least one common tip among all the sleep books: *Routine*. It doesn't matter if you're totally for sleep training or can't stomach hearing your baby's cries. Each and every expert recommends establishing a short and consistent bedtime routine to make sleeping easier.

### Don't Ignore Your Own Sleep Deprivation

We've spent a lot of time in this chapter talking about how sleep training affects your kid. Now I want to shift gears and focus on how kids' sleep affects parents.

You're obviously a dedicated parent who is taking the time to read this book and give some thought to the kind of mom or dad or guardian you want to be. You'd do anything for your kid, including but not limited to enduring soul-crushing sleep deprivation or skyrocketing anxiety over establishing a perfect bedtime routine. Deep breaths. You don't have to stress yourself out over this. Take care of yourself. Be kind to yourself.

There's a reason why sleep deprivation is a form of torture. And if it feels like torture to you, I'm giving you permission to not endure it. It's hard to function when you're exhausted, and raising a kid is a marathon, not a race. If you're beyond sleep deprived and miserable, how can you positively interact with your baby, let alone have enough energy to keep her from sticking a finger in an electrical socket? Just go to bed. You'll be a better parent for it.

**#NoShameParenting Takeaway:** Maybe you decide a couple of days or weeks of hearing your baby cry is worth it for your sanity. Maybe you don't mind tending to your baby whether it's 3 p.m. or 3 a.m. Either way, and above all else, *you* are the best expert on raising your family. Once you find a method that works, you don't need to stress that you're doing it "wrong" just because some judgey Facebook group says so. And here's the thing: You can always change your mind. Let's say you don't feel right sleep training an infant who can't even crawl. Then don't. When you decide that you're too tired to deal, try one of the methods listed above. As the wisest woman I know (Oprah) once said: "There isn't anything in your life that you cannot change." This certainly includes the way you raise your kids.

# 5

## You Don't Have to Be Mary Poppins:
## Why Your Kid Will Be Fine If They
## Go to Daycare (or Don't)

After Everett was born, I considered quitting my job but we couldn't afford it. So Everett started daycare when he was fifteen weeks old. Brad and I picked a homey, licensed in-house center with nine babies under eighteen months old, two caregivers that reminded me of my kind and gentle grandma, and a third who reminded me of a bossy big sister with a lot of advice and opinions. Luckily, it was only a block away from our house, which is a bonus when you live in a city where you walk everywhere instead of commuting via car.

When Everett was ten months old, my husband quit his job and became our son's primary caregiver three days a week (Ev stayed in daycare the other two days). In a complete 180 from my back-to-work angst, I took a high-pressure position at my company that required me to lead a team, launch a digital product from scratch, travel, and regularly appear on live TV. After I settled in, Brad went back to work as a consultant—and we enrolled Everett into another licensed in-home daycare center with twelve toddlers and three twenty-something caregivers who hardly spoke English. (Within a couple months, Everett could speak a little Russian and the caregivers had picked up English—so it appeared to have been mutually beneficial.)

By the time I became pregnant with Otto, there were zero infant daycare options within a four-block radius of our home. (The building that housed Everett's infant daycare was sold and converted into luxury condos, which is a hazard of New York City living.) My husband and I knew we'd never make it to work on time if we had to drop off a two-and-a-half-year-old and an infant at two separate daycares in different directions while simultaneously carrying my work laptop, pump, and bottles . . . so we hired an amazing nanny, Alicia, and recruited another local family to do a "nanny share" from our house. When Otto was about twenty weeks old, I went back to work and Otto started spending his days with Alicia and baby Vena, who was only two months older.

As Everett neared four, he entered pre-kindergarten at a local public school that fortunately also had an after-school program on the same site. By now, I was a vice president at a major media company.

Shortly after Otto turned two, Brad's consulting job finally started offering benefits, so I quit my corporate job to write the very book you are reading now, and we sadly parted ways with our amazing nanny. We enrolled Otto at the same daycare Everett had "graduated" from a mere eighteen months earlier.

When I reread this, I think *chaos!* So many job changes, so many childcare switches over five years. But the truth is that my kids have thrived as we've adapted our work/life parenting strategies in real time to what functions best for our family at that moment. Your kids will flourish no matter what choice you make when it comes to childcare. You can ramp up your job, scale back your job, quit your job—and your kid will be fine.

I don't mean to downplay how difficult these decisions are. I understand that there are many factors that play into the "decision," if you could even call it that. Childcare is outrageously expensive and parents usually need to work to pay the bills. It's a privilege to even have a choice between options. Multiple parents have told me their salaries were lower than their daycare bills, so one of them quit their job to stay home.

Such is the case for Ari. After his family moved, he and his wife discovered their daughter, Maggie, missed the kindergarten cutoff by two days in their new town—meaning they'd need to pay for an extra year of preschool for her, in addition to childcare for their baby, Gary. "Measuring the cost of the daycare vs. my salary, we determined that it was basically a financial wash," says Ari, who left his teaching job shortly thereafter. "We decided I should stay home at least for a year, possibly more, as I can take up to three years unpaid and still keep my job."

✳

When it comes to childcare, this is the big question many of us have: Will our kids be okay if I'm not there all the time to take care of them? And when you break down the research (as I will for you), it's clear that as long as you have *high-quality* care—whether it's with a parent, in a daycare center, with a nanny, or some combination—you won't go wrong. You can't fuck up your kids. So don't worry about converting yourself into Mary Poppins—or hiring her!

When I use the phrase "high-quality," I'm not talking about only the fanciest Montessori center that's super far from your home, has a two-year waiting list, and offers baby yoga, Spanish classes, and math drills. Save yourself the drama! Daycare facilities should be licensed, which you can usually look up online. They should have an adult-to-child ratio of 1 to 3 for infants between six and eighteen months. Nannies should have sound references and/or a background check.

The National Institute of Child Health and Human Development conducted a groundbreaking study of more than 1,000 children during the course of fifteen years, and then extrapolated what happens to kids in different childcare situations. I'll get into it in more detail in the following pages.

Ultimately, this study was able to define "high-quality care." It all came down to "positive caregiving"—caregivers who show a positive attitude, have positive physical contact (such as cuddling or hand holding), engage the kid in conversation, and interact by doing things like singing and reading and helping him or her button their shirt, use a spoon, or other developmentally appropriate activities. If a caregiver does these things regularly, then your kid is in good shape.[1]

This doesn't mean you or the caregiver needs to be doing these things *all the time*. We are human. Sometimes we're tired, or busy, or otherwise occupied. But as long as the interaction between a caregiver—whether it's a parent, nanny, daycare provider, or other adult—and child includes many of those "positive caregiving" traits sometimes, you're golden. (After all, the study found that just 9 percent of children receive "a lot" of positive caregiving. Children in 53 percent of childcare settings receive "some" positive caregiving. Children in only 8 percent of childcare settings get "hardly" any positive caregiving.)

We shouldn't think of a childcare situation in a vacuum. Instead, let's think of it as part of a potpourri of experience our children have with adults who love them. Our children spend mornings, nights, and weekends interacting with their nuclear family, and usually an extended mix of relatives and friends and other people in the world. There are so many opportunities for "positive caregiving" that don't need to only come between the hours of 8 a.m. and 6 p.m. when your kid is with their sitter or daycare provider.

✽

Teddy is an adorable toddler with brown bangs that wisp at his forehead. He's been in daycare since he was twelve weeks old, his mom Claire, who lives in Texas, tells me. "Biggest takeaway: Before I was a parent, I thought my child should be presented with some type of educational curriculum almost from birth," she says. "What I now know is, the most important thing in the first months of life is feeling safe, nurtured, and loved. He got that in spades at his first [daycare]."

Claire says her now-twenty-one-month-old son is "really easy-going with changes in plans, and he is happy to play with anyone," which she credits to his early exposure to daycare. "He's not really shy. He also knows he can love and trust other people besides his parents, and I'm happy that is something he has learned at this young age. I think it will make transitions in life much easier for him."

"Socialization" is a reason why many parents (including me) want to enroll their kids in daycare, even though I realize three-month-olds aren't exactly doing puzzles together. One study found that children who attend daycare are slightly more ready for school and slightly more social,[2] but researchers admit that also could be due to the way they spoke to the children during the experiment, so I take that with a grain of salt.

So let's go back to the National Institute of Child Health and Human Development study I mentioned at the beginning of this chapter. This study followed more than 1,000 kids from birth to age fifteen to see how their childcare may have affected their social, emotional, intellectual, and language development, and their physical growth and health. And (spoiler alert), it found that childcare quality has little to do with social outcomes—and much more to do with what a child learns in their family.

Furthermore, this study definitively states, "Children who were cared for exclusively by their mothers did not develop differently than those who were also cared for by others."

Now let's all roll our eyes that only moms were studied. When you delve into the back end of the study, you see that the researchers disagreed about how to classify dads: Main caregivers or not? They eventually decided dad was a second-class citizen. We'll chalk this up to the study kicking off in 1991. Times have changed since then.

Despite the major issue that only moms were measured (dads were surveyed in later follow-ups), this study is a good one because it included families from nearly every continental state in America, at every income and educational level, of different ethnicities, and single parents and two-parent homes. It also declares that, "Most children in exclusive maternal care at just older than one year and at two and three years of age had cognitive, language, and achievement scores similar to those of children in childcare."[3]

The study did find some pros and cons of various traits supposedly linked to childcare. But the differences were very small, described with lots of words like *somewhat* and *slightly*. For example, kids in high-quality childcare had "somewhat" better language and cognitive development during the first four and a half years of their lives. But the study authors warn, "The link was not a strong one. Family and parent features were more important predictors of this development than childcare quality. So, the differences between outcomes for children in higher and lower quality care were small relative to the differences associated with family characteristics." And despite those language and cognitive gains, those same kids also were "somewhat" more disobedient at age two and in kindergarten, but not age three.

A researcher involved in the study cautions that you need to put the data in perspective. "It's not going to mean that each child is going to have 0.05 percent probability of being more aggressive," Aletha C. Huston, a professor emeritus at the University of Texas at Austin, told *Slate*.[4] "What probably is represented here is that some kids are responding in that way, and a lot of kids aren't." The study also found that childcare did not predict the future health of your kid.

Again, the *child's family* had the biggest impact on how they turned out at age fifteen—regardless of whether or not they attended childcare, and if that childcare was high-quality or not. "Parent and family characteristics were more strongly linked to child development than were childcare features. And, parent and family characteristics predicted some developmental outcomes that were not predicted by childcare. For instance, children showed more cognitive, language, and social competence and more harmonious relationships with parents when parents were more educated, had higher incomes, and provided home environments that were emotionally supportive and cognitively enriched, and when mothers experienced little psychological distress. Family and parenting experiences were as important to the well-being of children who had extensive childcare experience as family and parenting experiences were for children with little or no childcare experience." To put it simply, it doesn't matter where kids of relatively financially comfortable, educated, stable homes receive childcare.

So don't freak if your childcare doesn't have all the bells and whistles, or about using childcare overall. As long as your caregivers are attentive and warm, and you (and your partner, if you have one) are also mostly attentive and warm—your kid will be fine. "The more sensitive, responsive, attentive, and cognitively stimulating the mother was during observed interactions, the better the children's outcomes," the study finds. (Again, this study only looked at moms, but this also applies to dads.)

The research also calls out the benefits of routine, which, as you may remember, was the key to getting our kids to sleep too. Researchers wrote: "Families who had well organized routines, those with books and play materials, and those who took part in enhancing experiences both inside and outside the home (such as going to the library or attending a cultural festival) had children who were more advanced socially and cognitively."[5]

## How Much We're All Spending on Childcare

We've talked a lot about the importance of high-quality childcare, but very little of the insanely high price of childcare. When Otto was cared for by a nanny and Everett was going to full-time daycare, we were paying $50,000 a year. Yes, I am checking our privilege that we could afford to pay that, even if it was a huge dent in our budget. Brad helped me frame it in a way that makes sense: Look at childcare as an investment, not a sunk cost. If you want or need to continue to work, spending money on childcare allows you to keep on building your career. Your earnings should rise to help absorb the cost, and your childcare costs should go down as your kids enter public school. Indeed, Everett only needs after-school care now, and Otto goes to daycare for fewer hours. We're still paying a staggering $30,000 a year, not including the days my husband or I take off work when public schools are closed. Otto's daycare is the bulk of that, at nearly $22,000 a year, which is twice the average cost in the United States of $11,666 annually.[6] That's more than college tuition and, when broken down monthly, higher than many mortgages. Families who earn $1,500 or less a month spend an average of $938 a month on childcare.[7] The least affordable state for daycare is the District of Columbia, according to *New America* and Care.com's annual "Cost of Care" survey.[8] The most affordable state for childcare is North Dakota, followed by Utah.

The average nanny makes $18.65 an hour, according to a 2019 survey of 811 parents in Brooklyn. They work fifty hours a week and take home approximately $46,000 annually. Nationwide, the average annual gross salary of a nanny is $36,000.[9]

But there are lots of options parents may not think of to lower costs, such as a nanny share, which can be the best of both worlds: near-individualized attention at rates higher than daycare, but considerably lower than having your own nanny. Or in-home daycare centers, which are smaller and sometimes more affordable. If you have a flexible workplace, you could work from home so that you have a shorter commute and you don't need to pay for as many hours of childcare. Brad and I have always staggered our work hours, with one of us starting our workdays earlier and then doing pickup and the other starting later and doing drop-off. Or, you know, you could recruit your family to move nearby and care for your children for free! (If they can afford that unpaid labor themselves.)

## *Should You Choose Daycare or a Nanny?*

This question plagued me when I was pregnant with my first son. For Lisa, a quiet-spoken brunette who is raising two boys in New Jersey, her nanny has been a godsend. "We have a nanny, a woman with [her own] grown children," she says. "I was hesitant when I hired her because she didn't drive (we live in the 'burbs), but I was desperate. I'd hired someone else who bailed on me right before I was due to go back [to work]. Our non-driving nanny turned out to be a blessing beyond blessings for all of us. She is one of the kindest and also toughest (in a good way) people I've ever met. Even though my sons are fourteen and eleven now and I work at home, she still comes to us one day a week and I think to be honest it's for me more than them. She calls my kids every holiday. Just today she told me that my older son texted her on her birthday last week and it was her first birthday message of the day (he sent it after midnight—so much for bedtime!). I feel like having her as a third parent, someone from another culture who grew up on a farm in Jamaica, has enriched my kids' lives and understanding of the world in so many ways."

Angela, a whip-smart mom to a daughter and newborn son, wrote me about her daycare experience while on maternity leave. "Our story of how we chose the daycare is relatively run-of-the-mill; my husband and I both work, we toured a bunch of daycares, went through all the usual fears (about cost and leaving our daughter with strangers), but in the end chose one that was convenient, (relatively) affordable, had wonderful testimonials, and—most importantly, really—just felt right. What I can say about the experience is this: My daughter is an incredibly social kid now, able to walk up to anyone and talk to them, and very confident in herself as a person. She is able to sit still for a book, but also run wild and play in the most imaginative and creative ways. She loves art and music, and because of projects the daycare did, cares a lot about the environment and her community. Of course, my husband and I have worked to instill these values in her, but the fact that she spent all day, five days a week in this place means they had a real impact on her—and the adventures she had and the diversity of kids she met was absolutely incredible. We moved to the suburbs and she started a new preschool. I was so worried about the transition. There literally was none. New house. New school. New kids. No problem. As a painfully shy child who grew into a very outgoing person (the result of a public school drama class), to see my daughter not have to go through that because she was part of a group so early is a wonderful thing."

And then there are many families who have tried many different options. Alison, a high school English teacher, and Kevin, a business school professor, are raising their two daughters, now ages six and eight, in suburban Washington, D.C. "We did the nanny thing for a year with No. 1. I was able to take a year away from the classroom for No. 2," Alison says. When Alison went back to work, they enrolled both girls at the local Jewish Community Center for daycare, where they both stayed until heading off to elementary school. "While each decision brought its concerns, I am still happy with how we did it. What surprised me about being part of the JCC for those five years was how sad I was upon the final pickup. It was the first place we were a part of as a family, we all loved it, and when it was over it was a tiny glimpse into the goodbyes of my girls growing up."

There are pros and cons to both daycare and a nanny, but as long as your child is receiving high-quality care from a caring adult in their lives, you can't go wrong. With a nanny, you get one-to-one nurturing and attention. They can adjust when kids eat and sleep, and what their daily activities are depending on the kid's needs for that day. Daycare is usually more structured—the kids eat lunch, nap, and usually have the same schedule every day. This is by necessity as the ratio of adults to children is usually 1 to 3.

Nannies can also help take care of extra tasks around the house, which Sarah, a busy publishing executive with a long commute, is eternally grateful for. Her family's nanny cooks for her two kids, packs school lunches, straightens up their home, does her kids' laundry, and handles school drop-off and pickup. Sarah also gives her the family's credit card to occasionally go grocery shopping. "It lightens our load and lets us focus on the kids during the weekend, when we all need to decompress, since most of the custodial chores have been handled," Sarah explains.

If your kid gets sick, a nanny can still care for him or her so their parents can go to work. If a kid who goes to daycare gets sick, they have to stay home so they don't spread their illness to other kids— leaving parents on the hook for finding childcare or taking time off work. If a nanny gets sick, parents are also on the hook for finding childcare.

It's just a fact of life that kids who go to daycare get sick more often, especially during their first twelve months,[10] and that reverberates through the household. As I am writing this sentence, I am recovering from both a stomach bug (courtesy of Otto) *and* a cold (courtesy of Everett). Vomiting and blowing tissues full of bright green snot has made for a hellacious week. Baby Everett once got such a bad stomach bug, I had to spend a day squeezing breast milk into a spoon and feeding it to him to keep him hydrated. If I gave him a bottle or my actual boob, he'd throw up everywhere. So. Much. Laundry.

Even though it felt traumatic, and my husband and I missed *a lot* of work during Everett's first year of daycare due to sickness, it's not like he never would have gotten sick if he stayed home with me.

But eventually, their immune system toughens up and the sicknesses abate—until another of your kids enters daycare. (I wrote this book during Otto's first winter in daycare, and I am dying. Thanks for the new germs, kiddo! I lovingly refer to my children as germ buckets. Kids will literally cough into your mouth.)

Here's how my husband and I rationalize the sickness: It's now or later. We'd rather Everett and Otto get sick as babies or toddlers, when missing a day of finger painting really doesn't matter, than get sick as a school student, when missing a day of learning how to read might be a bigger deal. Unless you plan to homeschool your children or raise them in a giant, plastic bubble, they're going to eventually encounter a whole host of germs once they enter school—and research shows that daycare kids are less likely to get sick once they're in school (because they've already built up immunity from earlier exposure!).[11]

Ultimately, the daycare vs. nanny choice depends on your values and priorities—and, of course, how much money you're willing to spend. No matter what, you should feel comfortable with your caregivers. "When it comes to quality of care, it really boils down to the relationship between that child and the people who are taking care of that child," Yale School of Medicine associate professor of child psychiatry and psychology, Walter S. Gilliam, tells the *New York Times*.[12] "Regardless of what choice you make, you need to form a strong relationship with the childcare provider and feel okay about it, because your child will be reading those cues."

## Why It's Okay to Stay at Home

My sister Cassie, a pretty blonde with light freckles who lives near Cedar Rapids, Iowa, doesn't regret her decision for a moment to pause her career to care for her two children, Meredith, three, and Nolan, one—even though she was initially concerned it would strain her family's budget to the point of no extra vacations or dinners out.

"When I went back to work after my daughter was born, I listened to everyone tell me that it was normal to struggle at first but I would adjust in time. Instead I spiraled into what I discovered was postpartum anxiety triggered by my return to work. Who knew it could happen six months after she was born?" she says from her tidy home, where her kids do craft projects and watch *PAW Patrol* as their dog, Oakley, patters around in the background. "When my son was born two and a half years later, I again felt that same postpartum anxiety taking over when I returned to work, magnified by the stress of starting a new job I was not happy with. I left before the kids were awake most mornings and spent the hour or so before bedtimes too stressed to enjoy the little time I had with them. It was devastating to me. When my youngest was six months old, four months into my new job, I pulled both my kids out of daycare and became a stay-at-home parent . . . and I have zero regrets."

Still, Cassie struggled with the decision, even though it's proven a huge help to her family after her husband, Brian, was promoted at work into a position that required international travel and longer hours. "Despite my initial fears that people would think I was throwing away all the time and money I spent working toward my master's degree, I've realized that I'm gaining a lot from both experiences and one does not negate the other. Plus my degree comes in handy quite a bit now that I'm home with the kids! I still get comments about how my kids are too attached to me, but you know what, I take it as a compliment. I hope my very young children do feel attached to me with that sense of security I never had growing up. I was also nervous I was going to be judged for not being enough of a feminist by choosing to give up my career to be a stay-at-home mom. But I've always felt that the freedom to choose my path without judgment is what true feminism is."

Want to be a stay-at-home parent? Great! If you can afford it, and it's a good decision for your family, then shed the guilt and quit your job. The numbers of stay-at-home parents have been on the rise in recent years, according to a Pew Research Center report, jumping from 22 to 29 percent between 1999 and 2014.[13] (The same Pew report says stay-at-home moms actually get more sleep, which I believe a number of stay-at-home moms would disagree with!)

For many parents, it's not a choice at all; one parent needs to stay home to raise the kids. Brooke is a petite blonde who grew up as a gifted ballet dancer and later enrolled in the navy. Her husband is also in the military. "Childcare has been the single biggest obstacle to me going back to work and being comfortable with both myself and for my kids," she tells me. "As a military family, we have lived in three states over the past two years and anticipate moving again next summer. My challenge has been identifying how each area works with regards to childcare and preschools as well as identifying providers I am comfortable with. Since I work part-time as an independent contractor, I'm largely able to make my own schedule and choose my projects, so my childcare needs are inconsistent, which adds a layer of challenge because I try to keep them home with me when I am not working. Also, at our last duty station, childcare and school was too expensive to have them in if I wasn't working full-time.

"For the past few years, I have been able to use a combination of half-day preschool/mothers' day out programs as well as in-home care by fellow military spouses. At our newest duty station, we are actually having a hard time finding in-home care since this location tends to have a very transient population and is much smaller and economically disadvantaged (we are in a small town in Alabama). This is causing a delay in my returning back to work, but we will somehow figure it out," adds Brooke, who has two children. "As we get settled here, I expect we will be able to identify other places or means to secure childcare, but to say that it is stressful is an understatement."

YOU DON'T HAVE TO BE MARY POPPINS

I found an interesting study conducted by Stanford in Norway. It found that Norwegian children who stayed home with a parent for the first year of their lives did slightly better at school than kids who entered childcare earlier. Of course, their grade point averages only increased by .02 percent on Norway's grading scale of 1 to 6.[14] But what's unique about Norway is that its culture values caregiving, and that is reflected in its generous paid family leave policy (forty-six weeks at 100 percent of salary or fifty-six weeks at 80 percent of salary for moms; dads can take fourteen of those weeks[15]) and highly subsidized childcare. Perhaps U.S. children could improve their GPAs even more if they had access to quality interactions with their parents shortly after birth and were all guaranteed high-quality childcare thereafter.

✳

It's time for us to stop assuming that all parents who stay home to care for their children are mothers. Today, more dads are staying home to care for their children. In 2012, two million men were their kids' primary caregivers,[16] a number that has nearly doubled since 1989. (But it has since dipped from its high of 2.2 million between 2007–2009 at the height of the Great Recession, when many men stayed home because they did not have a job.)

In conversations before Payal and Nate had their son Neal, they'd decided that Nate would be the "lead parent," a less gendered, more nuanced way of saying that he'd be a stay-at-home dad, and she would return to work as the director at a major insurance company. "It just made sense," Payal told me as we sipped wine at a window bar one hot summer Friday afternoon when their son, Neal, was two years old. "I had my MBA, I was a lot more engaged in my career. Nate was a teacher who made $40K a year," Payal said. "I always knew I'd be the breadwinner in our relationship, but that didn't bother me. I kind of thought it was novel. Why would I give up my career? I wasn't meant to stay home."

Her parents were baffled by this. As first-generation immigrants from India, their marriage was a business arrangement. Her mom always had jobs here and there, but set up her entire life around raising Payal and her brother. So they didn't quite approve of Nate staying home. "Why would they encourage me to get a $150,000 business degree and then quit my career?!" she wondered. Nate was raised very differently. He's an only child with British parents who doted on his every move. "His view of risk and mine were very different. I always felt like I had to prove myself for everything," she said. Nate was more laid-back, figuring he could always find another job whenever he wanted. "Typical white male in America" laissez-faire attitude, Payal says wryly.

When Payal's maternity leave wrapped up, the conversation about who would be the lead parent had evolved. She wasn't completely ready to go back to work but had to be practical. They needed her job and her health insurance. Somebody had to pay the mortgage. They'd recently traded their 500-square-foot one-bedroom apartment for an expensive duplex with a roof deck located a couple of neighborhoods away. "We didn't have a financial alternative," she says.

So Payal went back to work four days a week and got a local coworking space so Nate could bring Neal over to breastfeed. After about a year, though, Nate decided that staying home full-time with their son wasn't for him, so he got a job that basically paid the nanny's salary. Their relationship got better when neither of them were the "lead parent." Their son Neal is blossoming with his nanny, who has built up a huge community for him. "Our nanny is a better caretaker than us," Payal jokes. "It's a huge mental shift. It was a pivotal point in our marriage."

Like so many parents, Payal and Nate's work–life arrangement is a constant work in progress. In a 2012 Pew Research Center survey called "Modern Parenthood," men were just as likely as women to say it was hard for them to juggle both work and children (yet women are still the only ones asked this question publicly!). Some 48 percent of working fathers and 52 percent of working mothers "said they would prefer to be at home raising their children, but they need to work because they need the income."[17]

## Childcare Shaming Is Nothing New

I'll never forget the time my kids were excluded from a playgroup by a woman who declared that only stay-at-home moms (or, as she infuriatingly phrased it, "real moms") were invited. Why was I being judged for earning an income for my family doing a job I actually liked?!

Whether it's me feeling shamed for going to work or my sister feeling shamed for walking away from her job, judgment over childcare is not a new phenomenon. Our culture handles so many parenting issues through the lens of gender, money, and race, and childcare is no different.

When our society was largely agricultural, it was easier for all members of the family to work equally while caring for children. "Native Americans strapped newborns to cradle boards or carried them in woven slings; colonial women placed small children in standing stools or go-gins to prevent them from falling into the fireplace. Pioneers on the Midwestern plains laid infants in wooden boxes fastened to the beams of their plows. Southern dirt farmers tethered their runabouts to pegs driven into the soil at the edge of their fields," writes Dr. Sonya Michel in her book *Children's Interests/Mothers' Rights: The Shaping of America's Child Care Policy.*[18]

But this began to change with market growth, Michel writes. Instead of one artisan creating a pair of shoes from start to finish and selling it himself, he would buy raw materials from a shop, fulfill a larger number of orders, sell those back to another shop, and then wait to be paid. Suddenly, people had less control over their work hours and environment, which affected women especially. We were no longer able to balance raising children with money-earning work so seamlessly, downgrading our status in the household. When women did work, we were paid much less because it was assumed our productivity would be much lower due to our childcare duties. (Apparently women have been trying to "have it all" since colonial times.)

This shift did not pose a problem for well-to-do families, as women just stopped working to care for the children, relying on their husband's incomes. But in poorer, minority, and immigrant families, quitting work wasn't an option and so childcare situations were stitched together haphazardly—leading to stigma for any woman who worked, and any child in childcare.

In the 1920s, an investigation by the United States Children's Bureau uncovered situations of infants and toddlers who were seriously injured, sick, or even killed after they were brought to dangerous workplaces or left alone as their parents worked. But the Bureau still declined to recommend federally subsidized childcare. Instead, the mostly male physicians of the time argued that "worn and wearied" moms would "stifle" their child's growth.

The idea that a woman should stay home to care for her child was codified into most state laws by 1930 with "widow" or "mother's pensions." But it wasn't easy to get one of these "mother's pensions," especially if you were black, as the criteria was so arcane. (It was believed that black women, unlike white women, "were accustomed to working for wages and thus should not be encouraged to stay at home to rear their children," Dr. Michel writes.) A group of progressive philanthropists had set up nursery schools at the turn of the century, but they couldn't meet the growing demand, and so the centers fell into disrepair—further increasing the stigma against childcare.

During the Great Depression, the government's Works Progress Administration installed out-of-work teachers into Emergency Nursery Schools, which were free and targeted to people of all classes. The 8.4 million people employed by the WPA used these childcare centers, where education was taken seriously because well-trained and well-paid teachers ran them. For a brief moment, the stigma of childcare eased. But the centers began to decline once the teachers started leaving to take more lucrative jobs related to World War II. The war also brought a record number of women into the workforce—and the cultural backlash against working moms was swift. A 1942 radio program introduced the catchy term "latchkey children,"[19] referring to kids arriving home from school to sad, empty homes. Other media dismissed working mothers as "selfish," while so-called experts—mostly men, given the time—warned of kids' "maternal deprivation."

As the war ramped down, Congress refused to continue funding any childcare efforts, and what was left of the WPA-era childcare centers either closed or became even more run-down. It wasn't until the early 1960s that government again considered universal childcare, with President John F. Kennedy's Commission on the Status of Women declaring that it was becoming the norm for women to work outside the home and suggesting government-subsidized childcare could help children developmentally and encourage social and racial integration, Dr. Michel writes. But that plan fizzled out.

Feminists, labor leaders, civil rights leaders, and early childhood advocates partnered with a bipartisan Congress during the course of three years to write a bill for universal childcare, which President Nixon vetoed.[20] President Reagan's policies helped spawn for-profit childcare centers. Any further childcare funding was tied to President Clinton's welfare reform—which continued to link childcare as something only "poor" and "other" people did.

This stigma continues today, but it is at odds with the reality that 70 percent of women with children under the age of eighteen have a job outside the home.[21] Sixty-one percent of kids under five years old have a regular childcare arrangement.[22] "Because of its long history and current structure, the American childcare system is divided along class lines, making it difficult for parents to unite and lobby for improved services and increased public funding for childcare for all children," Dr. Michel writes.[23]

There is honestly no reason why we should waste one more second of energy shaming each other over whether mom stays home, dad stays home, grandma babysits, baby goes to daycare, baby has a nanny, mom works, dad works. The reality is that we have to do what works for our family the best we can.

*

Calvin and his wife Belzie live in suburban Boston, where they're raising their two children, a son in second grade and a daughter in preschool. Calvin grew up in Iowa, moved to New York City for a couple years to be a teacher, and then quit to become a writer and move to Boston. He sees how his wife, who immigrated from Haiti, is treated differently than he is. And it goes beyond the mom who called him "dashing" at preschool drop-off despite his uniform of sweatpants and stubble.

"Belzie's been in groups of mothers, especially when she first went back to work, who've said things like, 'I can't imagine leaving my son.' I wonder if it's just people justifying their own decisions," he muses. (Um, yes, it often is!) "Work is such a big part of people's identity, and when they stop, they have to invest that identity in something else. I find myself judging people who do that. When their role and identity as a parent becomes so all consuming . . . It's fine if that's how people want to spend their time or the choices they make. But when they think there's something lacking with you if you're not doing the same thing . . ."

Belzie also faces issues of what I'll call "mothering while black." Shortly after she'd given birth to her daughter, a nurse questioned if she was her mom. "She was like, 'No, I'm not the mother, what the fuck,'" Calvin says drily. Other parents have assumed that she's a nanny when she's out with their children. "She's been asked how much she charges and told she's so good with the kids. She also looks really young, [so] I do the white person thing of finding a reason it's not racism. I especially did that seven years ago when our son was born. [But] I don't think that stuff dominates our lives and how we think of ourselves."

In America, mothers are judged harsher than fathers. For example, a study of more than 700 people[24] (a mix of parents and non-parents of both genders, and mostly white people) were given different scenarios in which kids were left alone, ranging from a couple of minutes inside their own home to a parent getting injured and unable to care for their child. They were then asked to rate how much danger the kids were in on a scale of 1 to 10. Mothers were judged harshly if they left their kids alone for even a couple of moments. But men were given a lot more leeway and empathy. Tellingly, study subjects didn't think kids who were left alone while men worked were in that much danger. But leaving a kid alone so a woman could work? Sound the alarm!

"I think people think of me as a professional first, and I don't feel like I have to prove myself," says Calvin, who works out of his home office dotted with toy robots and a folding treadmill he never uses. "I'm not just 'a stay-at-home mom who also writes.'"

Calvin doesn't think twice about mentioning his kids when he's dealing with work clients. "If I need to do a call, I'll say, 'I drop off my kid at this time.' I feel like maybe it's just me not giving a shit. Enough people work from home and have flexible schedules and have kids. It's not that weird. I'm not missing a board meeting or anything."

With Calvin working for himself and Belzie employed as a teacher, they "have the best possible situation," he admits. "She's got a full-time job with benefits and good health insurance and a decent salary, and I have the ability to take whatever I want off, or work like crazy and make a bunch of money. If I want to take a day off, I don't have to ask anybody."

And yet, even they struggle with getting their kids to school and juggling home and work. "It's still hard. I don't have any idea how people with rigid and unpredictable schedules or single parents do it," he says. "It's hard when it's 'easy.'"

**#NoShameParenting Takeaway:** In the end, the decision whether to stay home or enroll your child in childcare should be your own personal preference, not some study results or judgment from another person. (And of course, let's all check our privilege if we even have the option to choose.) But rest assured that your decision won't fuck up your kid. As the American Academy of Pediatrics's report on "Quality Early Education and Child Care from Birth to Kindergarten" concludes: "When care is consistent, developmentally sound, and emotionally supportive, there is a positive effect on the child and the family."[25]

# 6

# Time Out! How to
# Discipline Without Losing
# Your Sh*t (Or Your Kid)

Truth time: I was dreading writing this chapter. My book is all about empowering parents to raise our kids the way that works for us—so how was I supposed to say spanking is okay, when I don't really believe that myself?

Then I realized I'd been thinking about discipline all wrong. Discipline is so much more than threats, screaming, time-outs, and, yes, spanking (which, if it *occasionally* happens in an otherwise normal childhood, is fine. But after reading this chapter you won't have to resort to that!).

Discipline is really about shaping positive behaviors and traits in our children. It's about praising them for their good behavior—even more than coming down hard on them for bad behavior. We need to revolutionize the way we look at discipline altogether. It doesn't have to be something we dread talking about or instituting.

But I get it. Discipline is a loaded subject. The way we do it has changed so much throughout the years. And it's stressful when your kid is melting down at the grocery store, and every single eye in the store is on you, judging away as you're ripping the M&M packet from your toddler's flailing arms while juggling a full shopping cart. There's just something about whining, fake tears, and ridiculous temper tantrums that get. on. our. very. last. nerve.

I met a dad named Freedom on a sunny Sunday afternoon at a Brooklyn playground. Dressed dapper in a bowler hat and plaid shirt, he pointed out his six kids—five of which are boys under five. I asked him if he ever felt shamed as a parent, and he immediately replied, "When one of my children is crying in public, everyone is judgmental. In my heart and mind, I know it's fine, but everyone judges. I'm not afraid to discipline. But I hear it from two perspectives: People who think I'm disciplining too much, and not enough. I'm not just talking about spanking."

Freedom nailed it: Oftentimes it feels like we're being too permissive, or too strict. A crying kid in public will catch everyone's attention. Our kids know this. We know this. It's why discipline feels so damn complicated. It's hard to find a balance.

But, as I'll explain in the coming pages, we can actually do more for our kids' behavior by *doing less*. As long as we positively reinforce our kids when they do something right and avoid constantly screaming at them and/or smacking them around—our kids will turn out just fine.

To be clear, this chapter is not going to give you permission to discipline your kids with methods that inch toward emotional and/or physical abuse. But I'll reassure you that things like time-outs won't ruin your kid either. And please don't verbally or mentally abuse your kid in the name of discipline. Yelling all day, every day is not going to raise a heathy kid. If your first instinct is to hit or mock your child, you've probably crossed the line and need to step back and take a deep breath. But on the flip side, if you occasionally snap and yell at your kid, he or she will be fine.

Critically, though, don't refuse to discipline your kid because you want to be the "cool parent" or the "best friend." Science has shown that giving your kids limits may help them cope with troubles in life by "enhancing children's sense of the predictability of their environments . . . The consistent occurrence of expected consequences for misbehaviors may promote a sense of control, which could lead to higher levels of active coping and coping efficacy and lower levels of avoidant coping."[1] In real talk, when kids know there are predictable consequences to their actions, they feel stable. When they have stability, they are able to cope when life throws them a curveball. And raising resilient kids is something we all want, right?

*

"Discipline usually means punishment, but that should be recast," says Dr. Alan E. Kazdin, a founder of the Yale Parenting Center and professor of psychology and child psychiatry there. Kazdin has worked with severely aggressive and antisocial children—and families facing everyday issues. His methods are simple—no traveling to Yale or spending big bucks to try them.

First, he asks parents to ask ourselves, "What are the three or four characteristics I want my children to have?" (If you are married or partnered, you should do this exercise together.) For example, how about raising an honest kid? Then first of all, we need to model honest behavior. Then, we need to watch for instances of our child acting honest. When we see an example of that, point it out. That immediately reinforces the behavior and development of the trait as the kid grows up.

Now, Kazdin jokes that this "doesn't work fast enough" when our kids are losing it in front of an ice cream truck. So he recommends a "tantrum game"—which sounds ridiculous at first, but makes sense. He swears you can do it with kids as young as one and a half years old.

When you're at home and everyone is feeling calm, tell your kid that he or she is going to have a pretend tantrum. "Here's how it works: I'm going to tell you that you can't do something, but you really can. It's just pretend. When you have a tantrum, you're going to get mad, but you're not going to hit Mommy, and you'll get a point on this chart." (The point of having a tantrum chart? "The parents do better if we have a point system," Kazdin jokes. So obviously feel free to ignore the chart, because I certainly do.) The next step: "Mom or Dad leans over and makes a mischievous smile. The smiling is important," Kazdin explains, because it helps to set the tone that this is a "game." It also helps parents feel calmer when their kid starts freaking out, even if it is a game.

Then you tell your kid, "You cannot watch TV tonight," and watch him go nuts.

Now, it's very important for parents to do three things, according to Kazdin. One: Offer very effusive praise. "Great! That was great! You got mad and you didn't hit Mommy!" Next, you need to do something nonverbal, such as a high five, tap on the head, give a point. "Whatever works for your family," Kazdin says. I like to squeeze my sons' shoulders. Then the third step is to set up the behavior again, by saying something like, "That was great. I bet you can't do two in a row. No five-year-old can do two in a row. Okay, let's try another."

Kazdin says tantrums disappear or greatly reduce themselves within one to three weeks of playing this game occasionally. Kids are getting praised for not acting as crazy when they're upset. "What happens in the game can shape them," he says. When a tantrum does happen, be sure to say something like, "We're not even playing the game! That was fantastic!" Pretty soon, playing the "tantrum game" just dies out. "The parent gets a little loose, [the kid] gets praise, and it's not a problem anymore," Kazdin says. "I have done this thousands of times." The key is introducing the antecedents, behaviors, and consequences (or, aptly, ABC).

We have to ask ourselves: How are we praising our kids when they're doing something good? When my kids are quietly playing together, I used to be hesitant to say, "Wow! You guys are playing so well together. I'm so proud of you both," because I was afraid that would snap them out of the moment and thus end my brief respite from wiping noses, butts, and tears.

But I've recently started spending a lot of time verbally praising what my kids are doing as they do it. And it's working! Just this past weekend, Everett voluntarily let Otto play with a coveted train toy he got from a birthday party. And Otto shared his snack with Everett.

"The human mind has a negativity bias. We tend to leave them alone when they're doing something good," says Kazdin. Then when they're acting up, we're all over them—which actually has the opposite effect of nipping the behavior in the bud. We're giving them attention for doing something bad, and they're getting no attention for doing something good. So we're basically reinforcing the bad behavior and undermining our attempts at punishment in the process.

※

There's a myth that bad behavior is contagious. Like, if one kid starts biting at daycare, all the kids will start biting. That's a bit of a misnomer, though.

"It's not so much that misbehaving is contagious," Dr. David Anderson, a clinical psychologist and senior director at the nonprofit Child Mind Institute, tells me. "It's that behavior is contagious when it has a payoff."

Let's say you have a teacher or parent who doesn't pay much attention to positive behavior, but the kid who acts out gets all the attention. Pretty soon, the entire class will act rowdy because they've learned that's how you get attention. And that makes bad behavior feel contagious.

(Biting, by the way, is widespread among young children; the American Psychological Association reports that half of all children in daycare have been bitten.[2] Biting is normal, Dr. Jess P. Shatkin, vice chair for education at NYU Langone's Child Study Center, told Yahoo! Parenting.[3] "Toddlers are old enough to understand a lot, but they can't express themselves in sophisticated ways. So they grab,

YOU CAN'T F*CK UP YOUR KIDS

bite or hit." Toddlers bite their classmates out of frustration, to get attention, or even just to see what the experience was like.)

There are several main reasons why a kid misbehaves, Anderson says. The first: There's an internal sensation for the kid, which he calls "an occupational therapist hypothesis." Biting might fall under the category. Next: They've been given attention for their behavior. Last: It allows them to avoid an uncomfortable situation. For example: If a kid doesn't want to go to music class, he may bite because that means he gets to quietly color instead.

### What's Going On When Your Kid Is Having a Tantrum

Why do kids have tantrums anyway? It has a lot to do about where they are developmentally, and how parents adapt to those changes. When we have a child who's younger than one, we control everything in their world. "Now they get a little bit older and start to have a personality, a will, food preferences, and ideas of what they want to do," Kazdin says. "The parent continues to expect a certain kind of control. Now the child is normally developing tastes and preferences. The parent isn't being weaned very well on how to adapt to that. It's a battle of wills."

Don't use the phrase "terrible twos" to describe your kid—Dr. Kazdin says that's largely a myth. (Dr. Kazdin and I agree that three is actually more trying for parents. It's when a number of my friends' kids started "rage peeing" all over the floor.) "There is a new understanding that tantrums, oppositionalism, [and] negativism are not a sign that the child is terrible or that the child's age is terrible. It's a sign that the ability of the child to think through a situation has collapsed because of overwhelming feelings of fear and frustration that dysregulates their emotional composure. There is more of an awareness that when we say the 'terrible twos' we're really talking about the adult experience rather than the child's," child psychologist Dr. Alicia F. Lieberman says in *The Atlantic*.[4]

"There is something in psychology called reactant. When you're trying to force people to do things, they react in a way that's oppositional. One has to present things to humans in a very special way," Dr. Kazdin says. "You have this child who is dependent, and now he doesn't want to put on a coat. Once a parent goes to authority . . . 'I said so' exacerbates the negative reaction."

Our kids are less likely to throw a fit if they feel like they're given a choice. "If you want a human being to do something, it's much better to provide choices. 'Put on your red jacket or your green sweater, we're going out.' When we're presenting a choice, compliance is a lot more likely. In life, the perception [of choice] is much more important [than even having a choice]. The perception of control is really, really critical," Kazdin says. "It's not rocket science, but it is science." (This doesn't just work with your kids, by the way. Try giving your spouse or a colleague the "illusion of choice" and watch how quickly they'll agree with one of your options. It's basic human psychology.)

In addition to learning their own preferences, toddlers are also learning how to walk and talk. "Toddlers are wired to explore as much of the environment as possible. My two-year-old walks into an environment and he has to expand to touch the walls and open everything. That's appropriate. That's what we want in a small human being: To seek out novelty and look at everything going on in their environment before they settle in," Dr. Anderson says. "This explains why they're constantly opening every cabinet and climbing on top of and below furniture."

Of course, while kids are learning how to walk and talk, they're pretty terrible at both of them, which is frustrating. Tantrums happen because kids are uncomfortable and don't know how to deal with it. As Lieberman writes in her book *The Emotional Life of the Tod-*

*dler*: "If adults experienced and enacted the full range of feelings available to an average toddler in the course of a day, they would collapse from emotional exhaustion."[5] (As opposed to just collapsing in exhaustion from dealing with tricky toddlers!)

### Why It's Totally Normal That Tantrums Make Parents Crazy—And How We Can Protect Our Sanity

I had just spent the past forty-five minutes cooking and serving breakfast, cleaning up toys, doing the dishes, changing the TV show 800 times, getting my kids dressed, and brushing their teeth. Now it was time to go to summer camp. "Why can't Daaaady take us to camp?" Everett said, hands on his hips. "I want Daddy because I like him!"

"Oh," I said, bemused. "And you also like Mommy?"

"No, I like Daddy," Everett said, launching into 100 reasons he didn't want to leave the house, and starting to whine. Instead of me rolling my eyes and moving on, realizing he was just being a pain because he didn't want to leave the house for camp, I felt that sharp pang right in the gut. "Put. Your. Shoes. On. RIGHT! NOW!" I snapped, thus leading to full-on teary tantrum and making us all even later.

Claire Lerner, a licensed clinical social worker who helps train pediatricians, says my reaction was totally normal—if not recommended. "Kids get really provocative. They say all sorts of things that get you in the jugular, like 'I hate you.' It's bait that you could completely ignore. They're all trying to get attention. Any reaction is enforcing. You could say, 'I know you're disappointed.'"

We all know that's easier said than done. Sometimes in the moment, it's hard to keep perspective. That's why Lerner suggests having a couple of mantras to repeat to yourself when you're feeling stressed. That way, we don't immediately slip into a raw emotional state. "You can't fear the tantrum because your child knows you fear the tantrum and the tantrum becomes a very effective strategy," she says. "That's a very clever strategic child."

Lerner points out that we should think of kids as "strategic" instead of "manipulative" to keep our emotions in check. "If you see them as manipulative, you'll have a harsher punitive reaction. Kids are just reading the tea leaves" to find out how to get a rise out of their parents.

And then there are the parents who never want to discipline their kids for anything. There's currently a push in our culture to become best friends with our children. Think an extreme version of Regina George's mom in *Mean Girls*: "I'm not a regular mom. I'm a cool mom," she says as she eggs on her daughter's bad behavior; or those sappy Instagram posts with parent and kid in matching outfits and a letterboard claiming the kid is "my best friend."

I get we all want to be the cool parent sometimes, but that can get in the way of laying down the law. Lerner says she sees this time and again in her practice. But we shouldn't be afraid to have an upset child. A couple of tears will certainly not fuck them up. "Happy children are not always happy," Lerner says. "That's really it in a nutshell.

"While sort of intellectually in their left brain, most parents totally get that children need limits, that limits are loving, and that they help children learn self-regulation and disappointment and frustration. They want that kid who, when they can't get something, are able to cope," Lerner says. "But in that moment when a child loses it or protests, in that moment they get into right brain reactive mode and then they respond in ways that sort of escalate tantrums and power struggles, and it makes it very hard for parents to follow through on that limit."

When you feel yourself losing it, step away from the situation, like Raakhee, a mom who lives in New Jersey. "Sometimes I have to put myself in time-out so I have the mental capacity to deal with her!" she jokes of her spunky daughter, Satya, who is the subject of a book called *Super Satya Saves the Day*. Lerner wholeheartedly embraces this technique. "We need to provide kids with tools, but we as parents need tools. When your child is provoking and you start to feel yourself getting triggered, it's really important to take a moment," Lerner suggests. "You could say: 'I've asked you for the iPad back and you're not cooperating, so mommy needs a mommy calm time-out to help us solve this problem.' For parents who are naturally very reactive, this is very helpful."

The bonus? "Often a child is so freaked out that you're not reacting, that in and of itself can cause them to back off. It's like throwing a monkey wrench when you're not escalating by not being reactive."

This is a strategy Chad, a dad based in the suburbs outside of Chicago, uses with his daughter. "I've learned that putting her in time-out just got her more angry and she wasn't really thinking about what she did wrong. Instead, I tell her to take some time to herself, wherever it is that she wants to be alone and for as long as she needs. This usually ends with her coming to apologize for her wrongdoings, and a much calmer kid and parent. This has also worked for me when she is getting on my nerves. I think it teaches them to respect people's feelings and personal space." Chad learned the idea from a counselor he and his ex-wife visited during their divorce. "It has worked really well and I'm trying to use it for my stepchildren as well."

## Do Time-Outs Really Work When Our Kids Misbehave?

My pediatrician recommends starting time-outs as young as eighteen months old. This works just fine if you have a crib (or a cage?) to put them into. But try putting a two-year-old in the corner and telling them that they're in time-out. My son Otto literally laughs and runs away. Oftentimes, I put him in his bedroom and I have to hold the door closed so he can't get out. Then he cries like a maniac. It feels futile.

"Punishment doesn't work really well unless you have praise for the opposite behavior," Kazdin says. "Punishment suppresses behavior only at the moment. You increase [bad behavior] when you hit. Abuse doesn't make it more effective. Some parents say, 'I use time-outs.' Time-outs are better than hitting, but they won't work really unless there's a 'time-in' . . . Unless the parents are doing something to praise the positive behavior." In other words, time-outs will be more effective and work quicker if you're actively praising your kids' good behavior.

Instead of time-outs, here's a #NoShameParenting discipline method I can get behind: When your kid is acting up, walk away. "The key is to completely ignore your child," Dr. Burt Banks, a professor at East Tennessee State University, told *Parents* magazine.[6] "A lot of misbehavior in children is done to get attention. Scolding gives them the attention they are seeking." (Banks found himself researching childhood discipline after he felt like he was becoming a "cranky, loudmouth dad" to his four-year-old.)

We can't walk away from our kid after he's smacked another kid on the playground. (Even though, let's be honest, I have been tempted to do exactly that!) But you can adapt Banks's method of ignoring your kid, while not ignoring the situation. Instead of going straight to admonishing your child, rush in and give a bunch of attention to the kid who was smacked. Two birds, one stone: Your misbehaving kid gets no attention, and you are able to make sure the kid who was hurt is okay.

## Yes, You Can Threaten Your Kid

Threats can work—as long as you actually follow through. This means you can't scream, "If you don't pick up your toys, you're not going to the museum tomorrow with summer camp!" unless you actually intend to keep your kid home from summer camp. (Yes, this is an actual threat Brad and I recently used on Everett, and it was a bad one. Realistically, Everett is going on the field trip because neither his father nor I are taking a day off work as a punishment for our child who wouldn't pick up his toys.)

If you only deliver empty threats, they mean nothing. Don't say, "Clean up your toys or else I'll throw them in the garbage," unless you actually intend to throw them in the garbage, in which case I salute you for being a badass parent.

Here is a better example of a threat that actually works. "You say, 'Here's the deal. You've got two choices: If you clean up all your toys, you get to play with them tomorrow. And the toys you won't clean up go on the "next-day shelf." You can't have them for however long you decide,'" Lerner suggests. Then you actually put those toys your kid wouldn't clean into a clear bin just out of their reach. Yes, of course your child is going to be unhappy, but that's what motivates change. Next day when they can't have their Magna-Tiles, you can say, 'No. You chose not to put them away. Today you can make a different choice.'"

Kelly, who has three children under five, adopts a version of this for her son. "For behavior modification, I'm constantly changing the currency. For a while it was his Matchbox cars. He could get them taken away for not listening, but he could also earn them back for being a good listener. We tried a chore chart and it didn't resonate with him. He needs something more immediate."

Another option besides threats: Connecting action to time. Use timers or clocks that change colors to show that kids who act up get less time to do their favorite activity, such as reading a book. In my home, we tell our sons they need to go to bed at 7:40 p.m. Lights are out at 8 p.m. They have that twenty minutes in between to put on pajamas, brush teeth, and read books. But if they act up, they get fewer books, which we are able to illustrate by pointing at their "OK to Wake" clock, which turns color at 8 p.m. If they listen to us and get pajamas on fast, they have time to read a lot of books. (They also play quietly in the morning until their clock changes color at 6:20 a.m., meaning they can wake us up. Yes, I have very early risers.)

Learning to deal with limits is an important life skill for kids. If you don't provide boundaries, you'll avoid the tantrum in the short term and your child will be quote-unquote happy . . . but what happens when they're adults and are unable to cope with limits? The goal is to "connect their behavior to consequences," Lerner says. "That this is really how the real world works: If you do really good work, you get a promotion, you get positive feedback, you get more time off."

I set limits with my kids' pre-bedtime demands. They always try to delay going to sleep endlessly by asking for more snacks, a cookie, another cup of milk, and so on. Lerner suggests instituting a bedtime snack before bed and calling it "last chance food." If your child rejects that, but then screams as soon as you say it's bedtime, don't react. "Once parents are able to tolerate the child's protest and the child realizes they're really not getting more food, that's when children adapt. But it requires parents to withstand uncomfortable moments. It's horrible for parents," Lerner says, adding that it is perfectly normal for a kid to whine for twenty or twenty-five minutes the first day you change the rules.

Even if it leads to some initial struggles, I wouldn't call a last chance food rule crazy. In fact, as Lerner points out, it's a "really natural consequence" to not listening to you.

### Yes, You Can Yell at Your Kid

"Yelling is totally natural. If your kids don't piss you off to the point you want to throw the couch at them, they aren't doing their job," jokes Chad, the Chicago dad.

Let's say you snap at your kid because, dammit, you're already late and you don't have the time or energy for your three-year-old to put on her coat "all by herself." Don't beat yourself up. It's totally normal for us to lose our temper at our kids every once in a while.

"Parents are human, we experience normal human emotion. And when you combine that emotion with the stresses of parenting, then sometimes parents yell," Dr. Alicia Clark, a psychologist and professor at the Chicago School of Professional Psychology, told *Fast Company*.[7] "And if we don't talk about how to be frustrated as parents, we aren't prepared for frustration and then, we can be mean. And while yelling can be okay, being mean never is." There's a big difference between, "Get your shoes on right now!" and "You're a spoiled brat just like your Aunt Judy! Get your shoes on!"

I try not to scream at my own kids because I grew up in an abusive household, but I realize my kids' childhood is very different. So when I occasionally snap or raise my voice, I let it go. When I feel myself yelling more often, I fall back on mantras, or taking a deep breath, or even sometimes snapping my fingers three times. It seems to help me break the mood.

"The real problem of effective discipline is that it requires a tremendous amount of our own self-regulation and our own ability to take our own deep breaths and not be reactive," says Lerner. "So that we can take a second to think about our emotions and choose our response, and those a response that is going to be more effective."

Adds Dr. David Anderson, "When met with resistance, toddlers are likely to respond with some strong emotions. First and foremost, we try to get parents to get control over their own emotions. It never works to fight fire with fire. Gotta fight fire with water. We have to be cool in the case of what's going on with the toddler."

And, hey, yelling may even be helping our kids in the long run. "In highly competitive situations—the coach, the one you report to in a job you want to keep—may well have a style different than a caring and sensitive one," psychotherapist SaraKay Cohen Smullens, author of *Whoever Said Life Is Fair? A Guide to Growing Through Life's*

*Injustices,* told *Fast Company.*[8] "So as our children grow, with the right balance of love, limits, and letting go, the child learns to stand on his or her two feet, when to speak up and when to know that is not in his or her best interest." (As an aside, Smullens tells a funny story about snapping at her kids at a store when they wouldn't stop begging for candy. "Someone overheard me and said, 'Hey, aren't you a therapist?' And I said, 'Yes, but I am also a human.'")

And of course this means you shouldn't be emotionally abusive, which is very different than occasionally losing your temper. Emotional abuse is when most of your interactions turn into a screaming match with the purpose of manipulating somebody via their feelings, sometimes resulting in crippling anxiety or PTSD. (I feel like this should go without saying, but please know: If you are physically, sexually, or emotionally abusive, you are in fact fucking up your kids.)

"While yelling can be alarming, it can be a realistic consequence of hurtful, insensitive, aggressive behavior that needs to stop," Clark says. "Yelling is not in itself abusive, belittling, or emotionally controlling. Yelling is in the range of normal emotional expression, can be an effective parenting tool, and should not be off limits to any human, including those of us who parent."

### The Problem With Negotiating
### With a Terrorist—Er, Your Toddler

Elliot* was having a rough time at the end of a play date at our house. "All right, sweetie, it's time to go," Victor* said as his two-year-old crumpled in tears on the floor near our front door. "We have to get home for dinner. And you know we need to eat dinner every night. You would be starving without food! So let's stop crying. Yes, please stop crying. Do you want a cookie? Some pretzels? Do you want me to cook macaroni and cheese when we get home? Chicken nuggets?

Okay, how about we put on your shoes? No, you want to walk home? Well, you can't walk home if you don't wear your shoes."

Why is it that some of us try to have full-on conversations with our kids when they're totally melting down and don't understand half of what we're saying anyway? Wishful thinking. "I think all parents have a fantasy at some level that their kids will stop crying and say, 'You know what, you did tell me four times that the cabinet was off limits, and I shouldn't have poured flour on the floor. Now I will go back to developmentally appropriate toys," laughs Dr. Anderson.

I should note: It's very different to narrate the names of vegetables while you're calmly grocery shopping together than to narrate a child's tantrum as it's happening and they're flailing on the floor. While some research shows benefits of occasionally narrating your day-to-day activities for your kids, a tantrum is not the right time. When you start throwing a lot of words at an enraged toddler, you're just prolonging the tantrum. So make it easier on yourself and keep words to a minimum. "We talk a lot about common sense. Any behavior you engage in with any human usually makes sense across all levels of development," Dr. Anderson says. If you're fighting with another adult, it's natural to talk less and be more straightforward about what you're angry about—not give them a hundred options to make them chill out. "It's the same thing for parents in handling a toddler in tantruming. Your job is not to give them a whole slew of words."

When your kid is freaking out, use simple language, ask few questions, don't make tons of demands. For example: If you want to go to the park, you can either put on your sandals or gym shoes, or we could sit here and have a quick hug. Pause and stop. "What we're allowing them is the opportunity to feel their feelings, or to engage in some sort of coping mechanism," Dr. Anderson says.

This way, we're not squashing our kids' very intense emotions. But we're teaching kids important life lessons by de-escalating tantrums and reacting unemotionally to them. Their future boss or spouse will thank you. "One of the skills adults need later on: How to sit with emotions, cope with them, talk about them," Anderson says. "We want adults to avoid throwing, kicking, and screaming."

## *Bribing: Not So Bad*

Confession time: I am a huge fan of bribes. And, thankfully, they may not be such a bad thing. "Looking for a win-win solution that meets both our desires and our child's desires is not bribery," Laura Markham, the author of *Peaceful Parent, Happy Kids: How to Stop Yelling and Start Connecting,* has said.[9] "The key is to offer the 'reward' in advance, by looking for a way to make the situation work for everyone."

This way, you're not encouraging the kid to act up in order to get a bribe from you. For example, tell your kid at the beginning of the day that they can have ice cream if they run errands with you without complaining. This way, every time they start acting up, you can remind them about ice cream. In other words, don't wait until they're having a meltdown in the dressing room of Old Navy before you make the ice cream offer. Or else they'll associate having a meltdown with getting the reward, instead of the positive behavior.

There is a slippery slope to bribery (like with most things in life!). Don't let yourself fall into the trap of giving your kid a toy or treat every time he or she does something you want him or her to. "Cooperation is too complicated to be shaped by a simple habit, since it's driven by emotions and how connected your child feels to you at the moment. That means you'll have to keep bribing over time. Besides, your child will quickly learn this new game and bargain harder, so you're setting yourself up for extortion," writes Markham in *Psychology Today*.[10] "What's more, you're ignoring a red flag. Why does your child need a toy to cooperate with you?"

Markham suggests substituting bribes with "giggly roughhousing" or some other type of activity you do together every day for a week: "I predict that your child will feel so motivated by her deepened connection to you that her requests for bribes will just melt away. Because the reward your child really wants is you."

### Can I Spank My Kid?

Do you spank your kid every time he or she talks back to you? Is spanking your first and only form of discipline? If your answer to these questions is yes, then it's time to find another technique. The research is clear that parents should avoid daily spanking. The American Academy of Pediatrics strongly advises against it, and studies have found negative cognitive side effects of "harsh corporal punishment."[11]

But let's say you're facing an extremely stressful, anxiety-filled moment, and you swat your child, which is what happened when my friend Catherine* was flying solo with her two-year-old daughter, Zoey. Zoey had been acting up the entire flight; screaming, climbing all over the seats, and throwing her toys on the floor, as sleep-deprived toddlers tend to do when confined to a tiny airplane seat for hours. When Catherine turned around to open the window shade, Zoey sank her teeth into her mom's back. Feeling the searing pain and at her wits' end, Catherine instinctively smacked Zoey—and then immediately texted me with total remorse, afraid that she'd fucked up her kid.

A rare spanking—especially when we're provoked suddenly or when our kids are about to do something dangerous, such as run into the street—is not going to ruin your kid for life. "Most parents have some weak moments and have done something akin to spanking in attempting to move their child's behavior to a different direction," Dr. Anderson says. "What we're talking about [in warning against spanking] is injurious spanking. A very dysregulated parent trying to spank a child to get them to stop doing something to manage their behavior through fear."

And while spanking or whipping with a belt may seem retro, many parents still do it today. In a Yahoo! Parenting survey I commissioned, 50 percent of moms said it was okay to spank.[12] (Separately, Dr. Anderson says that 85 to 90 percent of parents to kids under three will admit anonymously they've spanked their kids.)

Results differed in the Yahoo! Parenting survey among parents of different races: 39 percent of Asian moms and 65 percent of black moms approved of the practice. White and Hispanic parents reported that they were less likely to discipline using physical punishment.[13]

I want to be careful to avoid sweeping generalizations about entire cultures, especially as a white woman, but some experts have explained different attitudes toward corporal punishment. "The Chinese believe I hit you because I love you. The harder I hit you, the more I love you," David Chen, the executive director of the nonprofit Chinese-American Planning Council, once told the *New York Times*. Added Patrick So, a psychotherapist for the New York City Department of Education: "In Asia, your child is considered your property and you can do whatever you want. In the Western culture, it's not the case."[14] Some black parents believe that "physical violence is needed to rear a child properly," writes Stacey Patton, founder of an organization that advocates for nonviolent discipline and the author of the book *That Mean Old Yesterday*.[15]

"In my travels as an activist teaching positive, nonviolent discipline in black communities, I get a lot of pushback from parents and faith communities. Many say they must hit their children so that they don't get into trouble outside the home by falling prey to gang violence or getting shot by police," Patton writes. "They also say that the consequences for a black child who steps out of line are more dangerous than for a white child. Black parents often tell me that they must toughen their children to prepare them for the harsh realities of being black in America."

Beliefs about spanking also differ by region, according to Elizabeth Gershoff, a leading researcher on physical punishment at the University of Texas at Austin. She credits families' more conservative religious background as making them more likely to spank. "Those parents are more likely to say they have very strong beliefs and their interpretation of the Bible leads them to believe that spanking is a good idea, that they need to do it," Gershoff told CNN.[16]

People who live in the South are 17 percent more likely to advocate spanking than those in the Northeast, one survey said. Westerners are slightly more likely to disapprove of spanking than those in the Midwest. Still, "majorities in all regions continue to say spanking is acceptable," the survey says.[17]

Spanking or paddling has been banned by all but nineteen states. But, thanks to a 1977 Supreme Court case that found it's not "cruel or unusual punishment," it's still pervasive across America.[18] A child is hit in a U.S. public school every thirty seconds, according to federal data.[19] At one Florida school, woodshop class students build and sand the paddles used to smack their classmates. "You can't buy them anywhere," said Eddie Dixon, the school's principal. "There's not a market for them, so yeah, students make it."[20]

The idea of physically disciplining your kids is not new. In the tenth century BC in the Book of Proverbs, Solomon advises: "He that spareth the rod, hateth his son; but he that loveth him, chasteneth him betimes." By the nineteenth century, though, spanking and whipping began to fall in popularity in the United States. In the 1870s, U.S. courts decided that a husband couldn't "physically chastise an errant wife."[21] More than 100 years later, in 1992, the United Nations Human Rights Committee spoke out against corporal punishment, including "excessive chastisement ordered as punishment for a crime or as an educative or disciplinary measure" used against children.[22] In 2006, the United Nations Committee on the Rights of the Child declared that physical punishment is "legalized violence against children" and called for "legislative, administrative, social and educational measures" to outlaw it. The committee was established by a treaty that was supported by 192 countries. Only the United States and Somalia did not ratify it.[23]

In my nearly six years editing Yahoo!, spanking always proved a highly controversial topic, with people arguing valiantly for and against it. In an appearance on *Good Morning America,* I didn't outright criticize spanking, and my Twitter feed was full of people screaming at me. While I personally don't believe in spanking, to set the record straight, I don't think a child who gets an occasional tap on his or her backside will necessarily have adverse effects in a typical childhood.

If you're an adult of a certain age, you probably have a funny spanking story, like Rebecca, who wrote to me on Facebook to share a memory about an experience with her three siblings. "The four of us were supposed to be cleaning our disaster of a playroom, but we were messing around," she says. "All sorts of dire consequences had been threatened, including spankings (the '80s, yo). The next time my mom comes to check on us. My brother suggests protecting our, ahem, assets. So when my mom comes down next, she finds the four of us with Little Golden Books in the seats of our pants. Confronted with these square little butts, she had to quickly improvise before going off to laugh herself silly." Replied another high school classmate from Facebook: "We also tried the books-in-bottom response. It remains a family story fave as well."

We can laugh about these rare incidences, but in all seriousness, frequent spanking and physical punishment that borders on child abuse is no laughing matter. If every form of discipline immediately leads to hitting—or threatening to hit—there can certainly be long-term negative consequences. The American Psychological

Association says frequent spanking can lead to increased aggression, antisocial behavior, physical injury, and mental health problems for children.[24]

"Physical punishment doesn't work to get kids to comply, so parents think they have to keep escalating it. That is why it is so dangerous," Dr. Gershoff says in a paper on the American Psychological Association's website.[25] "A child doesn't get spanked and then run out and rob a store. There are indirect changes in how the child thinks about things and feels about things. This includes continuing the cycle of physical discipline with their own children, and believing it's okay to resolve conflicts by hitting."

But not all researchers believe that spanking is so negative when it's used infrequently. Dr. Robert Larzelere, an Oklahoma State University professor who studies parental discipline, has rebutted the APA's recommendation against all use of physical punishment. He disagreed about the validity of the studies due, once again, to the difference between correlation and causation.

"The studies do not discriminate well between non-abusive and overly severe types of corporal punishment," Larzelere has said.[26] "You get worse outcomes from corporal punishment than from alternative disciplinary techniques only when it is used more severely or as the primary discipline tactic."

Dr. Larzelere recommends "conditional spanking," which he describes as "a disciplinary technique for two- to six-year-old children in which parents use two open-handed swats on the buttocks only after the child has defied milder discipline such as time-out." In a meta-analysis of twenty-six studies, which he described in the journal *Clinical Child and Family Psychology Review* in 2005, Dr. Larzelere reports this technique led to greater reductions in child defiance or antisocial behavior than ten of thirteen alternative discipline techniques, including reasoning, removal of privileges, and time-out.

Still, Dr. Gershoff thinks we should hold off on regularly spanking our kids. "I can just about count on one hand the studies that have found anything positive about physical punishment and hundreds that have been negative," she says. "Unfortunately, all research on parent discipline is going to be correlational because we can't randomly assign kids to parents for an experiment. But I don't think we have to disregard all research that has been done."

**#NoShameParenting Takeaway:** Don't feel like you have to be your kid's best friend or that you have to resort to spanking right away. Go easy on yourself. No parent is without flaws and no child is perfect. We are all going to lose our tempers. They will all have tantrums. These are facts of life. As long as you set appropriate boundaries and expectations, don't lose your cool too often, and stay well away from crossing the line toward emotional or physical abuse, we can't fuck up our kids.

# Embrace Technology:
## There's Literally No Way We Can Keep Our Kids Off Screens Anyway

"Is it okay if I turn on the TV?" I've taken to asking this question every time I host families at my home. I grew up tuning into *The Price Is Right* or whatever was on (because we didn't have cable!), but today I don't assume kids are allowed to watch even the most educational shows, no matter their age.

As parents, we are exceptionally hard on ourselves about what kinds of technology our kids interact with or screens they watch. Perhaps we're afraid they'll develop attention issues, become anti-social, be exposed to something scary or obscene—or any number of potential outcomes that the Internet tells us could happen.

But this fear and reluctance to expose our children to technology is at odds with the reality of today's world, where I use an app to order toilet paper. This disconnect between outdated screen-time advice and reality is what causes us so much stress.

Luckily, the American Academy of Pediatrics (AAP) is catching up with the way parents live today and has relaxed their recommendations. Later in this chapter, though, I'll explain how even the doctor who wrote the new rules occasionally breaks them with her patients and her own kids.

And I think we're beginning to grapple with and understand how our smartphone addiction could be affecting our lives and our kids.

"The experience of having to deal with technology on a daily basis is normative now, and that's okay. The idea that every once in a while I have to be on my phone a whole bunch, that's okay, that's not going to ruin your kids," says Dr. Brandon McDaniel, an Illinois State University professor who studied something called "technoference," or instances of our phones interrupting our interactions with others. (We'll talk more about "technoference" later in this chapter.) Dr. McDaniel says a lot of technoference can have "detrimental effects over time," mostly because very young children can't cognitively understand that *Dad has a really stressful job so he spends an hour on Twitter when he gets home to unwind, but that doesn't mean he doesn't love me.*

"Not that we need to be feeling guilty," McDaniel tells me. "This is the world we live in now. Just like every generation has different challenges, [smartphones are our challenge]. How can we help our children to understand why we're on our phone? How can we prioritize [our children]. How can we not do all our interactions on the phone?"

∗

Calling ourselves a "low-tech" or "high-tech" parent has become "an increasingly judgmental discourse," University of Michigan pediatrician Jenny Radesky, who cowrote the AAP 2016 guidelines on screen time, told the Dana Foundation, which funds brain science research. "So much of what people are talking about does more to induce parental guilt, it seems, than to break down what the research can tell us about screen use—and that's a real problem."[1] Case in point: Even Apple cofounder Steve Jobs bragged about how his kids didn't use iPads.[2]

We need to look at screen time with common sense: It isn't really possible for parents to *completely* shield children from screens in 2020 (and beyond); nor is it advisable to let them spend ten hours a day playing Pokémon on our smartphones. In this chapter I'll share simple, stress-free tips for finding a reasonable balance that definitely *won't* fuck up our kids. And I'll reassure parents that we're not terrible and disengaged if we're not directing playtime with our kids 24/7, or if we can't find some magically age-appropriate TV show that *all* our kids of different ages will love.

Let's simplify how we look at screen time by focusing on two factors: the number of hours our kids are tuned in, and what they're consuming.

The AAP recommends only video chatting for kids younger than eighteen months, and only an hour a day of screen time for kids aged two to five years old. This isn't a hard-and-fast rule. There are plenty of exceptions: If you are flying with kids, the limits go out the window. Let them binge on movies and apps to save your sanity. If you need to work, or take care of a task around the house, or just zone out for a little, a couple of episodes of a kids' show won't hurt them. And if you're at a restaurant and the kids start acting up, I don't think there's anything wrong with occasionally handing over your phone to keep them occupied. After all, we deserve a warm meal and some decent conversation, too! On weekends, we often let Everett watch an afternoon movie while Otto is taking his nap—everyone needs some midday quiet time. We should look at the averages over time: If our kids watch a lot of screen time on weekends, maybe encourage them to play with toys or in the backyard on weekdays.

When it comes to what our kids are watching, experts recommend that we make sure our kids are having relatively high-quality experiences. This doesn't mean our kids can't watch YouTube. It means that we should ask them questions about what they're watching and try to engage them in discussion before or after. Yes, I've actually found teachable moments in those boring videos featuring kids opening toys. "How does the car move? What color is that truck? What kind of feelings does that little boy have?" (Considering some of those YouTube stars make more than $10 million a year, I'm going to guess they're feeling pretty good.) Again, this isn't dogma—and I'll explain why in a little bit. We don't need to quiz our kids nonstop about every single goofy YouTube video. And we can rely on reputable apps and channels, like PBS Kids, to help us out here.

We can be creative when we think of how we and our kids interact with screens. Melissa, an author of young adult novels with catchy, angsty names like *Why Can't I Be You*, has found an innovative way to incorporate technology into her parenting that delights her daughter and preserves her own sanity. She created an entire project around her five-year-old daughter June's favorite TV show, *Octonauts*. At the end of each episode, the cartoon characters sing a "creature report," which explains what they learned on their "mission." June, a precocious brunette with lots of energy, will spend entire afternoons coloring her own "creature reports," which she researches online with her mom from their living room.

Melissa admits she's not a fan of playing with kid toys, but she still wants to have fun with her two daughters. So they invented their own game. Each day, they identify a word, event, or person they'd like to learn more about—whether it's at school, work, or just walking around their neighborhood. Every night, they spend thirty minutes after dinnertime researching it online together.

∗

Obviously, the way your kids consume screen time will change with age (newborns don't care about TV like preschoolers do), and when you have more than one kid. Everett was hardly exposed to any screens until he was two, while his brother Otto has been watching Netflix since birth. That's just the reality of juggling a household with a lot going on. But I'm not too hard on myself. Screen time makes my life easier. We try to consume media in a thoughtful way when we can.

I'd be lying if I said my kids only watch educational series on PBS, and after each viewing we have a smart conversation about what they just viewed. Let's be honest: Sometimes my husband and I are exhausted, or I have to get dinner on the table, or my kids are grumpy and neither of us want to chitchat about *Mickey Mouse Clubhouse*. This is okay. As long as our kids aren't staring mindlessly at screens 24/7, occasional screen-time junk food won't hurt anybody.

"When parents feel so overwhelmed about their circumstances that they use tablets as substitutes for themselves, then their children are essentially alone with these inanimate objects. They are not engaging in reciprocal interpersonal relationships," child psychologist Dr. Alicia Lieberman tells *The Atlantic*.[3] "But parents [can also] use screen time as an aid, not as a persistent substitute. I have seen children and parents who move back and forth between the use of the tablet, the same way that you use a book or a toy . . . something that will give the child time alone to enjoy an individual activity while the parent is doing something else, but not as a substitute for relationships."

✳

While my husband, Brad, and I have become more lax in our attitudes toward screen time over the years, so have researchers. In October 2016, the American Academy of Pediatrics loosened its recommendation for screen time from "nothing before age two" to "it's okay to have a little screen time starting around eighteen months." They declared video chatting was pretty much okay at any age.[4]

So why has the AAP chilled out so much? There are a couple reasons, according to Dr. Jenny Radesky, who cowrote the guidelines. Mostly: Screens are ubiquitous, and it's unrealistic to expect parents to completely shield their children from laying eyes on one until they're two years old.

"I know this is a very controversial topic. It's polarized. It makes parents feel guilty. [The AAP] wanted the guidelines to be more practical and action oriented rather than dictating from the top down," Dr. Radesky tells me, explaining that doctors' recommendations have evolved over the years to something called precision medicine: Is this approach going to work for you? Are you going to engage with this treatment plan?

"I remember in medical school, there was all this questioning about nonadherence to medication, and I thought the whole question was kind of silly. Why prescribe before exploring whether it was going to be relative or doable for that family? Medicine and pediatrics have kind of grown up a lot," Dr. Radesky says. "[Over time], I've seen pediatricians especially understand that a child exists within a family context."

"Are you saying medicine has become less paternalistic and more realistic?" I asked her. "Exactly," she replied with a laugh.

So how did doctors suddenly decide it's okay for children younger than age two to watch a little screen time? New research showed that kids as young as eighteen months could learn new words from a TV or other, more interactive, screens, especially if a parent was sitting and teaching as a child was watching—which debunked old research that showed watching screens was too "passive." Not to mention, media has become a lot more interactive over the years, evolving from just staring at a TV screen to apps that teach the alphabet.

But even the newer research is flawed, which is something to keep in mind with all parenting science. You can't experiment on kids, which is a good thing! But as Dr. Radesky explains, the new research relied on apps that were specifically designed by scientists and aren't available to download. "This is the disconnect between lab-based research and real life," she says. Now, she and her colleagues have started analyzing how the apps that kids are actually downloading affect their development.

Dr. Radesky recommends slower-paced apps that aren't filled with ads or ridiculous bells and whistles and that have been designed by those who know something about child development, such as PBS Kids. "When you're using that and you have a parent helping make sense and saying, 'Hey, remember how we played that music on the Daniel Tiger app and look, we have drums right here!' That's when evidence shows kids can actually learn the most from media," she explains.

Children learn even more if parents interact with them as they're watching—but don't feel like you have to chitchat through every episode of *Daniel Tiger's Neighborhood* or family movie night. That is crazy making. Just try to occasionally say things like, "Hey, there's an excavator on the street just like on *Stinky and Dirty*!"

Not everything our kids interact with needs to be perfectly educational. "We're so hyper focused on our kids learning ABCs," Dr. Radesky notes. "There's some degree of rote learning of new words, letters, colors that young brains can effectively learn from media, but that's not the entirety of early learning. . . . It's such a delicate balance between the cult of intensive parenting, [thinking] your child has to have unstructured play every day and go outside and build a fort. . . . What did you enjoy doing when you were a kid? And try to do that with your kids, and enjoy it as a parent, because that makes parenting more fun."

Dr. Radesky often sees families in her practice who run the gamut from being terrified of their kids absorbing any screen time to being overly lax to the detriment of their kids. "Parents afraid of letting their kids watch a little screen media is bananas," Radesky jokes. But, on the flip side, she once met with a family who was concerned about their child not getting enough sleep. She soon found out the problem: Endless screen time at night. "I've had parents say, 'I watched a ton of TV growing up. Don't tell me to stop putting my kid to bed with You-Tube!'" Radesky recalls. This is when even she does not follow the AAP guidelines she herself wrote. "Me just citing the guidelines are not as effective as me saying, 'You're here in my office, worried about sleep. Let's have a shared understanding about what your media goals may be.'" You can't have a conversation with written guidelines. So don't be afraid to have that dialogue with a medical provider you trust, or your own rational brain.

Dr. Radesky has no problem letting her own children watch screens. "I have an eight-year-old who's obsessed with soccer. He watches videos like the 'top 10 goals of all time.' There's an endless amount of soccer content. It's not problematic if it's like, 'Hey, I have a phone call, can you watch some YouTube for thirty minutes and then we'll go out and do something?'" Radesky says. "It's different than a patient with autism, for example, who will literally watch hours and hours of a topic they're interested in [to the detriment of their development.] That's a mismatch between individual user and content. For the other kid, it's a good match. That nuance is really hard to translate into guidelines. I think that's the struggle of translating research into something a pediatrician can say in a twenty-minute consultation."

*

As I mentioned, the AAP suggests the only screen time children younger than eighteen months should be exposed to is video chatting (but again, it's not the end of the world for babies to occasionally see a screen, especially if they have an older sibling). My friends Max and Alex have a rambunctious son named Andrew. Max's mom lives in St. Louis and Alex's parents live in Texas. They've been FaceTiming every day with grandparents since Andrew was born.

"Skype and FaceTime are awesome. I'm really sorry my kids didn't have it when they were younger. Especially when I was on business trips," says social worker Claire Lerner, whose kids are now in their twenties. "If you're connecting with another person and mom's away and you're sending pictures and writing back and talking to each other, then that's awesome."

Lerner often works with families in which one or both parents travel for work. She recalls one young girl who had terrible separation anxiety. "Her mom was going on a work trip to Africa. So [before she went], they looked at maps and researched all about Africa, and then did FaceTime when she was there," Lerner recalls. Not only did it greatly reduce the daughter's separation anxiety, she learned all about a region of the world, too.

Unlimited FaceTime or video chatting should not be confused with noninteractive screen time, or screen time that's not developmentally appropriate. (Aka, don't watch *Game of Thrones* with your four-year-old.) "Everything in moderation," says Lerner. "You want kids to have a full range of experiences in the real world: Playing, doing pretend time, having down time, having to make their own fun. Screen time is part of the mix."

Ask yourself what your kids are missing out on doing while they're zoning out on screen time. If they watch five hours of TV a day, then those are five hours they're not running around in the backyard or playground, chatting with friends or siblings, or generally interacting with the world. That's very different than a couple of episodes of a show here or there, or a binge TV day when they're sick.

\*

We think so much about what our kids are watching without realizing that we are often buried in our smartphones. American adults collectively check their smartphones nine billion times per day.[5] Naturally, our kids notice and want to model our behavior. How can we create boundaries so that phones, which are a pervasive part of everyday life, aren't included in every single activity we do? Showing our kids a healthy balance between interacting with each other and taking care of business or relaxing is a lifelong skill that they'll need as they grow up in a world where technology is only going to become more prevalent.

Much attention has been paid to our own cell phone addictions, and how that affects our children. One buzzy study from 2017 invented that word "technoference," referring to every time an electronic device blocked a parent interaction with a kid. (I personally prefer to call it "just taking a break to recover from the intensity of parenting very young children.")

The "technoference" study was completed by professors from Illinois State University and Brigham Young University. The study families were all heterosexual and mostly white, married, educated, and slightly more affluent than the average American family (I think it's important to give these details because the people who are studied impact the results). Subjects were emailed a survey link asking questions like (1) "When my mobile phone alerts me to indicate new messages, I cannot resist checking them"; (2) "I often think about calls or messages I might receive on my mobile phone"; (3) "I feel like I use my mobile phone too much." Moms and dads were given a score based on how strongly they agreed or disagreed with those statements; from this, 40 percent of mothers and 32 percent of fathers were found to have problematic behaviors on their phones.

The study found kids were more negatively impacted by mom's cell phone use than dad's. The study authors reason that this is because kids spent more time with mom than dad in the study sample. But I think you can read between the lines of this study and hypothesize that women are generally tough on ourselves when it comes to any activity that makes us seem like less than perfect "moms," such as cell phone usage, and men just aren't as hard on themselves. (In this study, parents self-reported their own behaviors instead of researchers more objectively noting their behaviors.)

I called up one of the study authors, Dr. Brandon McDaniel, to ask him if he thought women judged themselves more harshly in this study. "It might be. There's a possibility," he said. "I think overall in our culture, a mother's identity as a mother plays a great role . . . as opposed to a father's identity that he's a father." He also pointed to "a lot of other pieces of research in comparing mothers and fathers. On average, fathers are less in tune with a lot of the family processes going on. That doesn't mean they're bad dads. It doesn't mean there's not good dads out there." (Again, many studies make sweeping generalizations that don't always take into account nuances in individual families. That's what happens when you take results from a survey and then report the average.)

Parents who self-reported more cell phone usage also said their kids were more likely to whine, sulk, have easily hurt feelings, become easily frustrated, throw temper tantrums, or be hyperactive. Please note: The average age of children in this study was three years old. It's not exactly out of the ordinary for children this age to have any or all of the above behavior.

The researchers' conclusion contradicts itself; they write that it's "premature" to definitively declare that there's a strong connection between cell phone usage and cranky kids, but "our findings contribute to a growing literature showing associations between greater digital technology use and potential relationship dysfunction or changes in interpersonal interactions."

Again, we have the correlation vs. causation issue here. Maybe kids are just acting up because they're three years old. Maybe parents are connecting behavior issues to their cell phone use because they were taking surveys every couple of months quizzing them about it. Hindsight is 20/20. It would make sense for a parent to think, *Johnny had that crazy temper tantrum last week*, and *I was really busy at work and checking my email nonstop. Maybe my phone is to blame.*

I'm not saying that the phone wasn't a factor—maybe Johnny wanted more attention in that moment and so he acted out to try to get it. But also, maybe he was acting up for any number of reasons that cause three-year-olds to lose their temper! (My sons lose it for reasons including the following: They don't like their shirt, they want their shirt back, they want to wear snow boots when it's 100 degrees outside, they want to wear sandals in the snow, they want a snack, they don't want *that* snack, and so on.) We'll never know: No study has been done to see if the children's behavior changed once mom or dad stopped looking at their phone.

I do think it's important to look at how our use of cell phones can affect our children—especially on the extreme end. Parents were asked if their devices interrupted a conversation or activity with their children (aka "technoference") more than twenty times a day. They were able to say if their kids watched devices (such as a tablet, smartphone, video games, computer, TV) more than seven hours a day.

I think many parents realize that kids should not watch seven hours a day of YouTube or play Roblox for seven straight hours. On the flip side, I think it's rare that a parent would interrupt playing with their kids twenty times a day, every single day to scroll Instagram— although Dr. McDaniel disagrees with me. He says studies have found that people check their phone up to seventy times a day. (If you're curious how many times you check your phone, download an app like Moment, which meticulously tracks it.) His study found that 48 percent of families reported three or more instances of "technoference" a day.

But "in the end, it's not necessarily the number that we worry about, it's whether it's really changing the quality of parenting on a frequent basis," Dr. McDaniel says. "We're not doing this [study] to try to make parents feel guilty. We're trying to get parents to realize that we live in a media saturated world. That's just the reality. We're just trying to get people to pay attention to things they may not be paying attention to," such as how much their phones could be interfering with their interactions with their kids, spouses, partners, friends, and family.

Look, if your kid feels loved, interacted with, and has an otherwise normal healthy life, your scanning Facebook occasionally while they watch the same episode of *Dinosaur Train* for the fiftieth time isn't terrible. Even if your phone usage ramps up for a period of time—for example, you have a big project coming to a deadline at work, so you spend a rare Saturday checking your phone way more than usual— your kid will be fine.

A generation ago, kids grew up watching their parents reading a physical newspaper or book, picking up a phone to call their friends, looking in a phone book to find a person's phone number. Now, parents use their smartphone for all those things: reading, texting with friends, researching whatever they need to find—and more. But kids may not understand what we're doing so it doesn't hurt to occasionally narrate. Dr. McDaniel seems to be saying the same thing.

Think: "Daddy is on his phone right now answering a question from a coworker. Daddy is reading an article from the newspaper about the new playground opening up in our neighborhood. Daddy is finding a recipe to cook for dinner. Daddy is texting with Uncle Joe about getting together for a barbecue tonight." (No pressure to go crazy narrating every single thing you do. Emphasis on the "occasional" explanation.)

My family bans phones from the dinner table most nights. It doesn't matter what kind of crazy deadline we're on—taking thirty minutes out to eat together is a realistic goal. I also block my calendar at work from 5 to 7 p.m. each night. My team knows to call if they urgently need to get in touch with me during those hours because otherwise I'm with my kids and not paying attention to emails streaming in on my phone.

One thing to note: If you find yourself turning to your phone instinctively every single time you're experiencing uncomfortable emotions, or to avoid dealing with real-world situations, there may be a bigger issue. "The parent should be paying close attention as to why they're using their phone," McDaniel says. "Are they feeling bored? Feeling lonely? Feeling anxious? Are they using their device as a way to regulate emotions? In a sense, are they interrupting family interactions and not engaging with their child because they're feeling stressed? I'm not saying you shouldn't use your phone when you're stressed. But it starts to become a pattern where things get stressful and parenting gets hard, and you turn to the phone." In that case, he recommends asking for more help from a spouse, partner, or therapist.

*

In a world where headlines blare that screen time is "digital heroin" and ask if touch screens are "melting kids' brains," I think we need to stop and take a deep breath. Are we overreacting? Probably, science says. The brain science nonprofit the Dana Foundation has an excellent article chock full of academic experts explaining all the issues with studies of screen time.[6] Namely: Most of the studies are self-reported surveys, as it would be unethical to split up a group of kids and see what happens to their brains if they watch fifteen hours a day of YouTube. And good luck finding a "control" group of kids who have never seen a screen in a world where even refrigerators are "smart."

"The majority of studies looking at media effects are correlational. They look at the brain structure in kids who spend more time playing computer games than other kids," MIT neuroscientist Robert Desimone says in the article. "Because of that, it's always a bit of a chicken-and-egg problem. Is it that kids whose brains are a little bit different are more attracted to playing these games? Or are games causing these differences in the brain? There's no equivalent of a controlled clinical trial, where you take a group of kids and randomly assign them to play computer games or not. I'm not sure you could even ethically do that. So, distinguishing cause and effect is extremely difficult.

"Parents are worried about how their kids spend time on entertainment. They have always been worried about this," Desimone continues. "We know that music education and reading can be beneficial to general learning. So, parents are willing to let their kids be randomly assigned to a piano or a reading group. But chances are, they aren't going to be so willing to allow their kids to be assigned to a Minecraft group. It's a huge practical problem."

"It's important to remember that screens are a tool," Abigail Baird, a Vassar neuroscientist, also tells the Dana Foundation. "Think of a hammer. Yes, you could murder someone with a hammer, but most people don't. They use it to build and create and fix. There isn't enough good science to tell us when, or even if, technology as a tool is going to be a problem yet."

Then there's that fear of our children getting addicted to screens. I've certainly seen my two-year-old stare like a zombie at YouTube before. But despite scary headlines, we don't have much to be worried about, according to Iowa State University developmental psychologist Douglas Gentile. "Issues of addiction are potentially a very serious concern, but they aren't all that common," he says. "There are immense individual differences in how kids respond to different media."

This is why, as I am writing this book, experts are emphasizing the importance of what kind of content kids consume versus the idea of staying away from screens altogether. After all, many apps are designed to suck us in (have you ever noticed how you can go down the rabbit hole of Instagram pretty easily?), while others are interactive and can teach important lessons.

"A little TV, app time, or computer session is not going to harm your kid. And there's nothing wrong with allowing some screen time of quality media that's age appropriate," Caroline Knorr, the parenting editor of Common Sense Media, a nonprofit that is focused on helping kids and parents navigate media and technology, tells me via email from her San Francisco office. "The risks come in when kids are over-exposed to media; if they're on it or around it constantly, and if the media isn't appropriate for their age (too violent, sexy, mature, etc.)."

If you need some suggestions about what to watch, Common Sense Media has a unique rating system[7] tailored to kids of different ages, tracking everything from education value and positive messages to "sexy stuff," violence, and scariness. They apply that rating to everything from TV to movies to YouTube. I used this before taking my two-year-old to his first movie, *The Grinch*.

For a child under four years old, Knorr recommends "gentle shows with short episodes, little to no advertising, pro-social messaging, very simple (like, two or three steps to convey), very concrete (not abstract) ideas are best. Shows for young kids are most effective at conveying ideas when they use what's called a 'para-social' character. A character that kids can relate to on a social level (such as Elmo), who guides the viewer through the content, improves comprehension. Young children will imitate what they see on screens, plus they'll learn the songs and repeat the language—so that's a good reason to make sure you approve what they interact with."

She also says to minimize ads "because kids under seven don't understand that ads have persuasive intent (i.e., they are trying to sell something), making them more susceptible to advertising claims." She also recommends avoiding virtual reality because "no one knows what the impact of the lens is on developing eyes." As for the pervasive report that shows like *SpongeBob SquarePants* can make young children less attentive, she says more research is needed to learn how fast-paced media impacts kids' brains . . . so you can take it with a grain of salt.

"There are multiple brain networks involved in attention and they change quite a bit in early development. Screens could have effects on the span of attention, especially if you are constantly switching from one thing to another, but it's all a manner of how the device is used," Michael Posner, who studies cognitive neuroscience from the University of Oregon, tells the Dana Foundation. "There's also evidence that different computer games or activities can actually help with attention."

\*

If your child is watching a lot of YouTube or Netflix, it helps to check in every once in a while, especially as one video ends and another begins to autoplay. Everett once requested videos of "muddy jeeps." Brad found a bunch on YouTube and then, feeling satisfied with fulfilling our son's random request so well, jumped into the shower. When he emerged from the bathroom fifteen minutes later, Everett was watching videos of naked women playing mud volleyball thanks to YouTube's wacky algorithm.

"If you are going to expose your child and have them engage, content matters a lot," Claire Lerner, who also serves on the AAP's Committee of Early Childhood Development, told me. "Make sure the content is developmentally appropriate and designed for a child your age. I have worked with families who say, 'PBS is a hugely trusted resource; as long as they're watching it, it's fine.' That's true if what they're watching is designed for their age."

That is all well and good, but any parent with more than one kid knows that a two-year-old and five-year-old (cough, mc) won't always agree on what to watch. In that case, Lerner suggests putting limits on how long you let your kids watch any media and being more interactive at times to explain what your kids are watching, especially the younger ones.

Knorr also says not to be too hard on yourself if your kid occasionally binges on media. "Strive for an overall weekly—not daily—balance," she says. "If your three-year-old is sick and watches three hours of *Daniel Tiger* one day, just make sure the next day is less screen intensive."

Each of my children have their own Kindle Fire Kids tablet. I bought them on sale on Amazon Prime Day. They stay hidden unless we're traveling, one of the kids is sick and needs to sit quietly to recuperate, or my husband or I need to work and keep the kids chill. (In fact, many of the experts in this book spoke to me while my kids were entertained with the painting app on their Kindle Fires!)

Screen time "is more [damaging if it's] every day for hours a day. I say the same thing to parents when they're going on a long plane flight. Kids are very adaptable so they learn quickly," Lerner says. "You say, 'We're going on a flight now, and there's not a lot we can do. So on this flight you get to play on a phone for a really long time. That's what we do on planes.' They may push for it when they get home. And that's when we get comfortable, [thinking] 'I let him sleep in my bed on vacation . . .' and saying it's fine. It's a slippery slope. So get home [and say], 'That's what we do on vacation.' They'll push. As long as you stick with it, they'll adapt. They have to hit the brick wall. They have to see that you mean it, no matter what they do, or how big of a fight they put up, they're still not getting the phone."

*

There are some interesting benefits to screens, such as opportunities to connect with children from whom they are different.

"There is a lot of judgment of screen time these days, however, for my family, our screens have been an important lifeline," Hillary wrote to me from her home in rural New York state. She'd just gotten home from New York City, where her daughter, Esmé, who has significant disabilities, was able to participate in a dance program created especially for children who use wheelchairs to get around. Esmé is nonverbal and medically fragile.

"We began using screens in physical therapy when she was three months old. Since then, they have been ways to show Esmé the world, to teach her, to connect with her," Hillary explains. "With the help of screens, she's taught herself to read, learned about friendships from Muppets, communicated her desires, and seen things she couldn't in person. Additionally, screens have allowed me to share my daughter with the world and connect with other families like ours, even as we've been isolated due to Esmé's health. They have also given me a chance to connect with my daughter in ways I thought might never be possible. I want children to be able to connect with my daughter in these ways as well. However, the push toward screen limited (or screenless) childhoods have led to a number of Esmé's peers saying things to her about screens being 'bad.' I find this sad because I don't want my daughter to be ashamed of the thing that empowers her so much."

Judith Newman wrote a book called *To Siri with Love*, about how her son, Gus, who has autism, is "BFF" with Apple's interactive voice. "*Just how bad a mother am I?* I wondered, as I watched my thirteen-year-old son deep in conversation with Siri," she opens an essay in the *New York Times*.[8] The fact that she equates her son's usage of Siri to being a terrible parent is a damn shame. Especially as she goes on to list all its benefits to her son: He now speaks more clearly so that Siri can understand him, as opposed to usually sounding "as if he has marbles in his mouth." Siri has helped Gus learn about social cues. "Siri's responses are not entirely predictable, but they are predictably kind—even when Gus is brusque." Siri has taught Gus to be polite. Siri is teaching Gus how to have conversations with others. "My son's practice conversation with Siri is translating into more facility with actual humans. Yesterday I had the longest conversation with him that I've ever had," Newman writes, recalling a "back and forth" talk about turtles that "followed a logical trajectory. I can promise you that for most of my beautiful son's thirteen years of existence, that has not been the case." Siri is a "nonjudgmental friend and teacher."

Newman brings up a good point: "In a world where the commonly held wisdom is that technology isolates us, it's worth considering another side of the story."

Ron Suskind writes in his book *Life, Animated* about how Disney characters dramatically helped his son, Owen, who was diagnosed with regressive autism at three years old, causing him to lose his ability to speak and interact with the world. At age four, while watching *The Little Mermaid*, the family had a breakthrough: Owen was able to communicate by repeating lines from his favorite movies.[9] Over the years, he regained his ability to speak and interact and express empathy by comparing real-world situations to scenarios his favorite Disney characters had endured. (Owen currently lives and works on his own, and researchers from around the world study him, calling his story an inspiration.) "'A Whole New World' from *Aladdin* seemed to ground and center him as he walked into a world that seemed new to him every day," Ron tells the Associated Press.[10] "All of these kids do have obsessions and affinities. The difference is, we used his affinity as a tool, to not only reach him by singing songs, watching movies together, playing with characters and being the characters, but then we took it further and started to use it to help him with academics and social growth."

Does this mean that if you've decided not to give your kid a tablet or phone, they're missing out on a developmental milestone or empathy chip? No! "We want to empower parents that they don't need to go out and buy a tablet to put their child ahead. You can do what feels good to you," Dr. Radesky says.

\*

"There's no reason to ban" screens, Knorr says. "While it's important to limit screen time (again because there's nothing better for kids than interacting with loving caregivers and exploring the world), there are tons of great TV shows, games, and apps for young children that it would be a shame to miss them! However, it's not carte blanche. You do have to be mindful that the media that they are exposed to is high quality (check reviews of products before buying), age-appropriate (check an independent ratings board like Common Sense Media), enjoyable (don't force your kids to watch, say, shows about science because you want them to get STEM careers), and to the extent possible, enjoyed alongside a loving caregiver who actively co-views and co-plays. There's some evidence that kids actually understand screen media better just by having a parent present. But don't kill yourself to do this every single time.

"The risk comes in when you use it as your default method of soothing, relieving boredom, ending a tantrum, or some other negative-behavior reinforcement that you do without thinking. It's okay if you need to get dinner on the table to let your kids play on an app you've approved. It's okay to let your kids watch cartoons on Sunday mornings while you have some Mommy and Daddy time," Knorr says. "Just don't hand over the device every time your kid indicates she's fussy or you need a 'babysitter.'

"And you shouldn't let other parents guilt you. Every family is different," Knorr adds.

Donna is a petite, freckled brunette whose rapid-fire speech betrays her Texas roots. She's hilarious and makes friends with everyone from the celebrities she interviews for work to the bartender at the local watering hole. She's also a single mom; her husband died of brain cancer when their son was one year old. Today, her son is a rambunctious second grader.

"The other day, I was picking my son up from a birthday party and as we sat on the stoop, waiting for our kids, another mom and I began chatting. Somehow, we got onto the fraught topic of screens. 'Roblox will never, and I do mean never, be allowed into my home,' said 'Principled Mom,'" Donna jokes. "I didn't even bother to respond because without the marauding zombies of Roblox, I'd never be able to take a shower in the morning. As an only parent, the screen has become my stuffy, my nanny, my pacifier. In all honesty, I do think my son is way too attached to his iPad. He launches into full-throttle tirades if the battery dies. Or if I make him read a book. But here's the thing—he's a stellar reader, at the top of his class. He's a whiz at math. And he can concentrate, spending hours meticulously building Lego droids. He has heaps of friends, many of them going back to their time in diapers. When he was an infant, I was as likely to sit him in front of an iPad as I would be putting Southern Comfort in his bottle. But slowly, reality chipped away at my fanciful notions of parenting. I needed time to brush my hair. To cook dinner. To do a phone interview that sometimes fell late in the day. And since I didn't have another able-bodied adult who could take over, the iPad filled that place. Sometimes, I feel guilty. Not a lot, but enough. But we don't live in a bubble and kids have to know how to navigate that alternate universe on their screens. What alternative is there? As for me, these days, I even find time to condition my hair."

Screens have benefits and drawbacks. Like with anything in parenting (and in life!), it's important to keep in mind that everything in moderation is fine. You don't need to completely throw out every screen or feel guilty about scrolling through your phone at the end of a long day—but unplug every once in a while.

## How Social Media Affects Parents

I imagine if you're reading this book, your kids are probably too little to be very active on social media yet. (I mean, maybe your two-year-old has an Instagram account. My kids have a private Tumblr account to share photos with long-distance relatives. Obviously you know I'm not judging.)

Studies have largely found that sites like Facebook can stress out some parents, especially moms, who are under more societal pressure to be "perfect parents." The reason is pretty obvious: If you compare yourself to other parents endlessly on social media and seek a lot of validation, then you're more likely to feel bad about your own parenting abilities.

So, when you open Instagram and that familiar feeling of anxiety starts rising, take a deep breath. Give yourself limits on social media apps. Maybe even delete them off your phone if they're stressing you out. One of my friends deletes all social media apps off her phone whenever she's feeling particularly overwhelmed or when she's super busy at work. Or, if she still needs access to social media apps for work, she'll regularly log herself out. This way, every time she wants to scroll Facebook, she has to stop and log back in. She says this makes her feel more mindful about using Facebook as an emotional crutch during stressful times because she has to pause, recall her password, and take the time to type it in. She says this extra thirty seconds has been hugely insightful; she's realized how much time she used to spend mindlessly scrolling and taken steps to limit herself.

The New Parents Project study examined how both moms and dads use Facebook after having kids.[11] It found both positives and negatives to relying on the social media network.

The study found that mothers who visit Facebook more often and update more content may be more stressed out. (Which directly contradicts another study that found mothers who joined an online parenting community benefited from interacting with other moms.[12]) "It is certainly possible that the new mothers in our study who were experiencing the highest levels of parenting stress were more likely to use Facebook intensely in an effort to seek social support or information. Longitudinal research is needed to detect whether use of online social networking sites or communities has a beneficial or detrimental effect on parental adjustment or whether individuals who have more to share about their parenting experiences—both good and bad—are simply more likely to take advantage of these venues," the study authors write. In other words, every parent is on Facebook and every parent is stressed; who knows how they're related.

The study authors find that new parents are using Facebook to "build social capital" with both friends and acquaintances, and thus, "enhance communication with more traditional social support networks (i.e., family and close friends), and these uses may be most beneficial for parental adjustment. Although speculative, this could be an especially important function of Facebook for parents who live far from family and friends." These connections may be helping us adjust to parenthood, researchers say, adding that parents who connect to other people—whether it's online or in person—are happier because they feel more supported.

But we don't need a study to tell us this: The happiest parents are those who connect with friends and family in real life as well as online. Still, study authors found that "Facebook can function as a strong-tie network where users derive trust, intimacy, and emotional support. Thus, it is possible that Facebook serves a similar function for new parents, providing them with a platform for maintaining strong ties like those with family and close friends that are vital at the transition to parenthood."

The caveat: Like so many family studies, those who participated in the New Parents Project were affluent, mostly white, educated, and married. What if Facebook provides greater support for other populations, or those who don't sit in an office all day, or those who don't live near other family members? Those benefits could easily cancel out the negative side effects of using it.

So, once again, we're looking at science with an asterisk. If Facebook makes you happy and your kids don't light your house on fire while you're scrolling, then carry on. If Facebook makes you anxious and less happy, then give yourself limits, log yourself out, or delete the app from your phone so you're more conscious about how you use it. You can always change your mind: If you're feeling less anxious, log back on.

Or, better yet, start a conversation on Facebook about the true experiences of parenting. I guarantee people will respond; after all, despite the perfectly posed photos, there are very few moments that are flawless in real life. It's those moments that make memories. (In fact, if you check out @NoShameParenting on Instagram or Facebook, you'll see a bunch of honest, real-life stories from parents around the country.)

**#NoShameParenting Takeaway:** Don't do anything to the extreme. Allow for moderation. You definitely won't fuck up your kids if they catch a couple episodes of *Daniel Tiger's Neighborhood* while you cook dinner or unwind at the end of a long day. So stop stressing—enjoy the rare moments of quiet while Elmo takes over as your home's chief entertainer. You also shouldn't feel bad about scrolling through your phone over the course of the day. Realistically, screens and technology are a part of our lives now. But take time to unplug, too.

# Technically, French Fries Are a Vegetable: How to Get Meals on the Table and Make Dinnertime Less Stressful

"No dinner! I want milk! I want granola bar!" hollered my son Otto, stomping around our dining room and refusing to come to the table. As Brad and I tried to ignore him, his screams got louder before he finally gave up and crumpled in tears on the floor. Reader, let me admit: My two-year-old ate a granola bar for dinner that night. Later in this chapter, though, I'll share a technique that has led to Otto eating dinner without complaints almost every single night!

You don't need me to tell you that food is loaded. We feel a lot of shame over what our kids are—and are not—eating. And many of us feel pressure to feed our children quote-unquote "healthy" meals that also look great on social media.

One of my favorite Instagram moms, @vegansmoothiemama (run by Tally, a mom of two sons who lives in Montreal), captures this perfectly. Under one photo of an artfully composed bowl of ketchup, plain white rice, and a single pea, she writes: "The DRAGON KETCHUP BOWL is back! You guys have flooded me with requests for an update to the Ketchup Bowl and it's finally here! If you've been following me for awhile, you'll know that this is the bowl that started me on my journey to inspirationalness. People asked for more greens so they could feel less guilty about giving it to their kids and I've addressed that. I also gave it an Asian-sounding name because everyone knows that makes it seem healthy. I've tinkered with the proportions, we're now at 2/3 ketchup (vegetable-ish) and 1/3 rice. If you like gluten, by all means swap out the rice for macaroni or your empty carb of choice. I've added one green pea for greenery to satisfy those of you who don't want your kids ketchup-loading. For the newbies: Green peas are available in the freezer section of most grocery stores . . . as if anyone ever eats bags of them, hahahahaha. For ketchup, any brand should work! . . . Let me know what you think and as always, tag a friend who needs a dinner plan."

All jokes aside, as long as we feed our kids *something,* we won't fuck them up. Allow me to put our complicated feelings about food into perspective. Parents put unrealistic expectations on themselves to serve perfectly balanced meals, while we don't always eat the ideal mix of veggies, fruits, and non-processed carbs ourselves. (I'll never forget one of my friends joking that the worst thing about her baby starting to eat solid foods was that she and her husband now had to start cooking and eating vegetables for the first time in their adult lives to model it for their daughter.) The reality is that as long as children eat a mix of food and they're introduced to new foods, we don't need to worry about a weird stage where they refuse anything green. Fussing over food is a waste of time and may in fact cause our kids to become compulsive adult eaters. Have fun with food. Not everything needs to be cooked from scratch. The act of eating together is more important than what we're serving. We don't need to stress about dinnertime as much as we do.

And when I say "introduce" your kids to new foods, that doesn't mean you need to insist that they take one bite of everything you serve. They just need to see you eating the food. Eventually, they'll want some, too. You have to think about feeding as a long-term goal: You want your kid to have a lifelong relationship with eating a mix of foods, instead of stressing out over every single thing they put in their mouths.

"Research shows us that pressuring kids to eat doesn't help at best, and makes kids eat less and grow less well at worst. The good news is that the less parents push and beg kids to eat, the more the family can actually enjoy each other and mealtimes," Dr. Katja Rowell the co-author of *Helping Your Child With Extreme Picky Eating*, tells me.

What kids notice more than the meal on the table: the atmosphere surrounding food. What their parents are eating. The fact that some members of the family are eating together. So why not be a little more chill? "Turns out that enjoying the time at the table is probably a big factor in helping children learn to like a variety of foods," Rowell says.

There's an oft-cited study that says kids need to be exposed to a food more than fifteen times before they like it.[1] But many times this is translated into the idea that parents need to shove this food down their kids' throats fifteen times, when kids just need to see somebody eating it fifteen times.

"I prefer to advise parents to keep serving the foods parents want children to learn to like over time. Serve family meals and snacks with tasty foods, with something the child is likely to eat, and parents, enjoy your food!" Rowell says. "Parents find it a relief when they can bring back their own favorites after feeling stuck only serving foods the child already likes."

### When You Grew Up as a Picky Eater, and Don't Want to Pass It Down

Having perspective is helpful. Just ask PJ, who today is a successful lawyer in Virginia of a healthy weight. But he grew up with super-picky eating habits: one phase included only hot dogs and Jell-O, then only plain chicken breasts—cooked with white pepper because he'd refuse a meal with any sign of black pepper. He loved tacos with only a plain white tortilla, lettuce, and cheese. He didn't eat a cheeseburger until he was in college because the texture grossed him out.

After he graduated from college in rural Illinois and moved to Washington, D.C., he slowly started eating more adventurously. "Being young and single in an urban area after college helped me. One, I had to make my own food, and two, I was exposed to all the different restaurants available. You get Ethiopian food down the street, I could get Indian food whenever I wanted. I could get sushi," PJ told me as he navigated the streets of Washington in his car after a business lunch. "It became as much about discovering myself as discovering food."

Then he met Cary, who would go on to become his wife. She only ate variations of meatloaf served with mashed potatoes, he jokes, which was largely what her family consumed in their small Michigan hometown. So now it was her turn to be exposed to different foods. The first time Cary ever ate sushi was in her twenties, on their third date. "She certainly eats a lot more than she did when I first met her," PJ says, but she still doesn't have a very varied palate.

Today, they struggle when their own two kids, Leighton, three, and Rye, one, go through picky phases. "There's a constant tension in the back of my brain that a lot of folks go through, who have means and understand food is a huge part of your health. Why don't they eat this food? I put all this good food in front of them," PJ says. "I would love to instill those great eating habits into them, but the truth is . . . I did just fine eating whatever, and while I certainly think it'd be important to instill good eating habits, I think it's the same challenge my parents had with me. You can only force it so much, short of only putting Brussels sprouts and nothing else on the table."

He laughs, but it's clear that his kids' picky eating bothers him— even though his palate drastically evolved in adulthood. "I would be lying to you if I didn't think about it every time I serve a meal that's chicken nuggets and French fries," PJ admits. "I put peaches out this morning, and they each took one bite and spit it out and then wanted a Nutri-Grain bar. That's okay, right, but they can't eat that every meal."

PJ's inner turmoil is familiar to me, and I'm sure it is to many other parents. I grew up eating Pop-Tarts (410 calories and 33 grams of sugar[2]) and Steak-umms ("chopped and formed emulsified meat product that is comprised of beef trimmings left over after an animal is slaughtered and all of the primary cuts, such as tenderloin, filet, and rib eye, are removed. . . . The emulsified meat is pressed into a loaf and sliced, frozen, and packaged."[3]) Despite consuming both of these things regularly—oftentimes on the same day—I also grew up to be an average-size, mostly well-adjusted human adult who eats a lot of vegetables and even relatively exotic things like octopus and bone marrow.

PJ's mom, Laurie, a strawberry blonde who lives in the Chicago suburbs, wasn't too hard on herself—or her son—about his particular eating habits. "The point of having this meal is that I have my kids together, and that we enjoy it and laugh or argue or cry or whatever it is," she says. Laurie had both her children young—at ages twenty-three and twenty-four, when she jokes that she and her husband were so broke, they bought their cribs at Goodwill and saved up pennies for diapers. She certainly wasn't buying $29/pound grass-fed beef. When Laurie's kids were in junior high, she went back to school to become a teacher, eventually earning her master's degree. Despite how busy their family got, mealtimes were nonnegotiable, even if they only had time to make hot dogs. "I needed some time to connect with my kids. It was not so much as to what I was putting on the table. I could create a consistent dinnertime and expectation that we all met there: That was my goal. . . . I didn't think a battle was worth it. My kids were growing healthy."

✳

When I was digging into the research for this chapter and interviewing experts, everyone pointed me toward family therapist and registered dietitian Ellyn Satter and her "division of responsibility" concept,[4] which basically says parents and kids each have simple roles when it comes to meals, which should be served family style: in bowls, plates, and dishes at the center of the table so everyone can serve themselves. These are the parents' jobs: The meal available for dinner and the time we eat. Here are the kids' jobs: What they want to eat from the bowls on the table and how much. One option on the table should be something that you know your kid likes. That's it.

I am telling you: Adopting the "division of responsibility" method (which is touted by the nonprofit Ellyn Satter Institute and in Satter's books such as *Child of Mine: Feeding with Love and Good Sense*) has revolutionized the way my family eats. Dinner is no longer a power struggle. I don't care if Otto only eats a scoop of strawberries and ignores the chicken. And because he no longer feels pressured to "clear his plate" or "take one more bite" or "just try it," he is much more likely to be curious enough to try everything. The one option that I usually always have is a small bowl of fruit because I know my kids like it. But, thanks to the "division of responsibility," now my kids have also tried a whole bunch of other foods: cucumbers, carrots, hummus, lettuce, pot roast . . . things they stuck their tongue out at just a month earlier.

You don't need to tell your kids that they have "roles," unless you have rule followers who you think should know this. And make sure the kids' plates are empty when they come to the table so they can serve themselves (or with a caregiver's help if they're too young).

"The key is to trust the child. This can terrify parents, most of whom don't trust themselves with eating," says Dr. Rowell. "This is absolutely revolutionary for many parents and even healthcare providers. The notion that children are born with skills around self-regulation, and that we need to support those skills, is critical. But, in a culture that thinks we need to rely on points, or our fitness trackers rather than our bodies to tell us how much to eat, the idea of trusting children seems even more dangerous or negligent. Virtually all children are born with the skills to become competent eaters if we support them. Unfortunately, our culture undermines this inborn skill at every turn."

## Lies We're Told about Food and Eating

Food is loaded in our culture. We place foods into "good" and "bad" categories. We admonish ourselves for putting on a few pounds and celebrate when we've lost those pounds. We're "watching our figure" and skip dessert, or having a "cheat day" and eat dessert. Or maybe we're just sad, bored, or angry, so we "eat our feelings." As Dr. Rowell says, "It's hard to model competent eating and feeling body positive when we struggle." So here's your permission to eat whatever you want, as long as it's in moderation and mixed with a lot of variety, and to find joy in your meals and sharing them with loved ones. To help you shed the guilt over "breaking the food rules," below are some of the biggest lies we tell ourselves about food— with explanations as to why they're myths.

1. Only from-scratch, "healthy" meals are worthy of sharing and making the time to eat together. *FALSE*. "People put so much pressure on family dinner. It doesn't need to be homemade," says Virginia Sole-Smith, the author of *The Eating Instinct*. "It does not need to have vegetables. Family dinner can be cheese and crackers and a banana. If we're all sitting down together, family dinner doesn't have to be mom and dad and kids. It can be mom and kids, dad and kids, any combination." She urges you to let go of the "perfection standard" and never look back. If you're somebody who likes to cook, then great—it's probably not too arduous to make family dinner. If you can't stand cooking, or work a lot, or don't have a partner to help clean up after the meal, "the convenience foods are there to help you," Sole-

Smith points out. "It doesn't make you a bad parent if you hate cooking. It's just a personal preference. I don't like watching basketball, and I'm not a failure as a human being. It's a choice, yet we've somehow decided it's not a choice. I think it's totally possible to feed your kids a healthy and varied diet and never cook a day in your life."

2. "Family Dinner" is the only meal that counts. *FALSE*. We tell ourselves that we need to gather every single night, with every single family member, for dinner—or else we failed. But that's so not true. Dr. Rowell will never forget when, after giving a speech, a mom approached her crying about how they couldn't eat as a family because the dad worked evenings. "I felt her shame and fear. That was a great lesson for me," Rowell says. "Family meals can be a shared snack time after school, break-fast or lunch on a weekend, a fast-food meal where everyone goes inside and sits and shares the meal together, take-out pizza with just dad and the kids. . . . Folks giving parenting advice need to be far more inclusive and supportive." Adds Dr. Anne Fishel, a Harvard professor, family therapist, and cofounder of the Family Dinner Project: "There are 16 opportunities over the course of the week for families to eat together: 7 dinners, 7 breakfasts, 2 weekend lunches. An intentional snack would also count: A little fruit, and hot chocolate, and talk."

3. Every single meal needs to be perfectly balanced, or else you suck as a parent. *FALSE*. "There is some research to suggest that all the benefits associated with family meals are more about the connection and less about the food. Put your ener-gies into enjoying each other first, and the rest will be easier," Dr. Rowell says. "There is so much fear out there over foods like sugar, which is the current evil now that fat is back in favor,

and flour and processed foods," Dr. Rowell adds. "But the pervasive anxiety and conflict around food can be far more toxic than anything the parents are trying to avoid." I jokingly asked Dr. Rowell what happens if your kid doesn't eat perfectly balanced meals three times a day, and she responded, "Um, they grow and are happy? Or there is a lot of fretting and pressure. Perfect is the enemy of good. The big lie is that children eat the way we want them to eat. My plate is not how most children eat." Still, Dr. Rowell says she hears plenty of parents who say a version of, "'I ate a variety when I was pregnant, I breastfed, I made homemade organic baby food with garlic and a variety of flavors, I cooked and we ate family meals, I vowed to ban all processed foods, and my kiddo eats five things and isn't gaining weight.' You can do everything 'right' and still struggle as a parent. It's not always in the parent's control, and parenting advice needs to be kinder and gentler." Like most weird phases, food included, this too shall pass.

4. Snacks will ruin dinner *FALSE.* There is nothing more stressful than rushing in the door from school or work with a bunch of whiny, hangry kids demanding to be fed right away, but you know dinner won't be ready for at least thirty minutes. Dr. Rowell recommends serving a balanced and filling snack after school and considering pushing dinner back to 6:30 or 7 p.m. "When kids aren't starving and pestering, that is a huge help. Use screen time when you need it most, which may be in that final meal prep push," says Dr. Rowell. "Say yes to takeout and convenience foods if it helps take the pressure off. When my kiddo was a young toddler, we were in a new city, and my husband worked insane hours. I had complications from a surgery. So, we ate a fair amount of takeout, enjoyed mac and cheese and a quick soba noodle stir-fry. We ate less variety. When things

calmed down, I got back into cooking more, which I enjoy most nights." And don't be afraid to just say no to after-school activities and sports. "Making choices to have a less frenetic schedule can benefit everyone," Dr. Rowell says.

5. Protein is hard to get enough of and must be eaten at every meal for your child to have enough energy. *FALSE*. "If your kid has milk three times a day, they're getting enough protein. You do not need to put them on a paleo diet!" jokes Amy Palanjian, who runs the popular *Yummy Toddler Food* blog and Instagram account. I dug into a number of studies looking for a recommended amount of protein for kids and asked every expert I interviewed for this book. None of them could say definitively; instead, all stressed how it's important to eat everything in moderation. (The estimates I did find didn't cite any sound science as support.) So don't stress out about forcing lean chicken on your toddler. Also don't think of protein as just meat; other good sources include beans, cheese, milk, yogurt, peanut butter, rice, eggs, and even many vegetables. Let's say your kid consumes one cup of milk, one mozzarella string cheese stick, and a tablespoon of peanut butter over the course of a day—that's a whopping 21 grams of protein. As for guilt that your kid is eating "too many carbs"? "Kids need carbs," says Maryann Jacobsen, who has her master's in science and wrote the book *Fearless Feeding: How to Raise Healthy Eaters from High Chair to High School*. "Carbs are related to growth in kids." She points to one study that shows kids crave sweets when they're going through a growth spurt, as evidenced by a marker in bone growth. "Some parents may try to do low fat because they eat that way, or no carbs because they eat that way, but kids are not little adults," adds Jacobsen. She doesn't recommend a diet of only buttery pasta, but don't beat yourself up if that's your kid's favorite dinner.

6. Children need to be taught portion control. *FALSE.* "I remember when I first watched my preschooler hand me a half-eaten ice cream, saying she was full. It was her favorite, but she could listen to her body," Dr. Rowell recalls. Your child does have the ability to regulate their consumption when we give them the space to do so, instead of sharing all our food hang-ups with them. Also, keep in mind that kids' serving sizes are tiny. A child-size serving of vegetables is just one tablespoon—meaning a kid who chomps on just one baby carrot has officially had one serving of vegetables.

7. Foods are "good" or "bad." *FALSE.* We should try not to put labels on food, even if they're more nuanced than "good" or "bad." For example, don't use phrases like "growing foods." Says Palanjian, "We're passing on a lot of mixed messages and a lot of confusion. A lot of the time, the things we're actually saying about food changes depending on the context. We may eat cake one day, and then say something negative about it the next time we see it. I think that can be confusing to a kid, when, to a kid, cake is just delicious and not out to get you!" Admit it: How often do you happily eat a piece of cake at a birthday party and then call yourself "fat" or "bad" for eating a piece after a meal later? "I think tying what we eat to good or bad is a tricky distinction for kids. When we use 'good' or 'bad' foods, I think kids jump to associate that if they eat it, they are also bad. That's problematic. It just brings in the whole guilt factor around food, which I think is a bigger concern," Palanjian says.

8. As long as the food is "healthy" kids can eat it whenever they want, and as much as they want. *FALSE.* Just like you wouldn't recommend your kid consume nothing but cookies for all his meals, you wouldn't recommend he only eat bananas all day,

every day. Also, if kids are snacking all the time, even if it's only on grapes and seaweed, they will be less likely to sit down for a family meal and thus lose out on an opportunity to be introduced to new foods and expand their palate.

9. Ordering off the kids' menu is a bad thing. *FALSE*. When I asked parents on Facebook to tell me about how their kids eat, more than one #humblebragged about how their kids *never* eat off the kids' menu. My response: "Why not! You're wasting money." I regret that many NYC restaurants do not have kids' menus, and I love ordering $3.99 chicken tenders when traveling. The smaller portions suit my kids better, and I can have an adult meal without hearing them complain nonstop about how they don't like red peppers in their rice, or that their food is too spicy. "If you're freaking out about wanting your kid to eat kale smoothies and all their friends are eating chicken nuggets, the world is set up against you there," Sole-Smith says. "All you're going to do is heighten the anxiety and give yourself a complex for feeling guilty or invite rebellion." And let's just be honest: Chicken tenders are basically a staple in the American diet. "It's not like you can keep them home forever, and I think that's something I have learned as I've had a child who has gotten older. When she was two and I was making all her food, I could control it. As soon as she started being in the world, I realized my job was to give her a solid foundation that lets her make mostly healthy choices on her own. That involves buying some school lunches because she doesn't want to miss out," Palanjian says. The key is to balance the chicken tenders from the kids' menu with more wholesome foods. How about grilled cheese and apple slices instead of French fries? Or, just get the French fries and eat some fruit later for a snack.

10. Teaching kids about "nutrition" will help them make better choices about food. *IT DEPENDS.* The idea of nutrition is so nuanced in America. A lot of it is tied to trends and the food business: Sugar, cholesterol, fat, and now gluten have all taken their turns being demonized or idolized. "In sixth grade, a visiting nutritionist came to my daughter's gym class and told them that bacon causes cancer and that they should all essentially eat vegan, with lots of scare tactics around health. Selling fear and headlines is part of the problem," Dr. Rowell says. "I had to explain to our daughter that eating bacon a handful of times a month is not going to raise our cancer risk, that we would need to regularly eat large amounts of cured meats for years to see an increase. We have whiplash from attention-grabbing head-lines; a drink of alcohol a day is good, a drink of alcohol a day is bad, yogurt is great for gut health but will give you cancer, eat paleo, no vegan . . . whatever it is, fear grabs headlines, and any nuance and certainly enjoyment is lost." And, when you dig into many of these studies, you see the correlation vs. causation issue again. Due to ethical reasons, no scientist is going to as-sign a group of people to eat three pounds of bacon a day and measure if they get cancer. So, once again, just help your kids to understand that everything should be eaten in moderation. French fries today, not tomorrow. Easy enough.

11. "Natural" or "honest" or "simple" food is better. *FALSE.* Those words "don't mean anything!" says Palanjian. She points to the Simply Balanced lunch kit at Target, which she jokes is "basi-cally a Lunchable, just the meat in it is hormone-free." Palan-jian says that allowing her daughter to bring them to school occasionally for lunch causes her to "lose her mind with ex-citement," which is kind of the point. "Allowing our kids to taste these foods they might see at school or go to a fast-food

183

restaurant and eat fries and not freak, or call the food bad or unhealthy, is a good thing." We spend *a lot* of money on things marketed as "natural." Roughly fifty-nine million Americans spend a combined $30.2 billion on "complementary health" products annually, according to the CDC;[5] $1.9 billion of that was on children. "There is no better consumer than an anxious mom!" says Dr. Rowell. "So parents might shell out over $500 for an organic mattress, or spend twice as much on a bottle that promises less gas, or unproven probiotic supplements, or buy a $5-a-pop organic 'healthy' snack bar made with organic honey. . . ." You shouldn't spend more money on food—or any product—that includes words like "natural" or "simple" or "honest" on their packaging because that is all marketing and means nothing about the ingredients included. The only word that is regulated is "organic," meaning there are no pesticides, genetic engineering, chemical fertilizers, or dyes, according to the USDA.[6] Organic foods tend to be more expensive, though, so don't feel like you're letting your family down or poisoning your kids if you don't want to spend more or can't afford them. Organic foods are not all created equally. Organic bananas, for example, are a waste of money because their skin is so thick that it blocks the pesticides from reaching the fruit, and then you remove it before eating anyway.[7] "There's this store near me that has the reputation of being the cheaper store. I shop there more often because their produce turnover is much better. I'm always telling my friends who will drive [an hour] to go to Whole Foods: You're crazy! I think shopping in a store with good produce turnover, whether or not it's organic, would always be my choice," says Palanjian, who lives in a small town in Iowa. It's fresher, which means it tastes better—making it more likely that your family will actually enjoy eating it. Palanjian also offered a tip I'd never thought of: If you don't see an item you're looking for in your local supermarket, ask the store to stock it. "Even a lot of smaller-town grocery stores have buyers who are really thoughtful," she says. Palanjian focuses less on splurging on organic and more on "whole foods," which she means as "something not turned into some other dish," such as beans, rice, fresh vegetables, and cheese. "This both keeps our grocery bill a little lower and gives me more control," Palanjian says. "You can buy those foods mostly everywhere."

12. Getting the "crap" out of the house means kids won't eat it and they won't develop a taste for it. *FALSE.* "This may be the case for some kids, but is also the set-up for sweets and forbidden food preoccupation that I've seen, or children sneaking, stealing and bingeing when they do have access," Dr. Rowell says. But by stressing so much over food, "we are teaching them that food is dangerous, and they need to be wary. We teach them fear and shame. When we teach them that sugar is 'poison' and we ban it, many will find it elsewhere. I've had clients eating entire bags of Oreos in a friend's bathroom, or sugar straight from the bag. The shame fuels disordered eating, which fuels weight dysregulation and lots and lots of suffering."

13. You're a terrible parent if you forget your kid's water bottle at home, or—gasp—leave it at home on purpose so you can travel lightly. *FALSE*. Kids don't need gallons of water every day. It's okay if they drink it only during meals, or when they actually say, "I'm thirsty," registered dietitian and chef Lindsay Stoulil told me as we handed out pizza slices to our kids. Reputable organizations have wildly different recommendations, ranging from "drink 8 ounces for every year of their life,"[8] meaning a three-year-old would need 24 ounces of water a day, to "5-year-olds need 34 ounces a day."[9] But there is little science

proving the benefits of one cup of water versus five. (Even the ubiquitous recommendation that adults consume eight cups of water a day has been debunked!) Two widely quoted studies that touted shocking numbers of dehydrated kids were funded by Nestlé Waters, which makes a lot of money selling bottled water. "There is no formal recommendation for a daily amount of water people need. That amount obviously differs by what people eat, where they live, how big they are, and what they are doing," pediatrician Aaron E. Carroll told the *New York Times*.[10] "But as people in this country live longer than ever before, and have arguably freer access to beverages than at almost any time in human history, it's just not true that we're all dehydrated." Don't forget that many foods, especially fruits and vegetables, have a high water content. If over the course of a day your kid drinks some milk, some water, and eats a chunk of watermelon, but otherwise doesn't ask for anything to drink, she's fine. Stoulil recommends that your kids mainly drink water, though, as opposed to only milk or juice. Milk is filling and can throw off meals, so we started limiting it to morning and before bedtime when my kids turned two years old. (If they ask for it at other times of the day, we don't normally deny it. But I don't offer it within an hour or so of meals.) As for juice, I don't care if my kids drink juice boxes at school or birthday parties—but I don't keep them in my house because I believe in sugar in moderation. A little apple juice never killed anyone, though. Sometimes I mix it with equal parts water. My kids don't know the difference, and it's an easy way to keep the sugar (and accompanying sugar high) at bay.

Now that we've debunked a bunch of myths, here are some things you should know to ratchet down the pressure: It's not abnormal for your kid to be a picky eater. A 2004 study of more than 3,000 infants asked parents to rate whether their kids were picky.[11] Only 19 percent of four-month-olds were deemed picky, but 50 percent were called picky by twenty-four months. And it's also very common for kids to eat erratically. "They may eat a large meal for breakfast, then almost nothing at snack. They might eat only pasta for dinner, and eat five clementines with lunch," Dr. Rowell says. "When I ask parents to look back over a day or two, they realize that their children are getting balance, just not at every meal."

Dr. Rowell cautions that there is no "one size fits all advice" when it comes to feeding your children. Again, their personalities play a big role—and you should keep that in mind. "Children are very different. Easygoing and adventurous kids tend to approach foods the same way and may like most foods after only a few tries. Children who are more cautious and hang back from new experiences approach foods with caution too." While the "division of responsibility" family-style meals changed the way my family eats, they may not work for your family. Try not to be so hard on yourself.

"That's the whole thing about developing a healthy relationship with food: If we're stressing so much about what we eat, it's not good for our health either. It counteracts some of the benefits we might be getting from eating certain foods," registered dietitian Maryann Jacobsen, author of *The Family Dinner Solution*, tells me. "When we take away that pressure and ask ourselves, 'What do I like to eat, how does this food make me feel?' then you're making the choices you want to, not to make sure everyone thinks you eat healthy or because it's the latest headline."

Knowing your kids' temperaments should take off some of the pressure on adults. A child who is adventurous with activities may be more likely to agree to "take just one bite." Her more stubborn sibling may turn the one-bite rule into a hostage negotiation. And is it really worth it to force your kid to eat a bitter vegetable like spinach? I didn't even like spinach until I was an adult!

"I had a mom email me saying she made her child try a food thirty-seven times and he still didn't like it. What so much feeding advice misses is that kids are different, and foods are different. Most kids don't need ten tries to like sweet foods, but might need dozens of exposures to like something like, say, artichokes, or they may never like them," says Dr. Rowell. Again, if our goal is to raise kids who eat a mix of foods, giving them a complex over one food at one meal is not how we achieve that.

## It's No Surprise That We're Struggling to Feed Our Kids

Even when we are trying to do our best, it's hard to know what's best for our kids. Food recommendations have changed so dramatically over the past several decades, it's no wonder that some parents are so confused and overwhelmed about what to feed their kids.

Take peanuts. In 2000, the American Academy of Pediatrics recommended no peanuts before age three.[12] By 2010, the number of kids with peanut allergies increased 100 percent, and peanut butter and jelly sandwiches became enemy No. 1 in school cafeterias everywhere. But Israeli kids seemed to be exempt from this trend—and studies into why revealed it's largely due to the popularity of Bamba, which is like a peanut butter version of a cheese puff. (And delicious, I might add!) I have many friends who Amazon Subscribe and Save these tasty treats because they're still not readily available in U.S. stores (although Trader Joe's now carries their own version of them).

In January 2017, the National Institute of Allergy and Infectious Diseases officially changed course, too, and recommended that parents start giving kids peanut butter at six months—or even earlier if they're prone to food sensitivities (if they have eczema, that may be a good sign they're at risk for food allergies) or allergies that run in families.[13] And now peanut butter allergies are on the decline.

But parents are still skittish about peanut butter. Both my kids showed sensitivity to it at first. Everett barfed the first time he had it, but probably because we didn't plan his initiation very well. (I gave him a bite of my peanut butter toast shortly before boarding an airplane, then let him crawl around all over the floor of the airport's dirty rug, and then he threw up on me as we were boarding.) Otto had his own bizarre initial response: His face turned red, especially around his mouth. Both times we waited another couple of weeks and gave it to them again, and neither developed an allergy.

Pediatricians give mixed advice, too. Some say to introduce a food, wait a week, and then introduce another food, so you can closely monitor reactions. My French pediatrician recommends feeding kids whatever you're eating to introduce lots of spices and flavors from an earlier age. This is also similar to a popular method called baby-led weaning, where you make no special pureed foods for your kids and just hand them over whatever you're eating, such as noodles or even a chicken leg.

I made some of my own food—but always in my old blender instead of some special baby food maker. I spent way too much money on those overpriced food pouches, because they're just so easy and it seems like a good way to sneak in some veggies. But I usually just served my kids whatever the rest of the family was eating. Of course, if you ask your parents what they fed you as a child, you'll probably not hear organic pouches or anything specially prepared.

I'm not dissing organic food. But let's be honest when we talk about how much we spend on food, and what it says about how we perceive ourselves. As Dr. Rowell says, food is "a marker of social status and education. If your kid has a $5 smoothie versus a can of Coke that can cost as little as twenty-five cents, that has a lot of larger societal baggage wrapped up in it."

Jessika grew up on food assistance and writes in *The Guardian* that she'll never forget cashiers searching her mom's hand for a wedding ring, or muttering "trailer trash" as her family checked out.[14] "A cashier once berated my mom for buying a box of cake mix for my brother's fourth birthday as my worried brother looked up at them. Adults sneered at my sister and me if they spotted the large bag of potato chips and five two-liter bottles of off-brand soda in our cart. But we bought non-perishables in bulk like that because our neighbor only gave us a ride to the store once a month, when new food stamps arrived."

Some 45.8 million Americans rely on the Supplemental Nutrition Assistance Program, which is also called SNAP or food stamps—and two-thirds of those are children, elderly, or disabled. It's a legal requirement that adult SNAP recipients have jobs.[15] Despite this, there is still plenty of stigma about the unemployed "welfare queen," which has been called "a vicious, racist stereotype"[16] of a woman who funds a lavish lifestyle of lobster and filet mignon with her food stamps— even though multiple surveys have shown recipients are a diverse mix of people from around the country, and that they end up skipping meals at the end of the month when their benefits run out. My family was briefly on food stamps when I was a kid. Headlines like "In the Shopping Cart of a Food Stamp Household: Lots of Soda"[17] further stigmatize SNAP recipients as unhealthy and lazy. When you read the article, you see that *all* American households spend nearly the same amount of money on sugary drinks, whether they use SNAP or not. The USDA, which distributes SNAP, reports that families who rely on the benefits buy roughly the same kinds of foods that people who don't use SNAP buy.

Yet, those of us who show off how healthfully our kids are eating are celebrated and seen as better parents. "Social media, and comparing ourselves to others, is awful," Dr. Rowell says. "I remember seeing a friend's post of her toddler drinking a green smoothie. She wrote, 'Mama must be doing something right!' The implication is if your kid isn't drinking green smoothies, you mamas are doing something wrong. I just have no time for that. Google mama and green smoothie. There are hundreds of posts, and extra health points if they are in a mason jar! By the way, smoothies don't have to be green to be yummy and packed full of nutrition. It's a great example of perfect being the enemy of the good. A child might love a smoothie with whole-fat Greek yogurt with berries and bananas, maybe even some flax oil, but would balk once spinach is thrown in the mix. I personally have no interest in drinking a green smoothie. I'll enjoy my spinach in a salad."

### "My Baby's Anorexia Diagnosis Changed My Mind About Food"

Virginia and her husband, Dan, are raising their two daughters in a neighborhood most would describe as peaceful. Their first years of parenthood were anything but. About one month after their daughter, Violet, was born, her pediatrician noticed her lips and fingers appeared bluish at a routine check-up. Her blood oxygen level was dangerously low. In an effort to save her life, Violet was rushed to the hospital in an ambulance and intubated before she was unconscious. Doctors soon discovered Violet had a heart defect that would require three open-heart surgeries before she turned three years old.

An unintended side effect of the trauma of having a tube crammed down her tiny throat while still awake: Violet stopped eating. "She started screaming any time something came near her mouth," Virginia tells me. She stopped breastfeeding, as she was physically too weak to do it. She lost the feeling of hunger. She was diagnosed with "infantile anorexia." For the first year of her life, she was completely feeding-tube dependent. It wasn't until she was older than two, and with a lot of effort from food therapists and hospital nutritionists, and Dan and Virginia's tireless resolve, that Violet's feeding tube was finally able to be removed.

191

That process informed Virginia's book *The Eating Instinct*, as Violet had literally lost her instinct to eat food and had to be taught it from scratch. It also caused Virginia to rethink her mind-set toward food. "I don't think I'd heard how I talked about food until I was really forced to examine it, because we were in this really intense situation," Virginia tells me. "It made me realize that all I wanted was for positive associations with food. The way we talk about food is very, very, very negative. When friends come over, they're always apologizing, 'Oh, I can't believe I'm eating this cheese' or 'I'm such a pig for eating this piece of pizza.' We're always berating ourselves over food, talking about things we can and can't eat, what plan we're on, if this is okay with the 'rules.' How could I expect this baby to develop a positive relationship with food when I was caught in this other place myself? I had to really get ahold of these voices. I told myself, 'I'm not going to food shame in front of her,' and then once I started following that rule, it was hugely liberating."

While she had freed herself from the negative self-talk, she suddenly heard "everybody else do it all the time," Virginia says. Whenever she hosts friends for meals, somebody inevitably apologizes for eating what they think is too much. "I just want to bang my head against the wall. Please stop! I made dinner, I want you to eat it!"

Today, Violet is an assertive five-year-old who has strong opinions about what she wants—and doesn't want—in all categories of her life. She's the big sister to baby Beatrix, who has had no heart issues or eating struggles. "With Beatrix, I'm taking things out of her mouth twenty-four times a day," Virginia notes. "Violet didn't put toys in her mouth."

Their family also relies on the division of responsibility family-style meal, with no shaming about what their kids eat, or don't eat. "That's really what's at the core of how I think about food," Virginia says. "I want kids to trust themselves. Listening to your body is the most important way to take care of yourself. I offer the food and get the hell out of the way."

## *Dinner in My Home: What It's Like*

These days, I cook dinner almost every night. It's exhausting and sometimes it stresses me out, especially when my two-year-old is turning on and off the oven (he really loves the dials and I should probably childproof better) and my five-year-old is complaining about how he wants to watch something else on TV, and can I please bring him some milk, and where are his Legos?!

But I'm not hard on myself if dinner ends up being scrambled eggs and toast. The meals we eat together do not need to contain organic quinoa steamed with foraged mushrooms and eggs from chickens raised in my backyard. "I don't think it's so important for [the meal] to be nutritionally ideal," Harvard Medical School professor Anne Fishel, cofounder of the Family Dinner Project, tells me. "The point is not to be the food police."

Dr. Fishel got into cooking after her husband quit smoking, figuring she'd give him another form of "oral pleasure," she laughs. Her two sons were young and energetic, and they eventually got involved with food prep: Playing with plastic containers, banging pots and pans, picking basil leaves for pesto, stirring the soup. "That was the start of them being really game, adventurous eaters," she says. Eventually, she wrote her own book, *Home for Dinner*, and then cofounded the Family Dinner Project in 2010 to empower parents and explain some of the benefits, all while encouraging families to keep the meals accessible and the pressure low.

"It's not about the great roast chicken, although that certainly helps," jokes Dr. Fishel, before growing more serious. "It's partly that kids and adults really do well when there are rituals that are predictable, times of the day or week that family can count on, or a certain sequence of actions that have some symbolic meaning attached to them: That can give a family a feeling of identity, or safety, it sets that time apart from the humdrum of everyday life. Family dinners really do it for a family, so I think that's part of what makes them so great. It's also one of the few reliable times that families really gather anymore. We don't garden. We don't farm. We don't play instruments together, we don't knit together, we don't do whatever nineteenth-century families did. So it's the most reliable time of the day to connect, to check in, to find out about small problems before they get bigger, to enjoy each other."

Meals shouldn't be an overwhelming activity. We shouldn't sit down at the dinner table fraught with fear that we're feeding our kids the wrong things. Focus instead on the benefit of eating together. Dinnertime conversation boosts vocabulary more than reading books. As the *Washington Post* reports, "Researchers counted the number of rare words—those not found on a list of 3,000 most common words—that the families used during dinner conversation. Young kids learned 1,000 rare words at the dinner table, compared to only 143 from parents reading storybooks aloud. Kids who have a large vocabulary read earlier and more easily. . . . For school-age youngsters, regular mealtime is an even more powerful predictor of high achievement scores than time spent in school, doing homework, playing sports or doing art."[18]

Despite my early complaining, I do actually love to cook. It's freeing to me to aggressively chop veggies after a long day working. Cooking uses a different part of my brain. I crank up jazz for me and *PAW Patrol* for my kids, and unwind over my stovetop almost every night.

Here are some of my secrets and tips to getting dinner on the table:

1. *An app where I can organize all my recipes neatly in one place.* I like Paprika, which costs $4.99, but there are plenty of others. My husband and I share logins on one account, so we're both able to access whatever recipes are needed for dinner. I

love how it formats book-length blog recipes into clean, easy-to-read directions.

2. *Share recipes with friends.* This can be done in person, on a Facebook group, or any number of ways. I like to follow @YummyToddlerFood on Instagram (run by Amy Palanjian, quoted earlier in this chapter) for easy recipe ideas. AllRecipes.com has a million ideas that are fast and easy. My friends and I tend to send recipes back and forth via our Paprika app any time we find something that our kids eat.

3. *Keep your recipes simple.* The end of a long, tiring day is not the time to use your last remaining shreds of energy to make beef bourguignon that your kids won't eat. I have a couple of fallback recipes that I can turn to if all else fails, such as pasta with butter, cheese, and frozen peas; or taco night, which my children will never tire of. I experiment with longer recipes on weekends.

4. *Go easy on yourself.* We do a ton of takeout in the summer because we're outside enjoying the weather. I have no problem picking up a rotisserie chicken from the grocery store on nights I'm not in the mood to cook. I normally have a couple of frozen pizzas on hand just in case something comes up and I don't have the time or energy to cook.

Here's the caveat you should employ so you don't feel like a short-order cook: Only make one meal for your kids. They won't starve to death if they don't eat it. In fact, if they are hungry every night because they refuse dinner, perhaps they'll learn to eat more. "I call it the Starbucks Phenomenon: The expectation that it's okay for each person in the family to order something different in the home,"

Dr. Fishel says. "That's just another burden on who is doing the cooking and could be another impediment. [People think] 'Oh, let's just go out, this is too hard . . . I can't figure out how to come up with a meal that everyone will enjoy.'"

My kids can be picky eaters. They don't love all vegetables, so there are always peas in my freezer. But I keep introducing foods. (Which I understand comes with the privilege that I can afford to throw away uneaten foods, and I know many families cannot.) And as a result, my five-year-old loves shrimp and lox, and my two-year-old recently compared carrots to potato chips. (Yeah, I'm just as confused as you, but I'll take it.) You never know what your kids will eat if you present options repeatedly and stop introducing your own learned fears and beliefs into food.

**#NoShameParenting Takeaway:** Relax. Not every meal needs to be home-cooked, perfectly balanced, or eaten with every member of the family present. You don't need to play food games. Your kids can drink juice boxes and eat cupcakes, as long as they don't drink juice boxes and eat cupcakes every single day. Procure a meal. Put it on the table. Allow children to eat as much (or as little) of what's on the table in front of them. Enjoy your meal. Repeat. The key is levity and togetherness. If your kids see that you enjoy a healthy, balanced meal, they'll turn out just fine.

# Busting the Myth of
# "Having It All": It Doesn't Exist
# (So Can We Stop Saying It, Please?)

"Hey, are you wearing a blue shirt today to match Everett?" Brad asked, and I burst into tears—surprising him, me, and our kids, who had otherwise been occupied with an episode of *Blaze and the Monster Machines*.

Why was I crying over a wardrobe choice? It was the morning of the "kindergarten opera," and the PTA copresident had sent an email late the night before recapping all the hard work other parents in the class had put into staging it, and urging us to dress in the same color as our kids' costumes. I was too busy with work to contribute to said opera and apparently to even remember to match my son.

"Oh my god, I was joking. You don't have to match Everett!" Brad said, pulling me into a hug. But of course, juggling *all. the. things* is what I am hardest on myself about, even though I get it's ridiculous to match my five-year-old, and he doesn't care anyway. And yet. I have to regularly take a deep breath and stop judging myself over dropping a couple balls.

Amelia finds herself in a similar boat, admitting she has been "low key judging myself and/or other parent friends" for living their lives differently than her. Amelia, who has short, wildly curly hair and lives with her family in Atlanta, says, "If we were discussing our preference for something—snacks, sunscreen, sleep training—I suddenly

197

felt very attached to whether they took my advice about a particular subject. I think it's because if my way wasn't the 'right' way and something else worked better for them, maybe their way would have been better for me, too."

Amelia soon realized her attitude was "just insanity" as she gained her footing as a mom and watched her daughter grow and develop. "Our NICU baby has quadrupled her birth weight in the first sixteen months of her life, sleeps through the night, and is a complete joy to be around (most of the time). Why would I retroactively judge myself for making parenting choices that worked for us?! It's like the choices we make become part of who we are and if someone else does it differently, our only options are to change their minds or take it as a personal attack. Now I just remind myself that I didn't take all the advice I received and it wasn't because I didn't think it was good advice. It just didn't work for my baby. End of story."

You can't scroll through social media these days without somebody bragging about how they "have it all"—this idea that we're supposed to be perfect parents in a loving, sex-filled relationship with equal chore division, have a spotlessly clean house and a size-zero body, a high-powered job that still allows us to be at school pickup and president of the PTA, a couple kids who never throw tantrums and always eat their vegetables and look adorable in their matching designer outfits that are never stained, and . . . the list goes on and on. The expectations we put on ourselves (and that society puts on us) are exhausting!

If you take away anything from this book, it's this: There's no such thing as perfection. It doesn't help your kids. It doesn't help you. A constantly stressed-out parent negates all the benefits of whatever lifestyle you've decided to strive for. Instead, the stress can spill over into every area of our lives, negatively impacting our relationships and our patience with our children, which can cause them to act out, explains Dr. Maryam Abdullah, the parenting program director of the University of California, Berkeley's Greater Good Science Center, which studies the keys to well-being.

On the flip side, "Happy parents are statistically more likely to have happy children—regardless of genetics,"[1] Dr. Christine Carter writes in her book *Raising Happiness: 10 Simple Steps for More Joyful Kids and Happier Parents*. So use this factoid as an excuse to take a deep breath and stop making yourself crazy with anxiety over baking cupcakes for the entire soccer team.

It's okay for parents to give up on the idea of a "perfect" arrangement (in other words, "having it all"), and acknowledge that finding a good system for "work/life balance" is going to be messy at times—but that we should be creative and assertive in finding the arrangement that works best for us. There's no right or wrong way, despite what your coworkers, neighbors, and our culture in America dictates—and however we make it work, we're not going to fuck up our kids.

✼

Dr. Anne-Marie Slaughter rocketed to viral Internet fame for her much-debated article "Why Women Still Can't Have It All,"[2] written after she quit her "dream job" working in the State Department to free up more time to care for her teenage sons. She'd been commuting from Washington, D.C., to her family's home in New Jersey, where she was a law professor and dean at Princeton, and it was taking its toll. She writes about the "blind fury" she felt when others judged her over her decision to scale back at work, while simultaneously implying she wasn't a good mother.

"All my life, I'd been on the other side of this exchange," Slaughter writes. "I'd been the woman smiling the faintly superior smile while another woman told me she had decided to take some time out or pursue a less competitive career track so that she could spend more time with her family. I'd been the woman congratulating herself on her unswerving commitment to the feminist cause, chatting smugly with her dwindling number of college or law-school friends who had reached and maintained their place on the highest rungs of their profession. I'd been the one telling young women at my lectures that you *can* have it all and do it all, regardless of what field you are in. Which means I'd been part, albeit unwittingly, of making millions of women feel that *they* are to blame if they cannot manage to rise up the ladder as fast as men and also have a family and an active home life (and be thin and beautiful to boot)." But she'd had a "rude epiphany" that she could not, in fact, "do it all."

Slaughter calls out Sheryl Sandberg, whose book *Lean In: Women, Work, and the Will to Lead* declared that women are holding themselves back by not dreaming big enough. "I am all for encouraging young women to reach for the stars," Slaughter writes. "But I fear that the obstacles that keep women from reaching the top are rather more prosaic than the scope of their ambition. My longtime and invaluable assistant, who has a doctorate and juggles many balls as the mother of teenage twins, emailed me while I was working on this article: 'You know what would help the vast majority of women with work/family balance? MAKE SCHOOL SCHEDULES MATCH WORK SCHEDULES.' The present system, she noted, is based on a society that no longer exists—one in which farming was a major occupation and stay-at-home moms were the norm. Yet the system hasn't changed."

Slaughter's article also shatters the illusion that women can do anything if they have a supportive partner, the idea you can "game the system" by timing the age you have your kids, and demands to know what's wrong with a woman who *wants* to spend more time with her family.

The first half of the essay scared the shit out of me, along with every other working mom I knew. The second half of the essay— where she details how to fix these issues—is one of the most inspiring things I have ever read in my life. I have internalized most of her recommendations as gospel. She suggests the following: More women in leadership positions. Forget the culture of office face-time. Regard childcare as valuable. Redefine what it means to be successful at work. Powerful women must normalize talking about parenthood in the office.

When I took a deep breath and quit my corporate job to write this book, Slaughter's voice rang in my head: "Women should think about the climb to leadership not in terms of a straight upward slope, but as irregular stair steps, with periodic plateaus (and even dips) when they turn down promotions to remain in a job that works for their family situation; when they leave high-powered jobs and spend a year or two at home on a reduced schedule; or when they step off a conventional professional track to take a consulting position or project-based work for a number of years. I think of these plateaus as 'investment intervals.'"

It's been eight years since Dr. Slaughter published her essay, where it became the most-read article on *The Atlantic*'s website and spawned a book called *Unfinished Business: Women, Men, Work, Family*.

I checked in with her to see if she thought anything has changed since her call to action. "I think the biggest thing that has happened since I wrote my article has been the rise in national awareness that 'care issues'—eldercare, childcare, care for the ill or the disabled—are on the national agenda in ways they simply were not before," Dr. Slaughter, who is also the CEO of nonprofit think tank New America, wrote to me via email. "They are politically salient in both parties; they are being recognized as a huge economic drag (childcare for two children is more than the cost of rent in all fifty states, which is driving women out of the workforce in ways that can affect economic growth); and they are affecting geographic mobility (often referred to as 'mojo'—willingness to move where the jobs are) because people are unwilling or unable to leave care arrangements that they have

carefully stitched together. Looking to the future, it is also notice-
able and being noticed that the care sector (now often referred to
as the care economy) is growing fast (the majority of job categories
predicted to grow in future are care-related) and will be changed and
improved by the addition of technology (robots to do the heavy lifting; AI to personalize learning styles, etc.)."

But she wasn't satisfied with the progress, adding: "That said,
we still have a *long* way to go with baby boomer bosses, who still
come out of a world in which care and women were synonymous and
don't understand the issues that millennial parents—men as well as
women—face, and we simply have not made up our minds as a society that investing in our children, from cradle to career, is as important as buying new weapons systems."

## Where Men Fit Into This Conversation

While Slaughter's essay largely focused on women, she did mention
how we need to bring men into the conversation. "Seeking out a more
balanced life is not a women's issue; balance would be better for us
all," she wrote.

Men are increasingly feeling overwhelming pressure. In the 1970s,
only six men in the entire country identified themselves as stay-at-
home dads, according to a *Huffington Post* analysis of census data.[3]
By 2015, that number jumped to 1.9 million—about 16 percent of all
stay-at-home parents. But professor Karen Kramer of the University
of Illinois, who has analyzed decades of census data, says only 20 percent of men who "stay home" do it by choice.[4]

Brian and his wife, Lori, moved from Kentucky to Virginia while
they were expecting their first child. She was starting a new job and
he was transferring within his company. Between all those changes,
and house hunting, they never found a daycare they liked and were
uncomfortable about their newborn daughter spending ten hours a

day there anyway. So Brian decided to take FMLA leave to see if he liked staying home with their daughter. They found that they could afford it financially, and it worked well for their family, so Brian quit his job to be a stay-at-home dad. Their daughter is now seven years old and has a four-year-old brother.

Brian says he doesn't feel judged by his community, but he has experienced the "mommy and me effect." "There was a moms' class that my wife went to some, but men really weren't invited. Too much breastfeeding," Brian says. "I started going to story time at our library when my daughter was about five or six months old. I was usually the only dad until one other started going. I met a few more over time, though. At story time, all of the songs and books that involved a parent would say mommy. The lady who ran story time actually said something about it after a few months. She said she felt bad that all of the stories and songs used mommy exclusively. She started adding in daddy or dad to a few of the stories after a while, but I was okay either way. We do live in a somewhat rural area and it is probably a newer phenomenon that there are stay-at-home dads. I have met about five over the last six-plus years that we have lived here."

Sal, a stay-at-home dad to Simone and Oliver, tells me he gets "occasional stares at the playground as if some wonder why I'm there, as well as the contrast praise from passerby that see me taking a primary role in parenting and award me with a smile. Honestly, I think it's all unnecessary and hope, as a society, we're able to move past the idea of gender roles and recognize that parents are parents as our children are our children."

Many men face mixed messages in our society, which still tells them they need to be the primary breadwinner. Yet, that's not always the reality, as women are entering the workforce in record numbers. They may also be shamed for admitting they face inner turmoil when they don't spend enough time with their children, and judged for staying home with their kids. "Being a man" has never been a more loaded phrase with today's machismo politics, but the reality is that fourteen of the fifteen fastest-growing job fields in America are primarily held by women, according to the U.S. Bureau of Labor Statistics.[5]

"I often think to myself that what I do is a wonderful thing, but it is no different than what my mother did for me. It can be a tough job, and some may consider it unconventional, but all I'm trying to do is raise my children to be good people and lead happy, healthy lives," Sal says. "In the early days of being a stay-at-home parent, I was more self-conscious about being one of the few—if not the only— men among mostly women out and about with our children. However, as I've grown into this role and embraced it, I'm less concerned about what others may think and try to focus on what's best for my kids. Most of my stay-at-home parent friends are mothers, but there is also a community of fathers out there too, and there is a general camaraderie among us all."

## Why You Should "Fake It" at Work

It can be tricky to navigate your career after having kids. When I returned to work after my maternity leave with Everett, I told my (male) boss that I would only be in the office forty hours a week instead of my usual fifty (or more) hours, but I would be available on email later at night and could finish up any outstanding work after my son had gone to bed. He responded by announcing to our entire team that I was now "leaving early" and forwarding me emails to interesting conferences with notes like, "I'd love to send you to this, but I know you probably don't want to travel right now!" It was infuriating. I quickly realized there was no room for me to grow in that role.

When I switched positions in the company, I took a different tactic. Instead of announcing the hours I would work, I simply blocked out the hours I couldn't work on my calendar. Most people are nonconfrontational, so this put the onus on my new boss to call me out if she disagreed with my work hours. But it never happened: I still hit all my goals (and then some), so the focus was on what I was achieving instead of the hours I was at the office.

I highly recommend this "ask forgiveness, not permission" method, and research backs me up. A study by Boston University's Questrom School of Business shows that men are more likely to "fake" an eighty-hour workweek by quietly scheduling their workday around their family.[6] (It doesn't hurt that our culture assumes a man who leaves the office at 5 p.m. is meeting a client, but a woman is probably going to pick up kids.) Men who didn't explicitly say they were heading to their kid's soccer game, for example, were just as likely to get promoted as men who actually worked eighty hours a week.

As I moved up the ladder to become a director at my company, I started speaking out about how I was leaving to spend time with my kids. It is the responsibility of high-ranking employees to set a culture that says it's okay to have a work/life balance—or else it will never change. After all, the CEO of my company at the time established an extremely generous (for America) paid family leave policy: sixteen weeks fully paid for birth moms, and eight weeks for dads or nonbiological parents. But then she never took advantage of that leave herself, which caused employees—especially men—not to take it either.

This is a cultural problem: America's system is broken when it comes to paid family leave. We are the only country—besides Suriname and Papua New Guinea—without a paid family leave policy. I believe both moms and dads should have the right to bond with their young children—but parents shouldn't feel guilty if one or both have to work.

When it comes to setting our own schedules, we are more concerned about our actions at work than most other people. While writing this book, I checked in with my former boss to see if she was annoyed that I arrived earlier than the rest of the office, checked out at 4 p.m. every day, and then ignored email until after my kids' bedtime. "I never thought that your schedule was unusual—you did an excellent job and were always available, no matter where you were or what you were doing," says Susan, who was a vice president. "Then again, I have always been open to people having flexibility if they were getting the job done on a high level."

While it can be hard emotionally, physically, and financially to drop off a baby, and then drag yourself to work, research shows long-term benefits for both your child and society as a whole when both parents work.

"Part of this working mothers' guilt has been, 'Oh, my kids are going to be so much better off if I stay home,' but what we're finding in adult outcomes is kids will be so much better off if women spend some time at work," Kathleen McGinn, a professor at Harvard Business School, has said.[7] "This is as close to a silver bullet as you can find in terms of helping reduce gender inequalities, both in the workplace and at home."

Of course, if "having it all" for you is quitting your job to stay home with your children and you can afford to do it, then you absolutely should. As long as our children receive quality childcare and we are at peace with our choices—whether it's to stay home, hire a nanny, or enroll them in daycare—our children will turn out great.

## Who Can We Blame for This Crazy Idea That We Need to "Have It All"?

The phrase "have it all" entered the popular lexicon in the late 1970s, used in ads to catch the eye of consumers of all genders. In 1980, the era of the shoulder-pad-wearing power working woman, *Having It All: A Practical Guide to Managing a Home and a Career* was published with no agenda; just hilarious, now-outdated tips like "let your nail polish set while you blow dry your hair," the *New York Times* reports.[8]

The legendary former editor in chief of *Cosmopolitan* magazine, Helen Gurley Brown, gets the credit for supercharging the phrase with her 1982 bestseller, *Having It All: Love, Success, Sex, Money, Even if You're Starting with Nothing*. Brown didn't have kids and hardly talks about them at all in the book. (After interviewing a tired working mom friend about her busy life, she even writes: "Isn't that a hard sell if you ever *heard* one?") The bulk of Brown's book focuses on how to stay thin ("You may have to have a tiny touch of anorexia nervosa to maintain an ideal weight . . . not a *heavy* case, just a little one!"), relationships, and career ambition (when it comes to sleeping with your boss, "Why discriminate against him?" she asks).

Brown reportedly hated the phrase "having it all" and fought hard to have her book title changed. " 'Having It All' sounds so [expletive] cliché to me," she wrote in a letter to her editors, according to the *Times*. "I've always, always visualized this as a book for the downtrodden, a book by a near loser who got to be a winner, instead of somebody who sounds—based on the title—like a smartass all-the-time winner from the beginning."

As the second wave of feminism was winding down in the early 1980s, just as Brown's book was published, "having it all" was becoming a politically charged phrase about "feminism's lie." This was written by a columnist in the conservative outlet *The Federalist*: "Women ask about having it all because they were told they could have it all . . . by women like Gloria Steinem."[9] Yet, feminists did not coin the phrase or claim it. Still, the former president of the National Organization for Women basically apologized for the phrase to the *Times*: "Twenty years ago, it was a triumphant phrase and also a demand, [but] the phrase has come to carry with it a sense of being overwhelmed."

As Jennifer Szalai, a book editor at the *Times*, notes, "We somehow took a puffed-up corporate come-on, one that made Brown herself chafe more than 30 years ago, and twisted it in the collective memory into a false promise of feminism. . . . To say that women expect to 'have it all' is to trivialize issues like parental leave, equal pay and safe, affordable child care; it makes women sound like entitled, narcissistic battle-axes while also casting them as fools. . . . This rewriting of recent history that blames the women's movement for women's troubles is just one part of the 'backlash.' . . . It is a self-perpetuating feedback loop of distortions and half-truths. The false accusation of betrayal has 'a way of turning women away from making demands on society.' The real betrayal lies not with the women's movement but with those who would rather keep us distracted by a never-ending sideshow than pay attention to the world as it really is."[10]

Food for thought the next time you're feeling guilty about not "having it all." The phrase was basically reinvented in modern history to sell people things, induce guilt, make women hate each other, and trivialize the very real struggles we face today. But you don't have to buy in to it! Define what "it all" means to you—don't let somebody else determine if you're "doing it all." How about we just rephrase it to "have what you want," so people can ask, "Do you have what you want to be sane?" instead of "Do you have it all?"

## *"Having It All" Is About More Than Work*

You don't have to be perfect. Your kids won't suffer from it. After I weaned Otto from breastfeeding, I struggled with postpartum anxiety. I was determined not to let it get in the way of me being a present parent, so I briefly saw a therapist (via an app—so that I could video chat from my bedroom after my kids' bedtime). I was anxious about dropping the ball now that I had another child, a demanding job, a marriage, and a busy household. The therapist eased my fears by saying: "You don't want to appear like a superhuman. You're giving your children a great gift: They will see you fail, be messy, be imperfect—yet get up every day and continue to try, continue moving forward. Hiding your day-to-day struggles does them a disservice. When they grow up and have their own struggles, they will feel confused, like their feelings are not normal, and ashamed that they can't easily brush them off like you appeared to."

That was one of the most important things anyone has ever said to me. I want my kids to face the day-to-day struggles, fail, and then get back up and try again. Building resilience in my kids is one of my greatest life goals. So I learned that I have to let some things go.

Entrepreneur Tiffany Dufu wrote an inspirational book called *Drop the Ball: Achieving More by Doing Less.* I met her in person when I was a vice president at a media company and was taken aback by her ruthless prioritization and calm demeanor. As she explains in a video for her book,[11] she used to wake up every day at 5 a.m., she was always exhausted, her to-do list was never ending. "I felt like I was failing and I broke down," she admits. Sound familiar?

She finally had no choice but to "drop the ball" even though it "terrified" her. I mean, this is a woman who helped found Lean In with Sheryl Sandberg, aka the woman who basically invented the idea of doing it all.

After letting go, the most magical thing happened to Tiffany: "The world didn't fall apart, so I decided to drop the ball on purpose. . . . I figured out what mattered most to me, what I really had to do to make it happen, and how to get more help from others. Suddenly, the less I did, the more I achieved."

Her book is hundreds of pages of very small type. Even Tiffany jokes that a woman approached her after one of her speeches and demanded a shortcut because she didn't have time to go through all the exercises and just needed to know what balls she could drop *right now.* So, as Tiffany says on YouTube, you can do this by creating a spreadsheet and listing all the tasks you're overwhelmed by in the first column. Then you need to ask yourself five different questions in the following columns. They should be yes or no responses:

1. Does this task align with what matters most? (She laughs that you don't want the person eulogizing you to say, "She got a lot of things done on her to-do list.")

2. Do I do this very well without a lot of effort?

3. Is this something that only I can do?

4. Would it be highly irresponsible or callous to delegate this task to someone else?

5. Does this task bring me joy?

After you're done, add up the nos. If you've got three or more nos, she advises trying to drop that task. She still thinks you need an overall framework about your priorities so you don't feel guilty about what you're dropping, but I find this simple exercise to be pretty eye-opening.

So what about those tasks like laundry that you may not be able to outsource? Well, now you have a visible to-do list. If you have a partner, you could ask him or her to pick up some of the line items you hate. If you ask your partner to make the same list, you may find that the tasks that annoy you don't really bug your partner, and you could swap them.

If this exercise sounds like too much work, I am also a fan of doing an actual gut check. Get in a quiet place. This can be while you're sitting in your car before going into the office, the shower, wherever you won't be interrupted for two minutes. Say out loud or in your head the thing that is plaguing you: "I didn't volunteer to be a class parent this year," pause, and then the opposite thing: "I volunteered to be a class parent this year," and then pause again. During the pauses, did you feel calm? Did you feel stressed? Did your stomach clench? Do the thing that didn't make your stomach clench after. This is how I make most of my bigger decisions in life.

Above all, don't be afraid or ashamed to ask for help. Learning how to ask for help has been a challenge for me—but I truly enjoy helping my friends when I can, so, keeping that in mind, I take a deep breath and reach out.

I have a huge village of people surrounding me, and that is how I accomplish anything in my life. My husband is a true partner who switches off daycare and school pickup and drop-offs with me. I am writing this while Otto is playing with loving caregivers Ms. Nerisa and Ms. Gigi at preschool and Everett is learning from Ms. Chandra and Ms. Kerry at a local public school. My house is relatively clean because we pay for a miracle-worker housecleaner, Daisy, once a month. I am forever in debt to Otto's former nanny, the incredible Alicia, who made him a group of friends, got him on a nap schedule, and even swept my floor every day! My friends help juggle babysitting and childcare. They're the ones listed on my emergency pickup forms, as our closest relatives are 250 miles away. There's no way I could do any of this alone, and you shouldn't feel like you have to either.

## So Then Why Are We So Afraid to Let Our Kids Do Anything Alone?

So many of us have a lot of anxiety about the pressure to *be everything* and *do everything* for our kids. It's a newish phenomenon. We've gone from the 1970s, when parents were the center of the family universe, to now, when our orbit revolves around our children.

When I was a kid, we played outside until the streetlights turned on at 8 p.m. in the summer. A pack of us roamed the neighborhood, and whichever parent was home would feed us lunch or hand out popsicles. As a parent today, I shudder at what would happen if I let my boys wander around outside by themselves, or even with a group of friends. There's a playground six doors down from my home, and I wonder at what age my children will be able to go there alone, or if they'll ever be able to. Parents Danielle and Alex let their children, aged ten and six, walk to a park in their suburban Maryland neighborhood together. The children were picked up by police and detained for five hours.[12] The parents were investigated by child protective services for neglect.

"Parents used to have milestones that were agreed on," Lenore Skenazy, founder of the Free-Range Kids parenting movement, tells me. But now, we don't. Our kids play inside. They go on "play dates" arranged by us. We don't let them out of our sight for fear that they'll get lost, or hurt, or we'll get judged or arrested. For example, Skenazy says, "My mom knew that kindergartners walked to school. She was a stay-at-home mom—she quit her job to stay home with me and my sister—and yet she didn't consider walking us to school. Nobody did."

Many schools do not let kids walk home without a guardian—forcing us to become overbearing parents. "If your child is not allowed to walk home in third or fourth or fifth grade, because the school won't let them self dismiss, because the principal thinks it's too dangerous . . . it's not me being a helicopter mom, it's not being a martyr," says Skenazy, who was dubbed "America's Worst Mom" after she let her mature nine-year-old son ride the New York City subway home by himself. Parents are "stuck with the decision that was made partly because of an inflated sense of danger and partly because of an inflated sense of liability. That means my kid can't walk home. And if my kid is walking home, and somebody calls 911 to say, 'I don't know why I'm even calling you, but it's so weird to see a kid outside, I wonder if they're safe?' And then CPS has an excuse to come over."

Skenazy, who wrote *Free-Range Kids: How to Raise Safe, Self-Reliant Children (Without Going Nuts with Worry)* and founded an initiative called Let Grow to give kids more freedom, adds: "Parents aren't crazy, because they're living in this crazy time. It's natural to worry about your kid. But it is obviously unnatural, this level of anxiety we have, because your parent loves you and didn't worry every time you left the house that you would never come home again."

Humans are living in the most peaceful time in our history, Harvard psychologist Steven Pinker has said. "The claim that we are living in an unusually peaceful time may strike you as somewhere between hallucinatory and obscene," Pinker wrote in his book *The Better Angels of Our Nature: Why Violence Has Declined*.[13] "I know from conversations and survey data that most people refuse to believe it."

Of course we don't believe it. We turn on the news, and it's all doom and gloom. We open up Facebook, and it's scary news stories, or people's "warning" posts like: "There was a weird-looking man following me and my children in the grocery store today," and everyone comments, "OMG! I'm so happy you're safe!" But what do you think are the chances of your child actually being abducted? Low. In 2010, there were 74 million children in America. Of those, 105 were kidnapped. Only half of those were by strangers. Ninety-two percent of the victims came home alive.[14]

I'm not trying to downplay what a horrifying ordeal it is when a child is kidnapped, or even worse. But we need to keep in perspective that the world is no less safe than when we were kids, and we were able to roam freely every once in a while. At the very least, we don't need to spend every moment hovering over our children or be so nervous that they'll turn out poorly because we failed to provide enough hand-eye coordination exercises while on maternity leave.

So how can we raise our children without so much fear? Baby steps. Let them play unsupervised in your basement, or maybe in the backyard. Let them resolve a fight with a sibling on their own. And sit back and watch with pride as your children learn how to handle their own problems.

### A More Chill Philosophy: Be an "Airplane Parent"

When parents were asked by a Pew survey which traits they most wanted their kids to have, they responded with these: being responsible, independence, creativity, and persistence.[15] How can our kids learn these skills if they're raised by overbearing parents who never give them an opportunity to work these muscles?

So let me introduce you to my idea of "airplane parenting," i.e., watching over our kids' actions from 30,000 feet above. We won't notice every single detail of their lives, but we can steer the overall direction they're flying in. We won't lose the forest for the trees—and that's a good thing. We know occasional turbulence is normal and will pass soon enough.

Airplane parents don't know every piece of food our children put in their mouths at daycare. But we know their overall attitude toward food because we set it during family mealtimes. We don't have nanny cams, because we trust our caregivers and feel good enough about our childcare situation. We don't beat ourselves up because we allow our children to watch a couple episodes of *Doc McStuffins*, because we know our kids also play many other different ways.

When you're an airplane parent, you parent with a lot less stress. And isn't less stress something we could all use?

### Just Say No

Power producer Shonda Rhimes, of *Grey's Anatomy* fame, wrote a whole book about how she said yes to everything during the course of the year.

I'd like to encourage you to do the exact opposite. Say no. Again and again and again.

There is so much pressure to volunteer for that thing at your kid's daycare, go to the gym a certain number of times a week, make small talk at every single play date you get invited to, and so on.

And yet, there is something so freeing about saying no and paring down the things that don't bring you joy. Check your energy after you hang out with that person you haven't seen in months. Do you feel drained? Just say no next time. Do you feel energized by volunteering at your kid's school? I do, because I think it's cool to occasionally be a part of my sons' school day. So I say yes a couple times a year. But I always keep in mind that there are only so many hours in the day. Every time I overbook myself, I get annoyed at myself, and then I'm that person canceling everything at the last minute or dragging tired kids along, and that's no fun either. I've gotten over FOMO. I make the events I can, and I skip the ones I can't.

I think the secret to "having it all," however you define it, is to be organized and scheduled during the week. I asked Brad to build another closet in our bedroom that we lovingly refer to as Target. I buy deodorant, shaving cream, shampoo, laundry detergent, toothpaste, and diaper cream in bulk and stock it up there so I don't have to think about making a toiletry run during the workweek. Brad and I share a Google calendar where we detail who is doing pickup/drop-off that day, birthday parties, events, doctor appointments. A couple times a week, we informally touch base and verbally go through the rest of our events for the week. I have some friends who swear by a more formal Sunday-night "family meeting." Another friend said her mom placed a dry-erase board in her kitchen, and she and her siblings wrote where they were, and how to reach them, every day. I plan out our groceries and meals a week in advance so I don't have to think about what to cook at the end of a long day.

### To Play or Not to Play:
### Why Extracurriculars Should Be Optional

Because much of my workweek is meticulously planned, I relish free weekends full of long walks, dinners out, and exploring random places. I like to text friends on the way to the playground and meet up, or bake a loaf of bread, or just take a nap. I hate having yet another set commitment on Saturday and Sunday.

We learned this lesson through trial and error. Brad and I first signed up Everett for soccer at age two. He didn't want to play. We spent the entire hour chasing him around Brooklyn's Prospect Park, urging him to get back in the game and "sit on the magic carpet," aka the yoga mat where the coach was trying to corral a bunch of toddlers. For some reason, we signed him up again at age three, this time with a crawling baby in tow. Everett still hated it, but Otto was desperate to play . . . scrambling onto the field just in time to get bonked in the head by a soccer ball. It was a waste of a couple hundred dollars, and it made our weekends feel too scheduled.

I don't feel pressured to fill my kids' days up with events, extracurriculars, music lessons, and sports teams—and you shouldn't either, if you don't want to. It seems like everywhere we look, there's a three-year-old doing ballet or playing piano. Perhaps you're already thinking how raising a tennis phenom from age two will really help with that Ivy League application. But these activities are expensive and time consuming, and they may not even benefit your kids if they don't enjoy them. Yes, a team sport can help develop social skills and graceful losing, two important life lessons. But your toddler doesn't need to play T-ball to reap the benefits—he could learn them both in free play with another kid or sibling.[16]

For every study touting the benefits of various organized activities, there is another study emphasizing the pluses of free play. A Harvard Graduate School of Education research paper says parents should look for three key signs that our kids are benefiting from play, whether it's structured or not: choice, wonder, and delight. "*Choice* looks like kids setting goals, developing and sharing ideas, making rules, negotiating challenges, and choosing how long to play. *Wonder* looks like kids exploring, creating, pretending, imagining, and learning from trial and error. *Delight* looks like happiness: kids smiling, laughing, being silly, or generally feeling cozy and at ease," the paper states.[17] We know that it doesn't take $500 gymnastics lessons to accomplish this. My kids display choice, wonder, and delight from simply playing with an empty Amazon box!

If you've signed up your kids for an extracurricular activity and it's stressing you out, plus your kid doesn't really enjoy it, forget it, and don't look back. If you're determined to get your kid playing a sport or an instrument, but your toddler isn't into it—back off, and try again in a couple of years. If your kid is still not interested in it, then forget it. "You know who did not hear Mozart in the womb, right? Mozart. And he turned into Mozart," jokes Skenazy.

It's no use forcing your kid to be somebody they don't want to be. Barbara, a curvy mom of two, felt pressured to be athletic when she was growing up. "My dad was a gym teacher. I liked reading and writing," she says. "He tried everything." The result? Barbara quit most physical activities for the rest of her childhood. It wasn't until she was pregnant with her first child that she was willing to try getting active again. "It took me a long time to find enjoyment in it. I remember trying prenatal yoga while pregnant with my first kid and being utterly shocked to find it kind of fun," she says. Today, she participates in 5K runs voluntarily.

I don't want to dis extra activities if you enjoy them, or if your kid does. Kara has been doing gymnastics since she was five years old, working her way up from the park district to practicing five hours a day by the time she was ten. Her mom went back to work to help pay for it.

Kara traveled the world for competitions and performed on cruises and inside the kinds of enormous arenas Beyoncé usually sells out. She won a full athletic scholarship to the University of Illinois. But there were also drawbacks: Kara skipped dances, clubs, and hanging out with friends so she could practice gymnastics. She also endured numerous injuries: a shoulder surgery, stress fractures in her back, broken bones.

Today, Kara owns a gymnastics club and still coaches. When I asked if she'd encourage her kids—who are five, two, and six weeks old—to do gymnastics, Kara replied, "I would truly say I would have mixed feelings. Sometimes I feel like it would be nice if they were just a 'normal' kid. Meaning, they didn't *have* to be somewhere that was basically as many hours as a full-time job. Other times, I think it would be great, because I'm pretty sure they would have such a sense of responsibility and drive that I wouldn't have to worry about them as much and they would be on the straight and narrow."

Still, she'll always believe that "the positives outweigh the negatives of being this committed to a sport." She speaks highly about her years training as an elite athlete. "Gymnastics has truly changed my life. It has always been an amazing part of my life. There will always be times when you want to quit. Whether it's a sport, job, friendship, relationship; gymnastics has taught me to take a step back and put in the work. If you love what you do, it's not work. I truly love what I do and enjoy seeing the progress the kids make in and out of the gym. I never thought I would coach gymnastics for a living but it just turned out I was able to do what I love and own a business doing that."

When you're deciding how you and your family spend your days, ask yourself an important question: Are we only doing this because other people are doing it, and we think that's what's expected? If the answer is yes, skip it.

## Don't Ditch Your Friends!

One thing that gets lost in the process of raising kids, running a household, schlepping to work, and, ya know, sleeping, is the idea that we should take time for friends. Randi Zuckerberg (an entrepreneur in her own right, but also sister to Facebook founder Mark Zuckerberg) famously said you can "have it all" if you pick three of the following: *Work. Sleep. Fitness. Family. Friends.*[18] The majority of the people I know drop fitness and friends.

Stop! See if you can combine family and friends. A close group of friends and I take turns hosting a monthly "family brunch." This entails filling up our home with four or five families and letting our kids run wild for a couple hours on a weekend morning. It's potluck style, so one family may bring bagels; another, coffee; the hosting family makes something like an easy egg casserole. The parents hang out and chat while our kids all play together. Fifteen minutes before leaving, it's all hands on deck to clean up the disastrous mess that the kids have made by that time.

Are you thinking any of the following thoughts? *My house is a mess. I don't have the energy to clean it up. I hate cooking, and I don't want to prepare a meal for fifteen people. My dining room table isn't big enough to host a ton of people.* Banish them now. *No one's* house is perfectly clean all the time, especially if you have young children. (I'll never forget my friend's nine-month-old daughter picking up crumbs from my floor and eating them. Sigh. HA!) Potluck meals are easy to do. Or tell people to BYOC (bring your own coffee . . . or bring your own champagne. As you know, I don't judge!). Spread out a blanket on your kitchen floor and tell the kids they're having a picnic—they'll think it's a lot more fun than sitting at a dining room table. This is the #NoShameParenting way to host a gathering.

I feel lighter, happier, and more supported when I spend time with my friends. And research proves that's not a fluke. Psychologists at Brigham Young University analyzed data across seventy studies and 3.4 million people in 2015, finding that having no social connections affects your lifespan on par with smoking fifteen cigarettes a day, obesity complications, and drug abuse.[19] Interestingly, the study found that it didn't matter your age or socioeconomic status, which tends to be a huge variable in many studies. As the authors declared in the study results: "Lacking social connections is detrimental to physical health." They also cited another study that equates loneliness on the same level as hunger and thirst, saying those who feel lonely will "alter behavior in a way that will increase survival . . . [to] reconnect socially." The study authors warn that "loneliness will reach epidemic proportions by 2030 unless action is taken."[20]

I'm not saying you're going to die tomorrow if you don't have a huge in-real-life social network, but I am giving you ammunition to hire a babysitter and meet your friends for that drink you keep putting off. Or invite your neighbor over and let your kids play while you enjoy some time together.

"A good friendship is a wonderful antidepressant," psychologist Janice Kiecolt-Glaser, director of the Institute for Behavioral Medicine Research at the Ohio State University College of Medicine in Columbus, told the *Washington Post*.[21] "Relationships are so powerful, we don't always appreciate the many levels at which they affect us."

This doesn't mean you need a hundred friends either. Think quality over quantity. Your health benefits will be stronger if you are able to connect in person, not just over social media. (I'm not against social media—I think it can be wonderful in many ways—but it can also be isolating when online relationships take the place of a physically close community. After all, we see our friends' struggles in real life when we hang out, but we probably don't see any of the shit show in those perfectly polished Instagram photos . . . causing us to question our sanity and feel even more alone when we face challenges.)

Ask yourself this: Do you live near somebody who would babysit your kids last minute if an emergency came up? Do you have a couple people you can text or call to meet in person for a walk or a beer? If the answer is no to both those questions, there's no time like the present to make some friends. Volunteer at a local church or your kids' school. Organize a block party. If you're short on time, try to get to daycare or preschool pickup five minutes early so you can chat with other parents. When Everett was about a year old, I asked his daycare caregivers who he "played" with most, and then I went home and actually wrote letters to those parents. They said something like, "Dear Judy's family, I hear Judy and Everett play together really well! Here's my cell phone number and email address if you'd ever like to come over for bagels one weekend morning." Believe it or not, every single parent texted or emailed me.

The big asterisk here is that I am an extrovert. I love hosting huge gatherings and meeting new people. My husband and I invited 114 people to Everett's fifth birthday party, which my dad pointed out is equivalent to a wedding. But being an extrovert doesn't mean that I never feel like an awkward weirdo when I approach people. I feel it, acutely. Most people feel like awkward weirdos putting themselves out there. Extroversion means I do it anyway, introversion means you probably have to work a little harder to overcome those *run away!* feelings.

There's no shame in not wanting to host 114 people for a birthday party. Find one friend. Invite this person over to your not-perfectly-clean house, or to a playground. Ask questions, and then follow-up questions. Make yourself a little vulnerable in conversations.

I met my friend Shannon in an unusual way. Her daughter, Vivi, is six months younger than Everett, and they've been attending the same daycare essentially since birth. One day, Shannon happened to be at daycare pickup earlier than her usual time, and she struck up a conversation with me outside the door. It just happened to be Everett's last week at that daycare, as he was transitioning to another location for toddlers, and I was an emotional mess. I think the conversation went something like this:

*Shannon: Hi, I'm Vivi's mom! I've heard she plays really well with Everett!*

*Me: OMG. It's so nice to meet you. I'm freaking out. I can't believe Everett is transferring daycares next week. I hope he is okay. I can't get pregnant. I've been trying for eleven months. There is so much happening in my life right now and I am so overwhelmed!*

I walked away feeling like a maniac, chastising myself for being *that crazy mom.* When I tell Shannon that now, she laughs and says her first impression of me was not one of an insane person, but I'm pretty sure she is just being nice. Anyhow, she decided I wasn't nuts and invited Brad and me to Vivi's first birthday party the following weekend. Even though we'd only met once, my husband, our son, and I decided to attend. And from that, a nascent friendship was born. (By the way, Everett was also totally fine at his new daycare, so my freak-out was for naught. I recently dug through my email and saw I'd written Shannon: "Wanted to let you know that the new day-care has been awesome so far—Ev seems to love running around with the older kids. There's been no tears, so I was definitely over-blowing things in my head.")

Fast-forward a couple years and Shannon and her husband, Joe, have become two of our closest friends. We see them most week-ends, we text multiple times a week. We've introduced each other to our friends, and all became friends in the process. Shannon babysat Everett when I went into labor unexpectedly with Otto (she came straight to our house from the airport after returning from a family vacation, no less), and I babysat Vivi when Shannon went to the hos-pital to deliver her second, Henry. We're both listed on each other's emergency pickup forms at our kids' respective schools. And all four of our combined kids are best friends, which is heartwarming to see.

Goes to show: You never know when a random conversation is going to turn into a lifelong friendship. So, even though you may pre-fer to zone out on Netflix than make uncomfortable small talk, put yourself out there. Accept that invitation to meet another family at the playground, or better yet: Invite another family to join you at the playground. Start a fantasy football league with some other parents, or a book club. It may save your life. Well, or at least your sanity.

✻

Don't fall into the trap of relying on only your spouse or partner for companionship. "Parenting is hard, and co-parenting is hard, and you can't put everything on one person. My husband's not my best friend. My best friend is my best friend, and I need somebody to complain about my husband to," jokes Rachel Bertsche, the author of *The Kids Are in Bed: Finding Time for Yourself in the Chaos of Parenting*, and *MWF Seeking BFF: My Yearlong Search for a New Best Friend*. "You get different things from different people. It's really hard to put it all on a romantic partner."

From 1984 to 2004, we've gone from an average of three confidantes to zero.[22] Men are less likely to have close relationships than women, especially if they're young (18 to 39), white, and educated (high school degree or more). And "the friendships they have, if they're with other men, provide less emotional support and involve lower levels of self-disclosure and trust than other types of friendships," sociologist Lisa Wade writes in *Salon*.[23] "When men get together, they're more likely to do stuff than have a conversation. Friendship scholar Geoffrey Greif calls these 'shoulder-to-shoulder' friendships, contrasting them to the 'face-to-face' friendships that many women enjoy. If a man does have a confidant, three-quarters of the time it's a woman, and there's a good chance she's his wife or girlfriend."

Still, despite all these studies showing again and again the benefits of maintaining friendships and our desire to socialize or take time to do the things that bring joy, the guilt about leaving our kids remains pervasive. I've certainly skipped that weekend Pilates class because I feel like I don't spend enough time with my husband and kids during the workweek. Even though I run my own business—giving me unprecedented freedom for the first time in fifteen years of corporate crazi-ness—I second-guessed myself about putting my kids into afterschool and daycare. *Why couldn't I pick Everett up at 3 p.m. dismissal?* I asked myself. The answer: Because I can't get that much work done between the hours of 9 a.m. and 2 p.m.—or have the flexibility for meetings and travel if that's my schedule. So I invest in childcare and banish the guilt. Besides, Everett lectures me when I pick him up too early because he's having so much fun playing with his friends at after-school. (Not to mention that it helps him meet kids from every class, which eases his transition each year because he always recognizes more familiar faces. The downfall is that he wants to invite literally one hundred kids to his birthday party each year, as I mentioned earlier.)

"Every parent I've talked to always feels like they're shortchang-ing their kid. 'I don't have time for my kids. I don't have enough time for my work.' There's this feeling of shortchanging everyone all the time," Bertsche says. Her book *The Kids Are in Bed* examines how parents feel pressure to accomplish everything on our to-do lists in the two hours between putting our kids to bed and falling asleep ourselves. Bertsche, who has coffee-colored curly hair and an inspir-ing amount of energy, was on my team at Yahoo! Parenting and we've been friends ever since. She's raising her two children under five with her husband in Chicago, working full-time and writing books.

"There is this sense right now—especially with mothers—that you can never do enough. So when you have free time, the question isn't: What can I do for myself? It's: What more can I do for my children, even though I have them in eight thousand classes and I'm tending to their needs all the time," Bertsche says. "It's never enough."

Why do people brag about being busy? Why is it a badge of honor that we don't have time for anything? "We live in a culture of pro-ductivity. The idea of relaxing and enjoying your life is not really val-ued self-improvement," Bertsche laments. "I've heard a number of women, especially mothers, say, 'I could indulge in a manicure and pedicure, or I could do something so much more productive.' Something else will always come up. If you wait until you get to the end of your to-do list to take care of yourself, it's never going to happen." Meanwhile, "if you're not taking care of yourself: It affects everything. Your stress level, your happiness, your health. Your kids notice."

There is no magical number of hours children and parents should spend together. And nowadays, research shows that we're spending more time than ever before with our kids. The average mother spent 54 minutes a day caring for her kids in 1965, and 104 minutes in 2012.[24] This is notable because, in 1965, more women stayed home from work; today more women are working *and* spending twice as much time with their kids. In 1965, middle-class and working-class mothers spent equal time with their children. By 2014, mothers with a college education were spending 30 minutes *more* with their children, despite their likely long work hours. The average man spent 16 minutes in 1965, and 59 in 2012. "Plenty of research has shown that more minutes with your children does not translate into happier kids or more successful kids," Bertsche says.

Again, focus on quality over quantity here. Kids don't benefit from a parent who is super stressed out and always distracted during playtime—instead, the kid sees a detached, anxious parent and internalizes what they did wrong. Meanwhile, forty-five minutes of playtime with a present, relaxed parent sends the message to their kids that they're worth it. Researchers agree. "I could literally show you twenty charts, and nineteen of them would show no relationship between the amount of parents' time and children's outcomes. . . . Nada. Zippo," Melissa Milkie, a sociologist at the University of Toronto, told the *Washington Post*.[25]

You shouldn't be a martyr and play with your kid all the time to the detriment of your own sanity. Take a break! Spend forty-five engaged minutes with your kid, and forty-five minutes taking a walk unwinding instead of ninety angry, distracted minutes together.

"Your children learn how they should take care of themselves from how their parents do it," Bertsche says. Do we really want our daughters and sons to think they should always be stressed-out parents themselves? No.

Your kids may cry when a babysitter first shows up, or the parent who usually puts them to bed is absent, but soon enough the change will become part of their routine. "Doing something for yourselves sets a very good example for your kids," Bertsche says.

*

Lindsey is the kind of friend you can sit down and talk with for three hours, even if you haven't seen each other in person for three years. She's a boss lady who runs her own consulting business, runs marathons, and runs a household of three kids—but also doesn't hesitate to share any of her own insecurities, putting anyone who meets her instantly at ease. To juggle their busy schedule, she and her husband have found all kinds of hacks. One includes skipping several performances of their ten-year-old daughter's many, many school plays. "We go to opening night and closing night. We never go to her two Saturday shows," Lindsey explains. One Saturday night, Lindsey and her husband, Pat, ran into a classmate's mom while out on a date. That mom was incredulous that Lindsey and Pat were skipping their daughter's show to have dinner together. "I literally held up my hand and said, 'Don't judge!'" laughs Lindsey, who recently moved from Kansas City to the Chicago suburbs for her husband's job. "My daughter knows our routine and is good with it! We are at drop-off and in the auditorium at the end of each show. It works for us and our family. And maybe that doesn't work for everyone, but it does for us."

It's a myth that you need to spend a lot of time or money with your spouse or friends to reap the benefits. To have a payoff on happiness, you just need to make the effort, whether that's a beer with your partner after your kids' bedtime or a quick walk with a friend to pick up your spirits.

I used to always sneak out or tell my kids I was going to work when I planned to meet a friend or go out with my husband. Everett and Otto were already used to me leaving for work, so they accepted it and didn't throw a temper tantrum if I missed bedtime or my husband and I left them with a babysitter. But recently I've decided to be honest with them so they see me as a multifaceted parent with lots of interests besides work. "Mommy is off to meet her friends" or "Mommy is going to exercise," I say. I always tell them I will return later that day or night, which eases anxiety.

I've also started occasionally dragging my kids with me to activities I enjoy instead of only dragging myself to activities I know they will enjoy. I love the Costume Institute exhibit at New York City's Metropolitan Museum of Art. It's a curated, themed display of over-the-top, gorgeous clothes—usually with tons of sparkles and lace and trains longer than my living room. I hate going on weekends because it's a mob scene. When Otto was a baby and I was on maternity leave, I packed him into my baby carrier and he napped as I browsed. Once, I brought Everett and his friend Vivi to the exhibit with me. (Yes, it was a ratio of two five-year-old kids to one adult.) And you know what? They loved it! We had a blast. I just had to temper my expectations, knowing that I wouldn't get to spend hours there examining everything and instead, we'd get about an hour to check everything out. That was fine.

Bertsche notes that "there has been this shift toward child-oriented leisure. In 1965, parents' leisure was mostly without their kids. Now parents use their 'leisure' time doing something fun for your kid, such as going to a movie for your kid. It's just a different experience of leisure." Think about this the next time you're rolling your eyes through another Saturday morning spent at the Thomas the Train exhibit at the local kids' museum. Why not take your kid with you to the farmer's market, or the gym, or whatever else you used to enjoy doing on a Saturday morning before you had kids? Sure, brunch may be chaotic at first with kids—but they'll get the hang of it eventually. If you never expose them to activities outside of their (and your) comfort zone, how will they ever learn to behave in those environments anyway?

"Kids used to be something we just had. You got married, you start having sex. Or perhaps you started having sex, and then got married. But kids were just part of life. So you had to deal with it, as opposed to fashion it," says Skenazy. "If humanity needed perfect parents all along, there'd be no humanity. Because throughout humanity, most parents started at age thirteen. And that doesn't leave you a whole lot of time to be a perfect parent!"

*

Don't want to spend money on a babysitter? Consider launching a co-op with some friends, where you take turns watching each other's kids so the other parent gets some free time. Or negotiate time with your partner, if you have one, for each of you to have some time with friends or solo. On public school holidays, consider sharing childcare with a friend so you don't all need to pay for a babysitter. My husband and I split childcare with our close friends the week between day camp ending and the school year starting—taking turns watching each other's kids so the other parents got a full day to work. It saved money and also made childcare easier because they had friends present.

Whatever activity you choose to do alone, with friends, or with your partner, put it on your calendar to make it more official. Recently, my husband seemed a little bent out of shape that he had to do school drop-off because I'd scheduled a once-weekly morning Pilates class. But I've decided the health payoff is worth it, and now he accepts it—and has also started putting drinks with his friends on our shared calendar. If it's on your calendar, it feels harder to blow off. Plus, it makes me happy to schedule things like date nights, exercise classes, and outings with friends well in advance so I have something to look forward to.

I'm a big fan of killing as many birds with one stone as possible. (God, that analogy sounds terrible.) I go on walks with my family after dinner, checking off the fitness and family boxes. One day while I worked on this chapter, I had my five-year-old son with me at work because his public school was closed for Yom Kippur. Family and work. The only thing you can't combine is sleep, which sucks. I've since accepted that if I get less than six hours of sleep, chances are high that I'm going to be a zombie the next day. I proactively arrange my workday so it's less intense when I can.

> **#NoShameParenting Takeaway:** Striking a balance that works for you can take some time. Sometimes it's difficult, messy work. You may try one thing, and then change your mind. But that's okay. I would even call it courageous. As long as you are loving and attentive to your children most of the time, even an unconventional arrangement won't fuck up your kid. There's no such thing as "having it all." Focus on what you want and strive toward that.

# 10

## Get It On:
## How Much Sex Everyone Is
## Really Having After Kids

It's a cliché —but we should all strive to make it a fallacy—that couples never have sex after having kids, between the recovery from actual childbirth and the pure stamina it takes to keep a child under five years old alive. Who has the energy? Just know: You're not alone. Every parent grapples with how much their relationships have changed after having a kid and adjusting their sex lives. It's totally normal. We can find an equilibrium again using some of the tips and information in the following pages.

The reassuring news is that there *is* a magic number when it comes to sex frequency and happy marriages: once a week, according to a study of more than 25,000 adults published in the journal *Social Psychological and Personality Science*.[1] More frequent sex didn't bring most couples more happiness. But sex less frequently made most couples a bit unhappier. One time a week was juuuuust right, like the Goldilocks of sex.

Mom Jancee Dunn wanted to end a long sex drought following the birth of her daughter. So she and her husband, Tom, got it on thirty days in a row, and she wrote about it in her book *How Not to Hate Your Husband After Kids*. Her exhausted parent friends at the playground could hardly believe their sex schedule. "I didn't feel judged as much as I felt like they were genuinely baffled—like, 'Why the hell would you do that?' They were more taken aback," Jancee told me a year after her book came out.

After the thirty days were up, Jancee and Tom happily stopped having sex every single day. But they both found their libidos had ramped up from their sexperiment. It turns out: The more sex you have, the more sex you want. They naturally settled into sex once a week, which is a number most parents have time for.

Jancee says reading the study that pinpointed sex once a week as optimal was a game changer for her: "I just loved how large the study was, and how it applied to new couples and those who had been together for decades. I also loved that the findings applied to both men and women—it sort of busted the old trope that men are up for sex all the time, and women are pushing them away. When we had a baby, Tom was as worn out as I was for the first six months."

Today, Jancee and Tom continue to prioritize sex, even when they're exhausted. "It's more than the physical connection—it's the emotional closeness, too," she says. "I know it's difficult, especially for mothers of multiple young kids who are 'touched out,' but usually you're glad you did."

Research shows we shouldn't worry about hitting a million different positions or otherwise staying up all night. A quickie is just as satisfying. Explains Jancee: "Another poll of sex researchers that I cite finds that the average length of time for intercourse for maximum enjoyment is thirteen minutes. That's not a giant time commitment, am I right? Thirteen minutes, once a week! That's do-able."[2]

I agree. Thirteen minutes, once a week is do-able most of the time. However, I completely understand that nagging voice that sets in when you have a moment of downtime: "Shouldn't you be doing laundry? Shouldn't you catch up on work email? Shouldn't you be spending more time with your kids? Um, can we just go to sleep?" Yes, these are all important things to do. But don't let your relationship fall into last place in the name of keeping a clean house that a toddler will destroy immediately anyway. (Of course, this doesn't mean every single sexual encounter needs to be exactly thirteen minutes long, once a week. That is a minimum recommendation to be built upon. Obviously, you need to do what works for you!)

## Getting Back in the Mood

Licensed social worker and relationship expert Rachel A. Sussman suggests couples get "back to learning how to flirt with each other. It's hard to feel sexy when you've got a baby with you, especially an infant. You have to feel sexy, you have to get away from your children. Even if you can't afford a babysitter, how about mom or dad or in-laws or trading with another family? Even if you can't afford to go out, how about a walk, or bringing a bottle of wine to a picnic?"

I also find that trying to squeeze in a hug or kiss reminds me that my husband is not just the father of my kids. Between packing school lunches, figuring out who is doing daycare drop-off, laundry, and running errands, it's hard to remember that you actually used to have romantic moments with your partner. . . .

The idea that it's difficult to move between a romantic and parenting relationship is a common theme among many couples I spoke to for this book. I set up a highly unscientific sex survey that I shared on Facebook, Twitter, and via email. To get honest results, I allowed people to answer anonymously—so the names following have been made up.

"One of the hardest things to overcome in our relationship post-kids was that somehow in the baby-stage we went from being companions to being business partners," Marcy* tells me. "It takes a lot of energy to get away from the transactional component of what needs to get done (the list is never-ending). . . . Between work and kids and life and everything else, I found it so hard to be emotionally open to my spouse. There was no time—and when there was, the last thing

I wanted to do was dig deep and share. It was so much easier to just watch TV or have quiet time, but that led to a huge loss in emotional intimacy that takes a lot of time to get back."

If you're not in the mood for sex, try cuddling or holding hands. "During times in the relationship when sex is less frequent, maintaining affection can help couples maintain sexual satisfaction," Dr. Amy Muise, the New York University psychology professor who authored the sex-once-a-week study, tells me.

Don't feel like you should rush into sex a minute after having a child. Your doctor may clear you for sex six weeks after giving birth, but you may not be physically ready—especially if you had a particularly rough delivery. That's when you should rely on affection until you are. "We try to have physical contact in little ways, a hug, a touch on the arm or back in passing, a physical reminder that we are still humans that are separate from the mom/dad identity we wear so often," Yvette* tells me.

Adds Yvette: "It has certainly changed and at times is hard to focus on the 'us' in the face of our family. So we ensure focus on maintaining us even when it may not be as romantic or thoughtful as it was before kids."

Part of the reason you may not be in the mood after kids: Science suggests that low libido after giving birth (and even longer if you breastfeed) could be caused by hormones. Women's estrogen levels dip, which can lead to vaginal dryness. Oxytocin is released during "let down" of breastfeeding (aka, when milk starts flowing), which is the "love hormone" that connects partners, and "may enhance feelings of affection between mother and child, and promote bonding," according to the World Health Organization.[3] (It also "induces a state of calm, and reduces stress," according to WHO.) Prolactin, which is the hormone that literally tells a woman's body to make milk, has been shown by studies to lower sex drives in both women and men.[4] It also may decrease the production of estrogen.[5] But,

234

the bonus is that prolactin "seems to make a mother feel relaxed and sleepy."

If you've been cleared by a doctor and you're still just not in the mood for sex, certified sex coach Gigi Engle (whose most popular web posts about sex have been shared more than 100 million times) suggests trying mutual masturbation or finding some porn both of you like and watching it together to "reintroduce desire into the relationship."

"Take intercourse entirely off the table," says Engle, who runs one of my favorite, slightly raunchy Instagram accounts, @GigiEngle. "There's this pressure and another sex myth that intercourse is the only kind of sex that counts. Unless there's penetration, it doesn't count or it wasn't good enough. That's a bullshit thing we have to stop telling people. Any way you experience sexuality with your partner is completely relevant."

Not to mention that "intercourse is a lot of fucking work," Engle jokes. "Sometimes it's just better to enjoy the intimacy of being together with your vibrator. And it doesn't matter if you have an orgasm. It doesn't matter how you experience intimacy."

She thinks studies that say things like thirteen minutes of sex is optimal "can be helpful, but add a whole layer of judgment. If you're not doing that, then you're broken. I think it puts these unnecessary boxes around what constitutes normal sexuality. There's no such thing as normal sexuality." So, again, don't stress out if *thirteen minutes* is not perfect for you.

Don't forget to be kind to yourself and your partner. "Understand that relationships change over time and the hormones and oxytocin and serotonin and craving and wanting at the beginning of the relationship . . . those hormones ebb and flow and change over time," Engle says. "If you expect to experience things the exact same way, it's unrealistic, and you're setting yourself up for disappointment."

This doesn't mean your relationship is doomed and will never be as giddy and fun as right in the beginning. It just means that it will change. Change is hard. Change is good. And there's no way you can avoid it in any area of your life—bedroom or otherwise.

And if you're all touched out and over it, there's no shame in saying no. You don't need to have sex every single time your partner wants to. You're allowed to be exhausted and only have the mental energy for an episode of the *Real Housewives of Whatever*. Just try to not let no be your answer every single time (assuming you're a consenting adult in a relationship). It is nice to remember our lives before kids, and more frequent sex is probably part of that.

### Ditching the Frigid Woman, Horny Man Myth

"Boys will be boys" is one of my least favorite phrases. It's false in all situations—including sex. The tired trope that women don't want sex but all men do has been debunked multiple times, most recently in anthropologist Wednesday Martin's fascinating book on infidelity, *Untrue*, which explores how society—more specifically the patriarchy (always the patriarchy)—conditions girls from a young age to expect monogamy and lets boys off the hook for cheating. Martin's book exposes how women are just as likely to cheat—and may in fact be wired to want more sex than guys. But we push down those desires (and often feel shame about them) due to society's expectations.

"Men and women might want sex equally, but I think women allow how they feel about their partners and how they're feeling about life to impact their sex drives," Sussman says. If women are exhausted and sleep deprived, we are less likely to be in the mood. (If that's not an argument for a more equal division of responsibility around the home, I don't know what is!)

Annika has chic, messy blonde hair and an infectious sense of humor, as she's described in Martin's book on infidelity.[6] She's Scandinavian but spent her teen years in an upscale Chicago suburb. At the beginning of her relationship with Dan, Annika tells Martin that she had a much stronger sex drive. Dan seemed "indifferent," so she began cheating on him. Dan proposed marriage multiple times, and Annika finally agreed, telling herself it would fix their sex lives. Eventually, hiding her cheating got too complicated, so she stopped. Then they had two children back-to-back. Annika couldn't justify the cost of childcare with her low salary, so she became a stay-at-home mother. Annika "was more comprehensively exhausted than ever. Sometimes her friends would come over to find her sitting on the living room floor with the kids, crying from sleep deprivation and frustration," Martin writes. Feeling trapped, "my sex drive just went into hibernation," Annika says. Around this time, Dan and Annika moved from the city (where all her friends lived) to the suburbs, where her feelings of isolation increased as her sex drive continued to plummet. Soon after, she discovered that Dan was lying about traveling for work. The man who once was completely "indifferent" about sex was actually sleeping with a long-time girlfriend. Meanwhile, Annika went from insatiable to zero sex drive due to being exhausted, isolated, and ignored by her husband. Our sex drive usually has less to do with "nature" than how much we feel supported by our partners (aka "nurture").

A social networking app called Peanut conducted a somewhat unscientific survey of 1,000 women ages twenty-two to thirty-seven.[7] The survey found that 56 percent of millennial moms think about sex "often or very often"—but did not specify what "often" means. ("We let our users interpret this; we weren't prescriptive on the meaning," the spokesperson says.)

Sixty-one percent of the women said they wanted more sex. Seventy-four percent of the moms said their sex life got better after babies. Forty-two percent said "being tired" was the number one reason why they didn't have as much sex, which I can certainly agree with. In my own highly, highly unscientific survey of a big group of my friends, exhaustion was also high ranking.

The survey found that 26 percent of millennial moms have sex once a week, just like the other study that pinpointed once a week as the optimal frequency. Twenty-nine percent of the women said they are intimate two or three times a week, while 19 percent of moms get down more often than that. Thirteen percent only have sex once a month, and another 13 percent have sex even less frequently than that.

(As an aside, some 70 percent of women surveyed by Peanut said they "use kegels to improve their experience in the bedroom." I have had numerous postpartum issues with my core, ranging from diastasis recti to pelvic floor weakness, and the physical therapists I have seen have all told me to kegel, kegel, kegel. I never remember to do it, and I'm not about to pull a Gwyneth Paltrow and insert a jade egg in my vagina. Once I was having lunch with a girlfriend who announced she was "doing kegels right now!" Certified sex coach Gigi Engle highly recommends kegels, too, telling me: "Do your kegel exercises—it's a great way to get back to feeling sexual and strengthen your pelvic floor, which will make you feel more like yourself again and that you didn't just push a baby out. Kegels help you have more controlled orgasm, more controlled clitoral function, better access to g-spots, and helps you not to pee your pants! You go to the gym and work out. Work out your vagina, too. It's a muscle!" To do a kegel, Engle recommends "squeezing your vagina muscles up to your belly button for five to ten seconds, and then releasing." Work your way up until you do one hundred a day, she says. I'm doing them right now as I'm writing, if that's not TMI.)

The idea that women aren't into sex has been popularized over recent centuries—mostly in the name of the patriarchy (of course). In 1886, psychiatrist Richard Freiherr von Krafft-Ebing released his book *Psychopathia Sexualis*. Though written in Latin and academic language to persuade lay readers, it's been used by judges and doctors for years. One key statement: "If a woman is normally developed mentally, and well-bred, her sexual desire is small. If this were not so, the whole world would become a brothel and marriage and family impossible." Or, as Martin writes: "Female passivity and sexlessness is the homeostasis that keeps the world in balance."

Engle says that even though many women believe today that sex is less taboo, many of us still feel shame for wanting more. "It's absolutely a myth that men want more sex than women. Women want sex just as much as men if not more," she says. "If you're a woman who wants sex, then you feel ashamed about that, and that doesn't feel good. This myth can have a lot of super-damaging effects on female libido."

This myth doesn't just hurt women. "If you're not hypermasculine and trying to have sex constantly, then you're less of a man," Engle laments. "These stereotypes are damaging both people.

"Some women have extreme increased sex drive while pregnant and after, and their libido is heightened after having children," Engle says. "Some say it's lessened. It's completely subjective. It varies so vastly from woman to woman. We can't make these overarching sweeping statements like, 'You don't want sex anymore after a baby.' That's not true at all, and it's not fair."

The pressure society puts on women to bounce back after having a baby is also a huge damper on libido. "I think there's this myth that if you are a new mom and just had a baby, that you're now in this mommy mode, that society doesn't want to see you as a sexual being anymore. They just want to see you as a mom and a caretaker," Engle says. "So your sex drive and sexual wants are no longer prioritized and you're supposed to put the child first. This is a big inhibitor for women. If you're in the mindset that you're not supposed to be sexual or having sexual feelings at this stage in your life, then you will naturally inhibit yourself from being sexual, which can really affect your libido."

The idea that we need to "flaunt" our "post-baby body" minutes after giving birth also adds to the pressure. "You're naturally going to put on weight, your boobs get a lot bigger and swollen—if you don't bounce back to this pre-baby weight right away, there are a lot of messages that you're no longer a sexual being," Engle sighs. "With all these messages raining down upon you, it's going to change the way you feel about yourself and your sexuality."

## A Trick to Find Time for Sex

Not everybody has the budget for lots of date nights. Or, even if you do, the idea of spending $25 an hour for a babysitter—which is the going rate in my neighborhood, not including the Uber home after the end of the night—makes it tough to stomach.

So here's another idea: Cynthia,* a mom of two with sandy brown hair who grew up in Kansas, and her husband, Sam, found an ingenious way to keep their romance hot and their childcare bills low(er): They took a day off work to go on a date while their kids were in school. (This of course assumes you have a job that pays you for personal days.)

"It was the best because we weren't exhausted after a long day, and could actually have a good conversation," Cynthia says. And of course, the sex was better, she laughs. "We actually had enough energy for that too!" (Later, when I asked her if I could use this anecdote in this book, she agreed, as long as I changed her name, and added: "If only I could follow my own damn advice . . . we've still only done it once!" with my most-used and favorite emoji, the laugh-cry.)

Amanda used to have sex with her husband five or six times a week. But after having kids, they just lost interest. "Neither of us really wanted it, even after that six to eight weeks [of postpartum recovery] was up. We were so tired and just overwhelmed with parenting, especially with our second—having two under two," she told *Huffington Post* in 2014.[8] "They're both so needy all the time. And how do you have any time for yourself, let alone your partner? So that initial period was really difficult to adjust to."

They found a solution that doesn't sound romantic, but actually works: scheduling sex. Specifically on Saturday afternoons during their kids' nap time. "Guaranteed. If you're looking at your clock and it's like noon-ish on a Saturday, we're doing it. I promise," says Amanda, a brunette based in Colorado who blogs frankly about her family life and wrote the book *2 Under 2 Pregnancy and Parenthood.*

Sure, scheduling sex is not as spontaneous as those pre-kid days (and, ugh, another thing to schedule in days full of wake-up times, school drop-off times, lunchtimes, and nap times) . . . but when you have it on the calendar once a week, it's a nice reminder, so my husband and I also employ this tactic. I find that anticipating that day's sex date helps with getting in the mood. It also takes the pressure off who initiates when you have a sex date on the calendar.

I checked in with Amanda again while writing this book to see if she was still scheduling sex and was pleasantly surprised that she and her husband were keeping up the same routine four years later. "We still have sex on Saturdays but it's not formally scheduled that way anymore . . . it just works out that way," she tells me. "Now that the kids are older, we set them up with a movie, craft or 'quiet time' in their rooms while we have our own 'grown up quiet time' in our room.

"Energy levels are still higher earlier in the day and we both look forward to an afternoon delight once a week at least," Amanda adds with a laugh. "We still rely on Saturday afternoons to be the consistent sexy-time each week and then sprinkle another one or two encounters into the week on top of that. I suppose that makes it a routine, technically, but it doesn't feel boring or predictable in a bad way at all."

The sex experts I spoke to for this book agreed heartily with the idea of scheduling sex. "Sex can't always be spontaneous. People are busy," relationship expert Rachel Sussman says. "We schedule everything else in the world. We schedule our doctor appointments, we schedule our girls' night out, boys' night out. We schedule our kids' play dates. People say, 'We shouldn't have to schedule sex.' Why? Then tell me how everything else gets done, but not sex."

Adds Engle: "It's very rare that you have sex with a partner who you trust and love and you regret it after. It's like when you go to spin class. The whole time you're walking there, you're like, 'I don't want to fucking go.' The entire time you're at the gym, you want to shoot yourself in the face. Then you walk out after, and you're so glad you did that. I don't want to compare sex to spin class, but it's kind of the same."

\*

It's important to talk about sex with your partner, even if it may feel awkward. "You talk about money and parenting style, why not sex? Just like anything else, if it's not talked about, the problem will fester and become a bigger and bigger issue in the relationship," Dr. Irwin Goldstein, president of the Institute for Sexual Medicine in San Diego, told *Parenting* magazine.[9] "Open lines of communication about wants and needs in the bedroom are key."

"I think a couple has to talk about what they're missing. . . . 'I miss our old life' or 'I miss you.' Send a funny text or a flirty text," Sussman suggests. "Even if you can't have a date night, meet for lunch or coffee. Find a way to re-create some of the flirtiness and spontaneity of your early life."

Just try not to bring up how much your sex life sucks . . . while you're having sex. "Couples should address their changing sex lives not in the heat of the moment or when one person might feel rejected, but rather when things are calm. Acknowledge any feelings that may have changed, any anxieties or concerns (such as child-care) that exist, and remember, you're a team so you should work together on this," psychotherapist Jonathan Alpert, who wrote (with Alisa Bowman) *Be Fearless: Change Your Life in 28 Days,* tells me.

Don't put off the conversation forever. "Issues don't go away by *not* addressing them," Alpert warns. "They usually will only become more problematic or people will resort to unhealthy ways of handling them—withdrawing, expressing with anger, frustration, depression, cheating even."

If you need more motivation to get back into bed, consider this: Sex may improve more than just your relationship. "Couples who engaged in regular sex were more likely to experience high-quality sleep than couples who didn't," according to a study by Laura Berman, director of the Berman Women's Wellness Center.[10]

Sex will also probably boost your overall mood. "They say exercise is like taking an antidepressant without an antidepressant. I think sex is too," Sussman says. "A lot of couples, when they haven't had sex in awhile, say, 'We kind of forgot how good that feels.'"

✳

Beyond sex, you shouldn't feel guilty for taking time out from your kids to focus on your relationship. E! News anchor Giuliana Rancic came under fire for announcing how she prioritizes her marriage over her son. "We're husband and wife, but we're also best friends, and it's funny because a lot of people, when they have kids, they put the baby first, and the marriage second," she once told *Us Weekly.*[11] "That works for some people. For us, I find, we put our marriage first and our child second, because the best thing we can do for him is have a strong marriage."

Another relationship you shouldn't abandon: The one you have with yourself. If you can't take some time to unwind—even if that means hanging out in the bathroom quietly for a liiiittle longer than you really need to (sometimes I sit on the edge of the bathtub for five extra minutes)—you will get resentful, and that will affect every area of your life, from your love life, to your parenting, to your work, and beyond.

I'm talking about a little #selfcare, which has been hashtagged more than fifteen million times on Instagram. But this isn't some expensive, time-consuming thing all the big marketing campaigns would have you believe. For me, self-care is always having something to read on my Kindle. So I spend $11 every couple of weeks to buy a book. For you, self-care may mean a cup of coffee every morning. Make time for it, even if that means you need to leave your kids with your partner, or a babysitter, or turn on a TV show. Try to find ways to do the little things that make you feel happy and like yourself—not just somebody's spouse or parent.

**#NoShameParenting Takeaway:** We're all tired. We're all stretched thin. So it seems counterintuitive to listen to my advice and do *more*. But taking thirteen minutes a week to have sex, and prioritizing your relationship with your partner (if you have one) and, most importantly, yourself, will make you a better, more present parent. And your kids will certainly benefit from that.

## There's No Such Thing as Normal: Embrace Your Family's Situation (Even If You Didn't Choose It)

Raise your hand if you grew up watching *Full House*. (Me!) In my head, those Tanners had the perfect family: loving parent, supportive extended family, siblings to fight (and make up) with, inspiring pep talks at the end of each twenty-two-minute episode. Yet, their family wasn't "perfect" by so many standards: Danny Tanner was a single parent. DJ, Stephanie, and Michelle's mom died when they were little kids. They were raised by mostly men until Aunt Becky moved into the attic. And every single one of the adults worked outside the home.

Why is it that we laud this fake TV family, but we're so hard on ourselves for not having our own two-parent home with 2.5 kids, a dog, a white picket fence, endless patience, and fresh cookies waiting on the counter every day after school? We think we're abnormal if we don't fit into a neat, little mold, thanks to outdated expectations within our culture. It's all good, though—you won't fuck up your kids no matter what labels society places on you.

Stats show there is actually no longer such thing as a "normal" family. "Different is the new normal," sociologist Philip Cohen told the *Washington Post*[1] following the release of his research paper for the Council on Contemporary Families.

"People often think of social change in the lives of American children since the 1950s as a movement in one direction—from children being raised in married, male-breadwinner families to a new norm of children being raised by working mothers, many of them unmarried," Cohen reveals in his research.[2] "Instead, we can better understand this transformation as an explosion of diversity, a fanning out from a compact center along many different pathways."

In 1970, about 70 percent of adults were married by the time they were eighteen years old, usually by age twenty-three (for men) and twenty-one (for women).[3] Fast-forward to 2018, and people are waiting a lot longer to say "I do" (on average, nearly thirty for men and twenty-eight for women[4]), which has driven down the marriage rate.

Alyssa skipped the idea of marriage altogether—becoming a mother on her own accord.

"There were hardly any 'single moms by choice' when I became one, and now it's become so basic," laughs Alyssa, whom I met up with at a hip coffee shop called Smith Canteen, on a busy street in Carroll Gardens, Brooklyn. Her hair was swept up in a perfectly messy ponytail, and she wore a peasant dress and furry Birkenstock sandals. Even though we hadn't seen each other in ten years, we fell into an easy conversation about parenthood.

When Alyssa was thirty-six years old and single, she decided she wanted to freeze her eggs. During the routine checkup before the procedure, though, her doctor told her she had fibroids, likely due to her age. "I had a huge wake-up call," says Alyssa, who always knew she wanted to be a "writer and a mother." She accomplished goal number one with her book *Apron Anxiety: My Messy Affairs In and Out of the Kitchen*. But a baby remained elusive.

A friend's sister had become a mother on her own, and Alyssa was enraptured after hearing about the process. And even though she considers herself a "scrappy . . . broke writer," she was thrilled she could afford the $10,000 fee. So she dove into the donor selection process. "I was looking for a genetically blessed human being," she admits. "I knew I could make my future child kind. I knew I could make him or her smart. I knew I could make them Jewish, which was very important to me. But why not give him a chance to be 6-feet 2-inches if it's a boy, or have striking cheekbones if it's a girl?"

She got pregnant on her second IUI. "I was in the best place," Alyssa says. Her confidence was contagious, and she dated all throughout her pregnancy. "I never cared what anyone thought."

She faced some judgment. A formerly close friend called her multiple times and told her she'd never find a partner and would end up alone. An Uber driver once lectured her about how a child needs a dad. "Those were the two instances that hurt my heart," Alyssa admits. But she knew: "When someone judges you, it's always about them, never about you."

Alyssa had an uneventful pregnancy. In casual conversations, acquaintances would call her brave. "I'd laugh and say, 'You're the brave one for having a kid with him!'" Then, growing serious, Alyssa says: "What's scarier is not living as my authentic self. I didn't get pregnant to make a statement."

When Alyssa was thirty-seven years old, Hazel was born into a familial village. At the time, Alyssa lived in the same building as her parents. "I'm so lucky to have the emotional and physical support of my family," she says. "It was like having live-in help. We joked that my dad was her manny." Not to mention that Alyssa is a freelancer with flexible work hours.

A couple of months later, while breastfeeding in the middle of the night and swiping Tinder, Alyssa spotted a man named Sam. "My Tinder profile was very clear: 'Single mom in uncomplicated situation.' Anyone who wasn't interested could just swipe right on by," she says. They sparked immediately in person. "We became pretty serious right away," Alyssa says. "It was the three of us against the world."

Now Hazel is three years old, and the three of them live together. "As far as I'm concerned, he's 100 percent her dad for life, as much as I hope he's my partner for life," says Alyssa, who has no plans to get married after two ended engagements.

When Hazel is older, she'll have the option to contact the sperm bank for more information about her biological dad—and maybe even the opportunity to meet him. "I would stand behind Hazel 1,000 percent if she chooses to do that," Alyssa says. For now, Hazel is too young to understand many details. Alyssa feels pride over the unique way her family came together.

"There are so many acceptable paths to find a career, to become a grown-up," Alyssa says, "but there's only one specific way to create a family. And that didn't work for me."

Today, more than 40 percent of children are born out of wedlock, according to numbers from the CDC. One-third of American children—twenty-four million kids—were living with an unwed parent in 2017, which has more than doubled since 1968. Just more than 20 percent of those kids were living with a single mom, and 7 percent were with cohabitating parents.[5]

Just as we saw earlier with the backlash against working moms: Any time there's a big societal shift, there's a lot of outcry that goes along with it. Some 48 percent of Americans said in a 2015 Pew research survey that "unmarried couples raising children was bad for society"—and a whopping 66 percent felt that single moms were "bad for society."[6]

But, with time (and a younger, more accepting generation), people tend to become more open-minded. An interesting comparison can be made with gay marriage. In 2004, only 30 percent of Americans approved of it. But 2019 polls show that 61 percent of Americans have shifted their attitudes in support.[7]

This coincides with same-sex parents, who are raising about nine million children in America, becoming slowly more accepted in our culture. [8] "I think there has been a very important and timely humanization of gay parents," Dr. Alicia F. Lieberman, a psychologist who specializes in childhood trauma, tells *The Atlantic*.[9] When she first published her book *The Emotional Life of the Toddler* in 1995, society was "not even giving gay people permission to be parents. It was like, 'Why would you want to be a parent?'" Lieberman recalls. "I'm a consultant for child protective services. I was in court several times to uphold the fact that gay parents that wanted to adopt a child had all the strength that heterosexual parents had. They were giving them the love, the understanding, the socialization. That giving a child for adoption to a gay couple did not endanger the child in terms of their mental health.

"People would say, 'Other children are going to tease them and bully them,' [or] 'Other parents are not going to want their children to play with them,' 'They won't have a community that they can belong to,' and the point that I and others were making is that that is not inherent to the condition of being gay. It is inherent to the prejudices of society in how they relate to gay people," Lieberman says. "I think gay parents really led the way in creating communities for themselves that were able to show the world that they were healthy, loving, joyful families. Twenty-five years ago that was by no means something that was understood or accepted."

Along with society chilling out about parents' love lives, science has also come around to support the obvious: As long as parents care about their kids, their sexual orientation doesn't matter. The National Longitudinal Lesbian Family Study found that kids who grow up with two moms have "no significant differences in measures of mental health"[10] at age twenty-five than any of their peers raised by heterosexual parents. Another study looked at gay parents of both sexes and found that "children with same-sex parents fare well, both in terms of psychological adjustment and prosocial behavior," Roberto Baiocco, of the Sapienza University of Rome, who conducted the research, wrote in a medical journal.[11]

Take Alan, who jumped through unbelievable hoops to become a father. "I always knew I was gay, but I never wanted to accept it because that also might mean I would have to accept I couldn't have children," he told Yahoo! Parenting.[12] "With no gay role models around, this idea became ever more disheartening for me." Thanks to his successful business, he was able to afford a $70,000, multi-continental odyssey that involved a Chicago-based agency, an American egg donor, and a hired surrogate in India. Alan traveled more than 8,000 miles to pick up his twin daughters, who today are thriving elementary-school students. "The best part of parenthood is just having a purpose," Alan has said. "Every day I wake up and I'm reminded that this is why I'm here on this planet. Everything I do is centered around them."

*

The divorce rate peaked in 1993 and has been on the decline ever since. Nowadays, fewer people get married in the first place, and those who do are waiting until they're older, more established in their lives, and more in touch with their needs.[13]

With the changing face of marriage comes the changing face of divorce. Couples who decide to separate may be fearful of how it will affect their kids, flashing back to our own experiences as children of hostile baby boomer divorces. But don't believe all the outdated stats that say kids raised by single parents won't fare as well. It's the quality of a kid's relationship with their parents—divorced or not—that counts, experts say. So there is no reason to stay in a terrible union for the sake of your kids.

"When the most major researcher in divorce, Mavis Hetherington, began studying divorce in the 1970s, she thought it was cause and effect: Parents get divorced, [which has a negative effect on] children," the child trauma psychologist Lieberman told *The Atlantic*.[14] "Thirty years later, she realized that it depends on: What are the mediating factors, moderating factors, social circumstances? How do the parents get along after divorce, how do they talk about each other to the child? [There are] all kinds of emotionally charged conditions that are much more predictive than the single factor of divorce."

Nile, a TV and movie writer in California, once wrote a *Huffington Post* essay called "Why I'm Happy My Parents Are Divorced": "Because I'm aware that saying 'my parents are divorced' elicits the same reaction as 'I have crabs,' I've learned to immediately clarify to people that no, I do not need a hug or a look of pity—the divorce is a good thing. . . . Divorce may not be a blessing, but it is not a curse either—nor is it a failure. My parents did not fail me, nor did they fail each other, by ending their marriage. I would have failed them, and they would have failed each other, had they stayed together unhappily. Instead, they were able to give me an awesome childhood while co-parenting apart, and I'm grateful for that."[15]

When I reached out to Nile to see if she still felt the same way five years later, she gave me an emphatic yes. "I don't think I've ever really felt any differently," Nile says. "I would say the closer I get to potentially getting married and having kids of my own, the more I can understand and appreciate how difficult it must have been for each of my parents, and the sacrifices they have to make—my mom got her PhD while raising me essentially as a single mom. She'd put me to bed and stay up all night writing her dissertation. My dad had to give up seeing me every day or even every week, and he missed a lot of big life moments simply because we didn't live in the same house. He called me every single night when I was a kid. My point is that perhaps what I've learned since I wrote the article is that divorce wasn't a failure; it also wasn't necessarily the easy thing to do—but they made the decision both to separate and to stay friends because it was the best thing for me, and for them, and thus, for us as a family, whether they were married or not."

She's found the silver lining of her parents' divorce. "It's certainly made me more independent, sometimes to a fault," Nile says. "But I think more than anything my parents' relationship (divorced but close friends/family) has taught me that there is no reason to settle or to feel pressured to get married, have kids, or stay with someone if you're unhappy. A nuclear family doesn't necessarily work for everyone. It doesn't really matter what a family looks like as long as it's a happy one and it's the one that's best for the individuals involved."

Nile isn't sugarcoating the idea of divorce. One of her earliest childhood memories is standing in the doorway of her kitchen while covering her ears with her hands watching her parents fight. She was three years old. That picture "makes me feel sad, of course," she says. "But it also makes me appreciate the choices my parents made in terms of separating—again, it was something they did for me. I also think/hope this makes me especially conscious of how I behave in front of my children one day."

Her healthy outlook today should free those parents who are staying together "for the kids," or concerned about how their kids will turn out after their divorce. When Nile's parents separated, she was relieved to have two calmer homes instead of one stressful one. "It doesn't really matter what a family looks like as long as it's a happy one and it's the one that's best for the individuals involved. A happy home with divorced parents can be so much better than an unhappy home with parents who stay together," Nile says.

The American Psychological Association agrees: "Healthy marriages are good for couples' mental and physical health. They are also good for children; growing up in a happy home protects children from mental, physical, educational, and social problems."[16] Unhappy marriages? Damaging for both the adults and children. "Divorce can be a traumatic experience for children, but research suggests that most children adjust well within two years following the divorce; on the other hand, children often experience more problems when parents remain in high-conflict marriages instead of splitting up," the APA notes.[17]

If you plan to end your partnership, "talk to your kids about what's going on," Nile says. "Kids aren't dumb, and they don't appreciate being treated as if they can't see what's likely right in front of them. Explain things in clear terms, and give them a chance to ask questions. Be honest without giving any of the gory details (that should go without saying, but you never know). And the golden rule: don't talk bad about the other parent in front of the kids."

I can't say this enough: Don't bad-mouth your ex in front of your kids. While it's so tempting to let it rip, save the bitch sessions for your friends or therapist or new partner. It sends a very mixed message to your kids if you tell them how much their mom sucks, and then turn around and drop them off at their mom's house. (Don't talk smack about your ex in front of your kids even if you think they're not listening. They are listening. One friend nicknamed his ex after a character in Harry Potter, so her name never came up in conversation if the kids were in the room.) In Nile's home, divorce "was always communicated to me and discussed in our family as a positive thing versus a negative thing."

These days, Nile has a great relationship with both her parents, and her parents have a pretty decent relationship, too. "I do think people are still shocked by the fact that my parents are able to stay 'family'—my mom still comes to the holidays in New York with my dad's side of the family, and my dad and his girlfriend at the time flew to Florida for my maternal grandmother's eightieth birthday. People have a hard time wrapping their heads around it, and I think it still tends to turn heads as much as it did in 2013."

Kids are happiest when their parents are happy. "Honestly seeing your parents happy is such a gift, and makes for a happy life for the kids," Nile says. "They deserve it and you deserve to see them like that. In my case, my mom and dad had to divorce to be the happiest, best they could be as both individuals and as parents."

✳

Tracy and Chris should get all the credit for "conscious uncoupling," as they did it years before Gwyneth Paltrow and Chris Martin. After their divorce, they split custody of their son Ryan fifty-fifty and even spend holidays with each other. "No matter how uncomfortable it was for us, we owed it to him to always make sure he knew we were a family—whether or not we lived under the same roof," Tracy says, admitting, "It wasn't easy in the beginning.

"Over and over again, I told myself that whatever happened between his dad and I, it had nothing to do with how we felt about Ryan—and without his dad, who is just a stellar man—my son would not be the kid he is today," Tracy says. "The three of us still spend every Christmas morning together, we spend Ryan's birthday together every year, and we high five that we've made it another three hundred and sixty-five days through this parenting journey together, and that we have this amazing kid."

They work together because "it's all about Ryan having the best life, and knowing that we still love and respect each other, even if we're not married anymore," Tracy says. "There will never be a time when his dad is not welcome in my new house and vice versa. Our kid deserves that security."

Yes, Tracy admits that she feels judged sometimes about her unique arrangement with her ex. "Mostly, it's by people who just don't get it, either because they are children of divorce and their parents never got along, or they have a terrible relationship with their own ex. I think people assume if you got divorced, you must hate each other," she says. "But I wouldn't change anything. I married the right man for me at that time in my life, we have an incredible child, he's a fantastic father, and that's not negated just because we grew apart and changed. Let them judge all they want. Chris and I have a beautiful story."

As for their son, he's now a happy, well-adjusted middle schooler. "Ryan is smart, funny, social, sensitive, goofy, kind—he's truly the best parts of both his dad and me," Tracy says. "I will forever be grateful to Chris, for giving me the greatest gift in my life—and even though he's not my husband anymore, I will love him for eternity. And I'm proud that Ryan will never have to doubt it." (It's amazing how well our kids turn out when adults act like adults.)

You don't need to spend Christmas with your ex if it makes you want to scratch your eyeballs out. But try to keep your interactions civil, for the love of your children. It goes a long way, says Rachel Sussman, relationship expert and the author of *The Breakup Bible*. When I asked her if divorce ruins kids, she responded with an emphatic "No!" and explained how to keep it healthy for your kids' sake: "If a couple has a healthy divorce, a conscious uncoupling, and does it right and the parents go forward and meet the right partner and have a fantastic relationship . . . those children have an opportunity to see what a [good] relationship works like," she says. "[And kids] have the opportunity to watch their family go through a hard time and survive. It builds resilience."

*

Some uncoupled parents have such civil relationships that they don't ask their kids to go back and forth between their houses. Instead, the kids stay in the family home, and the parents take turns staying in that home instead of shuffling them back and forth every other weekend or whatever the custody arrangement is. The parents then live in a secondary residence, like a rented apartment. It's called birdnesting. The idea is that it's much less disruptive to kids' schedules.

"It's really not the child's fault that you got divorced," *Sweet Home Alabama* star Josh Lucas told *People* magazine after he and his ex-wife, Jessica, decided to birdnest so their son Noah, five, could stay in his home.[18] "It's your fault and therefore it should not be the child's problem to go back and forth between two different homes. It should actually be the parents' problem."

Noah "loves" the arrangement, Josh tells *People*, before correcting himself. "He doesn't love us being separated but he loves that he has his bed and his toys and his dog. It's his life." The actor adds that it's a "remarkably complex period of my life and Jess' life that we're doing the best we possibly can to keep his life stable."

*

Interestingly, science shows that marriage affects men and women differently. Men, for example, tend to derive greater life satisfaction, improved well-being, and make more money at work after becoming fathers.[19] Women, meanwhile, are more likely to take on the "second shift," aka a full-time second job as the "on-call" parent.[20] After working a full day at the office, we'll come home and then put in the equivalent of another forty-hour-a-week job washing dishes, doing laundry, and basically being the overall "project manager" of the house. My girlfriends and I often bitch about how our brains are like Grand Central. We each have great, involved husbands or partners, but they don't always know when the school permission slips are due, who needs new pajamas because they had a growth spurt, and how much to pay the housecleaner.

I'm not trying to say that marriage is a terrible thing and we should be happy when it comes to an end. There are tons of benefits to coupling up, especially when it comes to having a live-in support system and being more financially stable. But I want to reassure parents who don't have a partner that their kids will be fine.

THERE'S NO SUCH THING AS NORMAL

*

Blended families are a reality for many Americans—40 percent of Americans have a step-relative,[21] whether that's a sibling, stepparent, or stepchild.

Ariel first met Dave in a bar at midnight. He told her he had a kid, but she forgot. "I was twenty-five. I had barely been with a responsible man at all, let alone one with a child," she tells me. On their second date, he told her again he had a son. Ariel didn't think much of it, figuring their relationship wasn't serious.

But it became serious fast. Ariel knew one thing: If she was going to be in Dave's life, she was going to have to have a good relationship with his ex-girlfriend, Melinda,* and their son, Owen.* At the time, this consisted of driving hundreds of miles between their home in Brooklyn and Owen and Melinda's home in Maryland.

A friendship blossomed between Ariel, Dave, and Melinda. Soon, Melinda invited Ariel and Dave to stay in her home when they were in town to see Owen. They'd arrive Friday night, giving Melinda a night off from parenting to hang out with her friends. Or sometimes all three of them would sip coffee or wine together in Melinda's kitchen while Owen played nearby. When Ariel and Dave got married, Melinda attended their wedding. Owen was the best man.

When Ariel got pregnant, she and Dave were surprised and delighted that Melinda agreed to relocate to Brooklyn, moving into a spare bedroom in their apartment as Owen was due to enter kindergarten. Shortly before Ariel and Dave's son Kai was born, Melinda moved one neighborhood away. They had no formal custody arrangement. Owen would go back and forth.

Ariel and Melinda continued their friendship, confusing many people. "We were class parents together. People didn't understand our relationship. They'd ask if we were sisters," Ariel says. "When we told them our connection, people were blown away."

Their carefree relationship became more complicated when Ariel got pregnant again, with Wyatt. "We had very little separation. Melinda was in a relationship. There were all these opinions. Our lives were so intertwined," Ariel reflects. They decided to put a custody arrangement for Owen in writing, which further strained things. "Transitions are never smooth." The formality of the legal process and the endless court proceedings frayed everyone's nerves.

Then, Melinda got married. As it was a tiny court ceremony, Dave and Ariel did not attend. Melinda's new husband had a daughter the same age as Owen. Shortly after, Melinda wrote Ariel a nice note: "I now understand the strange position you are in as a stepparent." Their relationship had come full circle. Ariel was so touched that Melinda acknowledged the "strangeness" of stepparenting that it brought them closer together again.

"It was really vindicating," Ariel says. "Everyone wants to be understood and to receive empathy." She sees both sides, though: "When you're a stepparent, you're an extra voice in the room that's not always wanted or considered when there are already two parents."

Now, both couples have created healthy boundaries in their relationship. They don't hang out at each other's homes all the time. But they're friendly and text each other. Recently, Owen's stepsister wanted to see Ariel and Dave's home, so Melinda walked her over.

Even during periods where they weren't getting along as well, Ariel says that they "never once said a bad word about each other" in front of their kids. "The relationship is too important in my life."

As for Owen, he has faced a series of adjustments during his young life—going from single child to having two half-brothers and then a stepsister and stepfather. But he's "so loving and caring" and surrounded by a village of adults who would do anything for him. And

Kai and Wyatt have also benefited from the extended family of adults who care for and love them. To them, their life is perfectly normal. It's all they've ever known.

Ariel wishes the "evil stepmother" stereotype would die, though. "People cringe when they hear the word *stepmom*, like it's a bad word," she says. Once, Ariel, Owen, and a stranger were in an elevator. The woman remarked how Ariel was his mom, and Owen matter-of-factly said, "No, she's my stepmom."

"The woman looked at me and cringed!" Ariel says. "Stepmother is not an insult. He has a mom. I've never understood society's obsession with shitting on stepmoms. Disney movies made it seem terrible. It's hurting us, and it's hurting kids. Kids get confused, thinking, 'I'm not supposed to like this woman.'" She's also extrasensitive of not being the "evil stepmother" herself. She once caught herself not disciplining Owen as harshly as Kai and Wyatt for that reason.

Ariel rarely feels judged by her family situation, except for older relatives who make offhanded comments about how she essentially became a stepmom before she was married. "It's just ingrained: First marriage, then baby," Ariel says. "But it doesn't always happen that way."

Doing things "out of order" has had some unintended benefits. "No one I knew had a kid at twenty-five. But now I'm almost thirty-five. I was so lucky to start young. It's a gift. I had so much energy then! [Before you get married or have kids,] you also wonder if your partner will be a good parent. But I'm lucky that I got to see mine as a dad, and know at age twenty-five that he's a great dad. It's been a unique experience. I'm grateful to have learned so much with Owen.

"Not that he's my 'trial child,'" she adds with a smile. But I know what she means when she says she stresses less when her little kids do something weird. "I'm not worried about milestones or missed meals," she says. Because she has an older son, "I know everything is a phase and works itself out."

She's realistic that the relationship between herself, Melinda, and Dave will continue to have ups and downs, but they're all committed to working through issues and being civil no matter what, much to the benefit of the extended blended family they have created.

*

Approximately 120,000 children are adopted in America annually,[22] such as Edie, who was adopted by Brian and his husband, Tim. "I can still see the look on my husband's face as we met her, and I don't think that I have ever loved him more," Brian writes on a blog named after their daughter called *Edie's Clothes*.[23]

"We want Edie to love herself," says Brian, a stay-at-home dad to his daughter, who is now four. "No small feat I know, particularly for a girl of color with two gay dads living in a world where racism, sexism, and homophobia are still rampant and viciously alive. This is part of the reason why I am a bit obsessed with Edie's clothes, wanting her always to put her 'best foot forward' for herself. I want her to be determined, confident, and brave. She already asks for straight long hair. This breaks my heart. We tell her every single day that her hair is perfect and that she is gorgeous and exactly right. We show her other people, famous and ordinary, with hair similar to hers. We hope that this sticks."

To counteract this, Brian, who jokingly calls himself a "middle-aged white guy," has learned how to expertly style his daughter's hair. "I wash, and condition, and co-wash. And I love it. I love it because it's an experience that I've never really had with someone who looks different from me who is also my daughter. I love it because it's intimate and relaxing and a time for bonding (and usually YouTube gymnastics videos). I love it because it slows down time and the day, for a minute. Mostly though, I love it because it's a time when my growing brown daughter sits on my lap and I can whisper, 'You are beautiful. You are perfect. You are exactly as you should be.'"

Because Brian and Tim have a different skin color from their daughter, "people do say some dumb shit," Brian writes. Recently, a TSA agent pointed at Edie and asked, "Is that yours?" which he says is one of his "favorites/gag/eyeroll."

Brian writes that his "biggest fear" is that Edie grows up feeling "unwanted due to her being adopted."

"I know that I have no real control over that, but in the meantime, I can make sure she knows how perfectly wanted she is by her two parents that need her. She makes our story so much fuller, so much better. She has changed our world, our minds, our hearts, and our lives," Brian says. "Her birth mother made a heroic and complicated decision that I am eternally grateful for in a way that I could never express to her or anyone else."

＊

Today's modern family consists of so many different combinations of parents, caregivers, and children, each dealing with their own struggles and triumphs. Before we become parents, we may have an idea of what our family will look like. Life usually has other plans. The only thing that matters is that we come to a good-enough peace with our individual situations.

We often face a chasm between two separate issues: (1) the action we've taken (such as going back to work, using formula, discipline, food, screen time, etc.), and (2) the stress we feel about that decision. And the stress we feel is more damaging than whatever decision we've made about raising our kids, the child trauma psychologist Alicia Lieberman has explained.[24] If we feel okay with the way our lives are set up, our kids get the benefits of that calming effect—we as parents are happier, more engaged, less anxious, and just overall more present.

Resist the urge to judge yourself—and other parents—over the way we live our lives. When we take the time to understand each other's stories, the more humanity we feel. Our situations are rarely black and white; we're all messy and doing the best we can. And that's more than enough.

> **#NoShameParenting Takeaway:** There is no such thing as a "normal" family today—so don't feel guilty if your life doesn't follow a path forged by *Leave It to Beaver.* Kids can flourish in all sorts of family situations. Their parents' marital status is not going to predispose them to having a good—or terrible—life. As moms and dads, what matters most is how we resolve disputes with each other, because research shows that our kids will fare much better if we settle our differences peacefully. But whether you decide to stay with your co-parenting partner or separate, raise your kids alone or with someone else, you're not going to fuck up your kids.

# The Bottom Line: Seriously, You Can't F\*ck Up Your Kids

I wrote this book as much for me as I did for you.

Before I even had kids, I felt confident that they would thrive. But there was that nagging voice from friends, scary headlines, experts: What if doing [one of a million things] irretrievably ruins my children's lives? I wanted to prove to myself, and the thousands of parents I've encountered during my career, that we are worrying too much. We cannot screw up our children if we buy them the wrong high chair, read them cereal boxes instead of kids' books, feed them formula, enroll them in daycare, divorce partners, and so forth.

We as parents need to let go of the idea that, from birth, we can mold our kids to attend Harvard, become millionaires, and live a so-called perfect life. And if we accomplish anything less than that, it's our fault for fucking them up. No. Our job is to give our children the tools to achieve their definition of success. We do this by loving, feeding, and housing them, and giving them healthy boundaries. We also do this by loving and supporting ourselves and each other in the crazy process of childrearing!

To prove why I believe this so passionately, I want to share the story of how I survived my own traumatic childhood. I'll start by saying that today I am a successful writer, corporate speaker, and media/technology leader. I would never consider myself anywhere close to perfect. But I still get out of bed every single day, striving to be there for my husband, for my kids, for my colleagues, and for myself. I have a strong marriage that we work very hard at, and two kids who seem pretty well adjusted. We all live together in an old house in my favorite city in the world.

It's the kind of life I only dreamed about as a child cowering in my bedroom as my parents screamed at each other. My most vivid childhood memory was when I was eight years old, forehead pressed against the cool glass of my bedroom window from my top bunk, watching my mom's shadowy figure dash off into the night. I tiptoed downstairs, barefoot and just wearing a long T-shirt, where my anguished dad spotted me and grabbed me by the arm, dragging me into the bathroom. Beyond the wood toilet seat floated a sea of blue pills. He flushed, and they swirled, swirled, swirled away. "Don't ever do drugs," he pleaded with me desperately.

That wasn't the first time drugs and drinking had seeped into my childhood. When I was seven years old, my dad placed me in the front seat of his Oldsmobile as we drove around to neighborhood bars looking for my alcoholic mother, me waiting in the car as he ducked in and out to check and then drive on to the next one. I can only imagine my sisters, then aged one and four, were in the backseat, but I don't have a clear memory of that. Around that same time, he sat me on the kitchen counter. "Do you want to move to Tennessee?" he asked me. That's where he was raised, one of ten children (of which only eight survived), in a rural town. We lived in suburban Chicago by then. I shrugged. No seven-year-old should make major family decisions.

Instead, we decided to move in with my mom's parents, my grandparents. My aunt flew into town to clean out our basement. She made trips to the dumpster again and again, until there was no more room and she had to stack toys—many unopened, purchased in sets of three from garage sales for my siblings and I—outside beside the overflowing garbage. "What's this?" I asked once, holding up a pretty glass thing in that same basement. "That's not for you," somebody said, grabbing it from my hands. When I was older, and thought back on this memory, I realized it was a bong. My mom dabbled in heroin, cocaine, and anything she could get her hands on. Pills were her favorite, though. "I love pills . . . and my kids . . . and pills," she once told me.

My mom entered rehab for the first time shortly before or after we moved in with my grandparents. Everyone at one of the family meetings thought I was "so cute" because I drew a picture that said my mom needed to do laundry instead of drugs. In hindsight, I have no idea why anyone would think it was adorable that an eight-year-old illustrated something like that, but I suppose we were all desperate for normalcy at that point.

Not that normalcy ever came during my childhood. My parents fought constantly, my mom often retreating to her room for days at a time. Once she slept with her eighteen-year-old drug dealer. "See him, that's the devil," my dad said, pointing the teen dealer out in our subdivision when I was eight.

It wasn't long before my parents were sleeping in two separate beds in our grandparents' home. Then they announced their divorce, and my dad moved out. After a couple of years of calm, thanks to my grandparents, we moved again. This time, my mom chose a tidy little townhouse on the wrong side of the tracks of another Chicago suburb. It soon became clear that she was too mentally ill to do things like parent or hold down a job. Our house became packed nearly to hoarder level, with laundry piled up to the actual ceiling, maggots crawling in the meat, and a dirty brown toilet that rivaled the grossest gas station bathroom you've ever seen.

My mom oscillated between spending days in her bed to days when she was screaming and even violent. She once punched me, causing me to fall backward into a brick wall. My father paid child support, but my mother wasn't so good at paying the bills. Sometimes the lights didn't work. Sometimes the phone didn't work. Sometimes there was no food, or just a giant bag of Burger King sandwiches in the fridge that my sisters and I would microwave for ourselves whenever we got hungry over the course of a week. My dad dutifully picked us up every other Friday night, spent a little time doing laundry, and then dropped us back off at that hell hole Sunday afternoon, as if nothing was wrong.

My mom kicked me out at sixteen, and I thankfully ended up with her sister, my aunt. Not long after, and most likely unrelated to me leaving, my mom made yet another suicide attempt, landing her in the hospital with thick bandages around her wrists. When my aunt took me to the psychiatric hospital to visit her, my mother threw a book at my head, leading us all to rush out of the room. I went away to the farthest college I was accepted into, to study journalism. My mom signed over custody of my two little sisters to my dad, right as they were entering junior high and high school in a brand-new town, with a brand-new house, with a brand-new stepmom and stepsister. When my sisters, then aged eleven and fourteen, struggled to find friends, to find a routine, to deal with their mom's suicide attempt, to get along with their new stepmom and stepsister, they found little support.

Things became even more complicated after my mom fell down the stairs and became quadriplegic, paralyzed from the shoulders down. Unknown to me, I was her power of attorney for property and health. Once again, I was thrust into the role of caretaker for her. I almost had to make the decision whether or not to pull the plug as she lay unconscious in the ICU with a broken neck and screws protruding from her skull. After she woke up, I sold her car and her home, and my extended family moved her into assisted living. And I returned back to my charmed life in New York. (Just to be clear, my parents are not terrible people. I suppose they were just doing the best they could in a complicated situation. I still have a relationship with them both.)

After surviving all this, having children was a scary proposition for me, even though I knew I wanted them. Luckily, I didn't realize how healing it would be to raise my kids with the basics that I never had: A safe home. Attention and love I could count on. Stability. Lights that always flickered on.

There's a resilience I've built by coming out on the other end of a childhood I wouldn't wish on my worst enemy. Every time that voice crept into my head questioning if the meal I was feeding my children was healthy enough, or if it was okay that my kids went to a high quality daycare while I went to work, or if it was okay if they spent a little time watching Netflix . . . there was an even louder voice saying, "Are you kidding me?! You experienced all kinds of shit and turned out okay! There is no way it matters if your kids eat chicken nuggets every once in a while! Be a little kinder to yourself!"

From that reassuring voice, I found my mission. How could I spread my self-assuredness to other families without them going through everything that I did? Furthermore, how could I use my journalism training to delve into the research to really *prove* to parents that their kids are going to be okay?

And now you are holding the result of that work in your hands. I know it's hard to quiet those inner, doubtful voices. I know being kind to yourself is easier said than done. I don't tell you my childhood sob story to invalidate your day-to-day struggles to do the best for your children. I also have those day-to-day struggles.

But my experience and the research I've done for this book and during my fifteen-year career allows me to say without a shadow of doubt: You can't fuck up your kids.

The one message all parents should know: You are enough. You can move on from the doubt and anxiety about your parenting decisions and regain your self-esteem.

It doesn't matter how many servings of vegetables your child eats with every meal, or if she's potty-trained by two, or if he knows how to do baby sign language. If you're divorced or married, a first-time parent at twenty-six or forty-six, raising your child on a farm or in a major city—they're going to turn out okay. A toddler who bites others isn't going to grow up to be a psychopath. It's just a phase. A baby who won't latch and thus drinks formula from birth won't have a lower IQ. She'll be nourished, physically and mentally.

It's time we focus all the energy we spend doubting ourselves on the one thing that matters: Loving our kids.

# ACKNOWLEDGMENTS

Writing this book felt like giving birth to a third child. I would not have been able to do it without the support, encouragement, tough love, real talk, endless text messages, and cheerleading from the following people:

My agents, Todd Shuster and Justin Brouckaert of Aevitas Creative Management, introduced to me by Albert Lee: Todd, you were an energetic supporter of this book idea from the first day we met, and I couldn't have shepherded it through to completion without your and Justin's thoughtful notes and guidance.

My editor, Sarah Pelz of Simon & Schuster's Atria imprint: Your excitement about this project made me want to work with you from Day One. You are in the trenches with me as a parent to young kids! I appreciate your kind words, support, and guidance throughout the process. Melanie Iglesias Pérez, thank you so much for being a helping hand. Thank you, Stephanie Hitchcock, for shepherding this project through to the finish line. Jon Karp and everyone at S&S: Thank you so much for believing in this book and the #NoShameParenting mission. I'm also so grateful for the tireless work of Bianca Salvant, Shida Carr, Dana Trocker, James Iocobelli, Libby McGuire, Lindsay Sagnette, Kristin Fassler, Suzanne Donahue, Emi Battaglia, Megan

Rudloff, Sarah Wright, Kate Lapin, and so many more at Simon & Schuster.

My former Yahoo! Parenting team, some of the smartest women I've ever known: Rachel Bertsche, Beth Greenfield, Elise Solé, Jennifer O'Neill, Julie Giusti, Melissa Walker, Lambeth Hochwald, Rachel Grumman Bender, and many other contributors whose work I loved. Esther Crain, Susan Kittenplan, Lori Bongiorno, Inger Carter, and Janice Min, you've taught me so much. Susannah Cahalan and Erin Carlson, you talked me through writing quandaries and answered my text messages and DMs about book publishing at all hours of the night. Thank you.

My first readers, who saw this book in all kinds of various states and offered suggestions and advice: Beth Greenfield, Elise Solé, Renee Spurlin Kornegay, and Shannon Meland. Thank you for taking the time.

My kids' incredible caregivers over the years: Alicia, Lena, Ana, Mariana, Amina, Vika, Ms. Debbie, Ms. Stephanie, Ms. Angela, Ms. Lori, Ms. Janet, Ms. Perri, Ms. Karen, Ms. Chandra, Ms. Kerry, Ms. Nerisa, Ms. Gigi . . . and countless others who have stepped in to help nurture my children.

My mom-support tribe, near and far: Renee Spurlin Kornegay, Nabiha Calcuttawala, Courtney Lane, Mindy Coronado, Shannon Meland, Nicole Di Schino, Alex Schneider Fine, Kathryn Patullo, Lindsey Burke, Julia Gilfillan, Julie Mead, Jacalyn Lee, Pam Colledge, Sara Gramling, Joanna Bock, Amy Vinciguerra, Cindy Kushner-Mancebo, Payal Maheshwari, Emily Rose-Blank, Anne Roderique-Jones, Andrin Mele-Shadwick, Nina Hoffman, Ann Casey, Cary and PJ Hoffman, Alison and Kevin Rockmann . . . xoxo.

All the people across the country who shared their stories via email, on Facebook, on Instagram, and in person—thank you! The Wing, Park Slope Parents, Li.St, Binders . . . Great, inspiring communities in which I'm lucky to take part.

# ACKNOWLEDGMENTS

My sisters, Cassidy Long and Allison Powers, I love you. Laurie and Keith Hoffman; Sue and the late Bob Casey; Susan and Martin Casey, thank you for being a steady presence in my childhood and beyond.

My father, David Powers, always supported and encouraged me to become a writer from a young age. My mother, Kim Powers, gave me a unique perspective of life. My stepmother, Bianca, sparked my love of cooking, and my mother-in-law, Mim's, entrepreneurism has always inspired me.

My firstborn, Everett, who never runs out of anything to say, and my baby, Otto, who keeps me on my toes. I've loved watching you both grow and discover the world.

Most of all, thank you to Brad Eichmann, without whom I would probably not be a functioning adult. You believe in me even when I don't. You've pushed me in all the best possible ways to make my work better. You've read uncountable versions of this book, always offering astute suggestions. You're an incredible role model for our sons, and an amazing husband. Thank you.

# NOTES

## Introduction:
### It's Time for #NoShameParenting

1. Mary Brophy Marcus, "Study. Breastfeeding Could Save More Than 8,000 Lives a Year," *CBS News*, January 28, 2016, https://www.cbsnews.com/news/breastfeeding-could-save-lives-babies-mothers/.
2. Stephen Solomon, "The Controversy over Infant Formula," *New York Times Magazine*, December 6, 1981, https://www.nytimes.com/1981/12/06/magazine/the-controversy-over-infant-formula.html.
3. Jennifer O'Neill, "Daycare vs. Nanny," Yahoo! Parenting, November 1, 2014, https://www.yahoo.com/news/daycare-vs-nanny-100297666807.html.
4. Carrie Craft, "How Many Children Have Gay Parents in the US?" Child Welfare League of America via *LiveAbout*, updated May 8, 2019, https://www.liveabout.com/how-many-gay-parents-in-us-27175.
5. Neil Shah, "U.S. Sees Rise in Unmarried Parents," *Wall Street Journal*, March 10, 2015, https://www.wsj.com/articles/cohabiting-parents-at-record-high-1426010894.
6. Jennifer O'Neill, "What Moms Really Think About Spanking, Judging Each Other, and Their Relationships," Yahoo! Parenting, October 5, 2015, https://www.yahoo.com/news/what-moms-really-think-about-spanking-judging-090037683.html.
7. David Crossman, "Simon Sinek on Millennials in the Workplace," Inside Quest via *YouTube*, October 29, 2016, https://www.youtube.com/watch?v=hER0Qp6QJNU.
8. "Myths: Smoking and Pregnancy," Smokefree Women, National Cancer Institute, https://women.smokefree.gov/pregnancy-motherhood/quitting-while-pregnant/myths-about-smoking-pregnancy.
9. Cheryl Oncken, Ellen Dornelas, John Greene, Heather Sankey, Allen Glasmann, Richard Feinn, and Henry R. Kranzler, "Nicotine Gum for Pregnant Smokers," *Obstetrics & Gynecology*, vol. 112, issue 4, October 2008, 859–867, https://www.ncbi.nlm.nih.gov/pmc/articles/PMC2630492/.

10. Vivian Chou, "To Vaccinate or Not to Vaccinate? Searching for a Verdict in the Vaccination Debate," Harvard University: The Graduate School of Arts and Sciences, January 4, 2016, http://sitn.hms.harvard.edu/flash/2016/to-vaccinate-or-not-to-vaccinate-searching-for-a-verdict-in-the-vaccination-debate/.

## Chapter 1: Drink a Little Wine!

1. Steven A. Shaw, "Chicken of the Sea," *New York Times,* July 15, 2007, https://www.nytimes.com/2007/07/15/opinion/15shaw.html.
2. "Food Safety for Pregnant Women," U.S. Departments of Agriculture and Health and Human Services, September 2011, https://www.fda.gov/media/83740/download; "Caffeine Intake during Pregnancy," American Pregnancy Association (2018), https://americanpregnancy.org/pregnancy-health/caffeine-intake-during-pregnancy/.
3. "Alcohol: Balancing Risks and Benefits," The President and Fellows of Harvard College, Harvard T. H. Chan School of Public Health, 2019, https://www.hsph.harvard.edu/nutritionsource/healthy-drinks/drinks-to-consume-in-moderation/alcohol-full-story/.
4. Loubaba Mamluk and Luisa Zuccolo, "Health Risks of Light Drinking in Pregnancy Confirms That Abstention Is the Safest Approach," *The Conversation,* September 12, 2017, https://theconversation.com/health-risks-of-light-drinking-in-pregnancy-confirms-that-abstention-is-the-safest-approach-83753.
5. Loubaba Mamluk, Hannah B. Edwards, Jelena Savović, Verity Leach, Timothy Jones, Theresa H. M. Moore, Sharea Ijaz, Sarah J. Lewis, Jenny L. Donovan, Debbie Lawlor, George Davey Smith, Abigail Fraser, and Luisa Zuccolo, "Low Alcohol Consumption and Pregnancy and Childhood Outcomes: Time to Change Guidelines Indicating Apparently 'Safe' Levels of Alcohol During Pregnancy? A Systematic Review and Meta-Analyses," *BMJ Open,* 7:e015410, August 3, 2017, https://bmjopen.bmj.com/content/7/7/e015410.info.
6. Mayo Clinic Staff, "Chronic Stress Puts Your Health at Risk," Mayo Clinic, March 19, 2019, https://www.mayoclinic.org/healthy-lifestyle/stress-management/in-depth/stress/art-20046037.
7. Emily Oster, *Expecting Better: Why the Conventional Pregnancy Wisdom Is Wrong and What You Really Need to Know* (New York: Penguin Books, 2013), 46–47.
8. Mahsa M. Yazdy, Sarah C. Tinker, Allen A. Mitchell, Laurie A. Demmer, and Martha M. Werler, "Maternal Tea Consumption during Early Pregnancy and the Risk of Spina Bifida," *Birth Defects Research Part A: Clinical and Molecular Teratology,* vol. 94, issue 10, September 2, 2015, 756–761, https://www.ncbi.nlm.nih.gov/pmc/articles/PMC4557736/.
9. "Food Safety for Pregnant Women," U.S. Food and Drug Administration, August 15, 2018, https://www.fda.gov/food/people-risk-foodborne-illness/food-safety-pregnant-women.

# NOTES

10. "Facts + Statistics: Mortality Risk," Insurance Information Institute, 2019, https://www.iii.org/fact-statistic/facts-statistics-mortality-risk.

11. "Frequently Asked Questions: Pregnancy," The American College of Obstetricians and Gynecologists, June 2018, https://www.acog.org/Patients/FAQs/Listeria-and-Pregnancy.

12. C. Tam, A. Erebara, and A. Einarson, "Food-borne Illnesses During Pregnancy: Prevention and Treatment," *Canadian Family Physician*, vol. 56, issue 4, April 2010, 341–343, https://www.cfp.ca/content/56/4/341.long.

13. Julia Moskin, "Sushi Fresh From the Deep . . . the Deep Freeze," *New York Times*, April 8, 2004, https://www.nytimes.com/2004/04/08/nyregion/sushi-fresh-from-the-deep-the-deep-freeze.html.

14. Harvard Women's Health Watch, "Going Off Antidepressants," Harvard Health Publishing, Harvard Medical School, August 13, 2018, https://www.health.harvard.edu/diseases-and-conditions/going-off-antidepressants.

15. Mayo Clinic Staff, "Antidepressants: Safe During Pregnancy?" Mayo Clinic, February 28, 2018, https://www.mayoclinic.org/healthy-lifestyle/pregnancy-week-by-week/in-depth/antidepressants/art-20046420.

16. Melissa Conrad Stoppler, "Updated Product Labeling Warns of Birth Defect Risk with Paxil," *MedicineNet*, June 13, 2018, https://www.medicinenet.com/paxil_and_pregnancy_possibilty_of__birth_defect/views.htm.

17. Harvard Women's Health Watch, "Going Off Antidepressants."

18. Oxford University Press, "Length of Human Pregnancies Can Vary Naturally by as Much as Five Weeks," *Science Daily*, August 6, 2013, https://www.sciencedaily.com/releases/2013/08/130806203327.htm.

19. Oster, *Expecting Better*, 142.

20. Hannah Barnes, "The 300-Year-Old Fertility Statistics Still in Use Today," *BBC News Magazine*, September 18, 2013, https://www.bbc.com/news/magazine-24128176.

21. David B. Dunson, Bernardo Colombo, and Donna D. Baird, "Changes with Age in the Level and Duration of Fertility in the Menstrual Cycle," *Human Reproduction*, vol. 17, issue 5, May 2002, 1399–1403, https://academic.oup.com/humrep/article/17/5/1399/845579.

22. Barnes, "The 300-Year-Old Fertility Statistics Still in Use Today."

23. Angel Petropanagos, Alana Cattapan, Françoise Baylis, and Arthur Leader, "Social Egg Freezing: Risk, Benefits and Other Considerations," *Canadian Medical Association Journal*, vol. 187, issue 9, June 16, 2015, 666–669, https://www.ncbi.nlm.nih.gov/pmc/articles/PMC4467930/.

24. USC Fertility, "Frequently Asked Questions About Egg Freezing," https://uscfertility.org/egg-freezing-faqs/.

25. Pam Belluck, "What Fertility Patients Should Know About Egg Freezing," *New York Times*, March 13, 2018, https://www.nytimes.com/2018/03/13/health/eggs-freezing-storage-safety.html.

26. "Can I Freeze My Eggs to Use Later If I'm Not Sick?" American Society for Reproductive Medicine, 2014, https://www.reproductivefacts.org/news-and-publications/patient-fact-sheets-and-booklets/documents/fact-sheets-and-info-booklets/can-i-freeze-my-eggs-to-use-later-if-im-not-sick/.

## NOTES

27. "Brief History of Egg Freezing," Global Donor Egg Bank, https://globaldo noreggbank.com/history-egg-freezing/.

28. European Society of Human Reproduction and Embryology, "More Than 8 Million Babies Born From IVF Since the World's First in 1978," *Science Daily,* July 3, 2018, https://www.sciencedaily.com/releases/2018/07 /180703084127.htm.

29. Christene Barberich, "After 5 Miscarriages, What's Next?" *Refinery29,* August 2015, https://www.refinery29.com/en-us/2015/08/92613/multiple-mis carriage-womens-fertility-story.

30. Ibid.

31. "Nearly 386,000 Children Will Be Born Worldwide on New Year's Day, Says UNICEF," January 1, 2018, https://www.unicef.org/media/media_102362.html.

32. Christene Barberich, "After 7 Miscarriages, The Surprise I Wasn't Expecting . . ."*Refinery29,* September 24, 2018, https://www.refinery29.com /en-us/2018/09/210343/recurrent-miscarriage-pregnancy-success-story.

33. Jaime Primak Sullivan, "'I Will Always Mourn That Baby,'" *Yahoo! News,* December 29, 2015, https://news.yahoo.com/i-will-always-mourn-that-baby -108828550802.html.

34. Melissa Dahl, "How Misconceptions Over Miscarriages Cause Needless Guilt," *The Cut,* August 4, 2015, https://www.thecut.com/2015/08/harm-of -miscarriage-misconceptions.html.

### *Chapter 2: C-Section vs. "Natural"*

1. Jorun Bakken Sperstad, Merete Kolberg Tennfjord, Gunvor Hilde, Marie Ellström-Engh, and Kari Bø, "Diastasis Recti Abdominis During Pregnancy and 12 Months After Childbirth: Prevalence, Risk Factors and Report of Lumbopelvic Pain," *British Journal of Sports Medicine,* vol. 50, issue 17, June 20, 2016, 1092–1096, https://bjsm.bmj.com/content/50/17/1092.info.

2. "A Typical American Birth Costs as Much as Delivering a Royal Baby," *The Economist,* April 23, 2018, https://www.economist.com/graphic-detail/2018 /04/23/a-typical-american-birth-costs-as-much-as-delivering-a-royal-baby.

3. Charlotte Hilton Andersen, "What It Was Like Giving Birth in Every Decade Since the 1900s," *Redbook,* July 28, 2016, https://www.redbookmag .com/body/pregnancy-fertility/g3551/what-it-was-like-giving-birth-in-every -decade/?slide=1.

4. Arlene W. Keeling, John C. Kirchgessner, and Michelle C. Hehman, *History of Professional Nursing in the United States: Toward a Culture of Health* (New York: Springer Publishing Company, 2018), 168.

5. "Achievements in Public Health, 1900–1999: Healthier Mothers and Babies," *MMWR Weekly,* vol. 48, issue 38, 849–858, Centers for Disease Control, October 1, 1999, https://www.cdc.gov/mmwr/preview/mmwrhtml/mm4838a2.htm.

6. Hilton Andersen, "What It Was Like Giving Birth in Every Decade Since the 1900s."

7. Quinn Rathkamp, "Childbirth Through Time," *WWU Honors Program Senior Projects,* 56, May 2017, https://cedar.wwu.edu/wwu_honors/56.

NOTES

8. S. Campbell, "A Short History of Sonography in Obstetrics and Gynaecology," *Facts, Views & Visions in ObGyn*, vol. 5, issue 3, 2013, 213–229, https://www.ncbi.nlm.nih.gov/pmc/articles/PMC3987368/.

9. American Association of Birth Centers, "Highlights of 35 Years of Developing the Birth Center Concept in the U.S.," https://www.birthcenters.org/page/history.

10. "Who Invented Ultrasound?" *CME Science*, 2018, https://cmescience.com/who-invented-ultrasound/.

11. T. J. Mathews and Sally C. Curtin, "When Are Babies Born: Morning, Noon, or Night? Birth Certificate Data for 2013," NCHS Data Brief, No. 200, May 2015, https://www.cdc.gov/nchs/data/databriefs/db200.pdf.

12. "More U.S. Women Dying in Childbirth," Associated Press, August 24, 2007, http://www.nbcnews.com/id/20427256/ns/health-pregnancy/t/more-us-women-dying-childbirth/.

13. "Pregnancy-Related Deaths," Centers for Disease Control and Prevention, February 26, 2019, https://www.cdc.gov/reproductivehealth/maternalinfanthealth/pregnancy-relatedmortality.htm.

14. Nina Martin, *ProPublica*, and Renee Montagne, "Black Mothers Keep Dying After Giving Birth. Shalon Irving's Story Explains Why," *All Things Considered*, NPR, December 7, 2017, https://www.npr.org/2017/12/07/568948782/black-mothers-keep-dying-after-giving-birth-shalon-irvings-story-explains-why.

15. Rob Haskell, "Serena Williams on Motherhood, Marriage, and Making Her Comeback," *Vogue*, January 10, 2018, https://www.vogue.com/article/serena-williams-vogue-cover-interview-february-2018.

16. Marcos Silva and Stephen H. Halpern, "Epidural Analgesia for Labor: Current Techniques," *Local and Regional Anesthesia*, vol. 3, December 8, 2010, 143–153, https://www.ncbi.nlm.nih.gov/pmc/articles/PMC3417963/.

17. Laura Geggel, "Epidurals: How They've Changed, and How They Work," *LiveScience*, July 19, 2016, https://www.livescience.com/55457-how-epidurals-work.html.

18. Emily Oster, *Expecting Better: Why the Conventional Pregnancy Wisdom Is Wrong and What You Really Need to Know* (New York: Penguin Books, 2013), 230.

19. B. L. Leighton and S. H. Halpern, "The Effects of Epidural Analgesia on Labor, Maternal, and Neonatal Outcomes: A Systematic Review," *American Journal of Obstetrics and Gynecology*, vol. 186, issue 5, suppl., May 2002, S69–77, https://www.ncbi.nlm.nih.gov/pubmed/12011873.

20. Y. W. Cheng, B. L. Shaffer, J. M. Nicholson, and A. B. Caughey, "Second Stage of Labor and Epidural Use: A Larger Effect Than Previously Suggested," *Obstetrics & Gynecology*, vol. 123, issue 3, March 2014, https://journals.lww.com/greenjournal/fulltext/2014/03000/Second_Stage_of_Labor_and_Epidural_Use__A_Larger.8.aspx.

21. Center for the Advancement of Health, "Epidural Leads to Less Pain, More Assisted Deliveries," *Science Daily*, November 22, 2005, https://www.sciencedaily.com/releases/2005/11/051122210414.htm.

22. Unzila A. Ali, MD and Errol R. Norwitz, MD, PhD, "Vacuum-Assisted Vaginal Delivery," *Reviews in Obstetrics and Gynecology*, vol. 2, issue 1, Winter 2009, 5–17, https://www.ncbi.nlm.nih.gov/pmc/articles/PMC2672989/.
23. Geggel, "Epidurals: How They've Changed, and How They Work."
24. The Pennine Acute Hospitals, "Headache after an Epidural or Spinal Anaesthetic: An Information Guide," NHS Trust, February 2006, https://www.pat.nhs.uk/downloads/patient-information-leaflets/anaesthetics/headache-after-an-epidural-or-spinal-anaesthetic.pdf.
25. Dr. Eugene Smetannikov, "Can I Get Paralyzed from Epidural?" allaboutepidural.com, 2015, http://www.allaboutepidural.com/can-i-get-paralyzed-from-epidural.
26. "Lightning Strike Probabilities," National Lightning Safety Institute, 2019, http://lightningsafety.com/nlsi_pls/probability.html.
27. "Births—Method of Delivery," Centers for Disease Control and Prevention, January 20, 2017, https://www.cdc.gov/nchs/fastats/delivery.htm.
28. WHO, HRP, "WHO Statement on Caesarean Section Rates," World Health Organization, April 2015, https://www.who.int/reproductivehealth/publications/maternal_perinatal_health/cs-statement/en/.
29. Amy Tuteur, "The Childbirth Lie That Will Not Die," *The Skeptical OB*, June 17, 2014, http://www.skepticalob.com/2014/06/the-childbirth-lie-that-will-not-die.html.
30. M. Wagner, "A Global Witch-Hunt," *The Lancet*, vol. 346, issue 8981, October 14, 1995, 1020–1022, https://www.sciencedirect.com/science/article/pii/S0140673695916962.
31. Amy Tuteur, "World Health Organization's Optimal C-section Rate Officially Debunked," *The Skeptical OB*, December 1, 2015, http://www.skepticalob.com/2015/12/world-health-organizations-optimal-c-section-rate-officially-debunked.html.
32. John Elflein, "Cesarean Section Rates in OECD Countries in 2016 (per 1,000 Live Births)," *Statistia*, August 9, 2019, https://www.statista.com/statistics/283123/cesarean-sections-in-oecd-countries/; Central Intelligence Agency, "Country Comparison: Maternal Mortality Rate," *The World Factbook*, https://www.cia.gov/library/publications/the-world-factbook/rankorder/2223rank.html.
33. American Academy of Pediatrics, "Breastfeeding After Cesarean Delivery," *Healthy Children*, 2009, https://www.healthychildren.org/English/ages-stages/baby/breastfeeding/pages/Breastfeeding-After-Cesarean-Delivery.aspx.
34. Joyce King, "Contraception and Lactation," *Journal of Midwifery and Women's Health*, vol. 52, issue 6, 2007, 614–620, https://www.medscape.com/viewarticle/565623_2.
35. Josef Neu and Jona Rushing, "Cesarean versus Vaginal Delivery: Long Term Infant Outcomes and the Hygiene Hypothesis," *Clinics in Perinatology*, vol. 38, issue 2, June 2011, 321–331, https://www.ncbi.nlm.nih.gov/pmc/articles/PMC3110651/.
36. Beth Greenfield, "Inside the Growing Practice of 'Seeding' Babies Born via

C-Section," Yahoo! Parenting, August 19, 2015, https://www.yahoo.com /news/inside-the-growing-practice-of-seeding-babies-127085374637.html.

37. James Gallagher, "Vaginal Seeding After Caesarean 'Risky,' Warn Doctors," *BBC News,* August 23, 2017, https://www.bbc.com/news/health-41011589.

38. Shuyuan Chu, Qian Chen, Yan Chen, Yixiao Bao, Min Wu, and Jun Zhang, "Cesarean Section without Medical Indication and Risk of Childhood Asthma, and Attenuation by Breastfeeding," *PLOS One,* 12(9):e0184920, September 18, 2017, https://www.ncbi.nlm.nih.gov/pmc/articles/PMC5602659/.

39. Evelyn Xiu Ling Loo, Jordan Zheng Ting Sim, See Ling Loy, Anne Goh, Yiong Huak Chan, Kok Hian Tan, Fabian Yap, Peter D. Gluckman, Keith M. Godfrey, Hugo Van Bever, Bee Wah Lee, Yap Seng Chong, Lynette Pei-chi Shek, Mark Jean Aan Koh, and Seng Bin Ang, "Associations between Caesarean Delivery and Allergic Outcomes: Results from the GUSTO Study," *Annals of Allergy, Asthma & Immunology,* vol. 118, issue 5, May 2017, 636–638, https://www.annallergy.org/article/S1081-1206(17)30125-4/fulltext; A. Maitra, A. Sherriff, D. Strachan, and J. Henderson, "Mode of Delivery Is Not Associated with Asthma or Atopy in Childhood," *Journal of the British Society for Allergy and Clinical Immunology*, vol. 34, issue 9, September 2004, 1349–1355, https://www.ncbi.nlm.nih.gov/pubmed/15347366.

40. Neu and Rushing, "Cesarean versus Vaginal Delivery."

41. Sheryl L. Rifas-Shiman, Matthew W. Gillman, Summer Sherburne Hawkins, Emily Oken, Elsie M. Taveras, and Ken P. Kleinman, "Association of Cesarean Delivery with Body Mass Index $z$ Score at Age 5 Years," *JAMA Pediatrics,* vol. 172, issue 8, June 11, 2018, 777–779, https://jamanetwork.com /journals/jamapediatrics/article-abstract/2684228.

42. Nicholas Bakalar, "C-Sections Not Tied to Overweight Children," *New York Times,* June 12, 2018, https://www.nytimes.com/2018/06/12/well/c-sections -not-tied-to-overweight-children.html.

43. Mayo Clinic Staff, "Vaginal Birth after Cesarean (VBAC)," Mayo Clinic, 2019, https://www.mayoclinic.org/tests-procedures/vbac/about/pac-20395249.

44. Kathryn Doyle, "Out-of-Hospital Births on the Rise in U.S.," *Reuters Health*, March 28, 2016, https://www.scientificamerican.com/article/out-of-hospital -births-on-the-rise-in-u-s/.

45. Anna Claire Vollers, "Midwives Can Legally Deliver Alabama Babies for First Time in Decades as State Issues Licenses," AL.com, January 19, 2019, https://www.al.com/news/2019/01/midwives-can-legally-deliver-alabama -babies-for-first-time-in-decades-as-state-issues-licenses.html.

46. Joseph R. Wax and William H. Barth Jr., "Planned Home Birth," American College of Obstetricians and Gynecologists Committee Opinion, April 2017, https://www.acog.org/Clinical-Guidance-and-Publications/Committee-Opin ions/Committee-on-Obstetric-Practice/Planned-Home-Birth.

47. Doyle, "Out-of-Hospital Births on the Rise in U.S."

48. Marian F. MacDorman and Eugene Declercq, "Trends and State Variations in Out-of-Hospital Births in the United States, 2004–2017," *Birth,* June 2019, vol. 46, issue 2, 279–288, https://www.ncbi.nlm.nih.gov/pubmed/3053 7156.

49. Neel Shah, MD, MPP, "A NICE Delivery—The Cross-Atlantic Divide over Treatment Intensity in Childbirth," *New England Journal of Medicine*, vol. 372, June 4, 2015, 2181–2183, https://www.nejm.org/doi/full/10.1056/NEJMp1501461.

50. Dianna Douglas, "Should More Women Give Birth Outside the Hospital?" *Morning Edition/NPR*, July 13, 2015, https://www.npr.org/sections/health-shots/2015/07/13/419254906/should-more-women-give-birth-outside-the-hospital.

51. "Key Facts About Late or No Prenatal Care," ChildTrends.org, 2019, https://www.childtrends.org/indicators/late-or-no-prenatal-care.

52. Douglas, "Should More Women Give Birth Outside the Hospital?"

53. Ibid.

54. Beth Greenfield, "Midwives and Hospitals: The Ideal Birth Combo?" Yahoo! Parenting, July 20, 2015, https://www.yahoo.com/news/midwives-and-hospitals-the-ideal-birth-combo-124591107097.html.

55. Oster, *Expecting Better*, 267.

56. CDC, "Epidemiologic Notes and Reports Perinatal and Maternal Mortality in a Religious Group—Indiana," *MMWR Weekly*, June 1, 1984, vol. 33, issue 21, 297–298, Centers for Disease Control, https://www.cdc.gov/mmwr/preview/mmwrhtml/00000345.htm.

57. "HELLP Syndrome: Symptoms, Treatment and Prevention," American Pregnancy Association, August 2015, https://americanpregnancy.org/pregnancy-complications/hellp-syndrome/.

### Chapter 3: Protein Is Protein

1. Donna Freydkin, "This Is My Love Letter to Baby Formula," *Today*, May 22, 2018, https://www.today.com/parents/baby-formula-saved-my-sanity-new-mom-t129503.

2. Gisele Bündchen, Instagram, December 10, 2013, https://www.instagram.com/p/hvz4wzntH_/.

3. Charlotte Triggs, "Gisele Bündchen Says She Had a Hard Time Adjusting to Motherhood: 'I Kind of Lost Myself,'" *People*, September 27, 2018, https://people.com/parents/gisele-bundchen-hard-adjusting-motherhood/.

4. American Academy of Pediatrics, "Breastfeeding and the Use of Human Milk," *Pediatrics*, March 2012, vol. 129, issue 3, https://pediatrics.aappublications.org/content/129/3/e827full.

5. "Frequently Asked Questions—Break Time for Nursing Mothers," U.S. Department of Labor, https://www.dol.gov/whd/nursingmothers/faqBTNM.htm.

6. Hanna Rosin, "The Case Against Breast-Feeding," *The Atlantic*, April 2009, https://www.theatlantic.com/magazine/archive/2009/4/the-case-against-breast-feeding/307311/.

7. U.S. Department of Health and Human Services, "2013 Poverty Guidelines," *Federal Register*, December 0, 2013, vol. 78, no. 16, January 24, 2013, 5181–5184, https://aspe.hhs.gov/2012-poverty-guidelines.

# NOTES

8. Ibid.
9. Rosin, "The Case Against Breast-Feeding."
10. Corinne Purtill and Dan Kopf, "The Class Dynamics of Breastfeeding in the United States of America," *Quartz*, July 23, 2017, https://qz.com/1034016 the-class-dynamics-of-breastfeeding-in-the-united-states-of-america/.
11. Sam Wang and Sandra Aamodt, "Breast-Feeding Won't Make Your Children Smarter," *Bloomberg View,* July 2, 2012, https://www.bloomberg.com/opin ion/articles/2012-7-2/breast-feeding-is-not-how-mothers-make-kids-smart; Amy Sullivan, "The Unapologetic Case for Formula-Feeding," *New Republic,* July 31, 2012, https://newrepublic.com/article/105638/amy-sullivan-un apologetic-case-formula-feeding.
12. "Diet Considerations While Breastfeeding," American Pregnancy Association, May 16, 2017, https://americanpregnancy.org/breastfeeding/diet-con siderations-while-breastfeeding/.
13. Emily E. Stevens, Thelma E. Patrick, and Rita Pickler, "A History of Infant Feeding," *Journal of Perinatal Education,* Spring 2009, vol. 18, issue 2, 31–39, https://www.ncbi.nlm.nih.gov/pmc/articles/PMC2684040/.
14. Ibid.
15. Rosin, "The Case Against Breast-Feeding."
16. Andrew Jacobs, "Opposition to Breast-Feeding Resolution by U.S. Stuns World Health Officials," *New York Times,* July 8, 2018, https://www.nytimes .com/2,017/6/7/health/world-health-breastfeeding-ecuador-trump.html.
17. Alison Stuebe, "Every Time a Baby Goes to Breast, the $70 Billion Baby Food Industry Loses a Sale," *Breastfeeding Medicine,* May 9, 2018, https:// bfmed.wordpress.com/2018/7/8/every-time-a-baby-goes-to-breast-the -70-billion-baby-food-industry-loses-a-sale/.
18. Jill Krasny, "Every Parent Should Know the Scandalous History of Infant Formula," *Business Insider,* June 25, 2012, https://www.businessinsider .com/nestles-infant-formula-scandal-2012-6/.
19. Stephen Solomon, "The Controversy over Infant Formula," *New York Times,* December 6, 1981, https://www.nytimes.com/1982/1/6/magazine /the-controversy-over-infant-formula.html.
20. James Bock, "Women Made Career Strides in 1980s: Census Data Show Marked Md. Gains," *Baltimore Sun,* January 29, 1993, https://www.balti moresun.com/news/bs-xpm-1993-0-29-993029154-story.html.
21. Rick Du Brow, " 'Murphy Brown' to Dan Quayle: Read Our Ratings," *Los Angeles Times,* September 23, 1992, https://www.latimes.com/archives/la -xpm-1992-09-23-ca-1113-story.html.
22. Anne L. Wright and Richard J. Schanler, "The Resurgence of Breastfeeding at the End of the Second Millennium," *Journal of Nutrition,* vol. 131, issue 2, 421S–425S, https://academic.oup.com/jn/article/131/2/4215/4686960.
23. Purtill and Kopf, "The Class Dynamics of Breastfeeding in the United States of America."
24. Patrick A. Coleman, "What Is the Cost of Breastfeeding Versus Formula Feeding?" *Fatherly,* November 28, 2016, https://www.fatherly.com/love -money/real-cost-analysis-breastfeeding-versus-formula-feeding/.

25. Phyllis L. F. Rippeyoung and Mary C. Noonan, "Is Breastfeeding Truly Cost Free? Income Consequences of Breastfeeding for Women," *American Sociological Review,* February 1, 2012, vol. 77, issue 2, https://journals.sage pub.com/doi/abs/10.1177/0003122411435477.

26. Centers for Disease Control and Prevention, "Breastfeeding Report Card," 2018, https://www.cdc.gov/breastfeeding/data/reportcard.htm.

27. Jamie Grumet, "That Time I Breastfed My Son on the Cover of *Time,*" Mom .com, February 3, 2016, https://mom.com/entertainment/27667-how-being -cover-time-changed-everything/.

## Chapter 4: Knock Yourself Out

1. Michel Cohen, *The New Basics: A-to-Z Baby & Child Care for the Modern Parent* (New York: William Morrow Paperbacks, 2004).

2. Stephanie Pappas, "Early Neglect Alters Kids' Brains," *LiveScience,* July 23, 2012, https://www.livescience.com/21778-early-neglect-alters-kids-brains .html.

3. Allan Coukell, "Dr. Ferber Revisits His 'Crying Baby' Theory," NPR, May 30, 2006, https://www.npr.org/templates/story/story.php?storyId=5439359.

4. Will Doig, "Enter Sandman: Suzy Giordano Will Solve Your Baby's Sleep Problems—Just $1,000 a Night. Babble's Infant Industry," *Babble,* March 8, 2007. Article has been removed after Babble shut down.

5. Kate Pickert, "The Man Who Remade Motherhood," *Time,* May 21, 2012, http://time.com/606/the-man-who-remade-motherhood/.

6. Cynthia Eller, "Why I Hate Dr. Sears," *Brain, Child,* June 4, 2015, https:// www.brainchildmag.com/2015/06/why-i-hate-dr-sears/.

7. Amy Tuteur, *Push Back: Guilt in the Age of Natural Parenting* (New York: HarperCollins, 2016), 315.

8. Bonnie Rochman, "Mayim Bialik on Attachment Parenting: 'Very Small People Have a Voice,'" *Time,* March 15, 2012, http://healthland.time.com /2012/03/15/mayim-bialik-on-attachment-parenting-very-small-people -have-a-voice/.

9. Human Rights Watch, "Romania's Orphans: A Legacy of Repression," *News from Helsinki,* December 1, 1990, vol. 2, issue 15, https://www.hrw.org/re port/1990/12/01/romanias-orphans-legacy-repression.

10. Vlad Odobescu, "Half a Million Kids Survived Romania's 'Slaughterhouses of Souls.' Now They Want Justice," Public Radio International, December 28, 2015, https://www.pri.org/stories/2015-12-28/half-million-kids-survived -romanias-slaughterhouses-souls-now-they-want-justice.

11. Mary Battiata, "A Ceausescu Legacy: Warehouses for Children," *Washington Post,* June 7, 1990, https://www.washingtonpost.com/archive/politics /1990/06/07/a-ceausescu-legacy-warehouses-for-children/137a4951-04b4 -42d5-957b-ed321609023c/.

12. Human Rights Watch, "Romania's Orphans: A Legacy of Repression."

13. Odobescu, "Half a Million Kids Survived Romania's 'Slaughterhouses of Souls.'"

14. Molly Webster, "The Great Rat Mother Switcheroo," New York Public Radio, WYNC, January 10, 2013, https://www.wnycstudios.org/story/261176-the-great-mother-switcheroo; Darlene Francis, Josie Diorio, Dong Liu, and Michael J. Meaney, "Nongenomic Transmission Across Generations of Maternal Behavior and Stress Responses in the Rat," *Science,* November 5, 1999, vol. 286, issue 5442, 1155–1158, https://science.sciencemag.org/content/286/5442/1155.

15. Darcia F. Narvaez and Angela Braden, "Parents Misled by Cry-It-Out Sleep Training Reports," *Psychology Today,* July 20, 2014, https://www.psychologytoday.com/us/blog/moral-landscapes/201407/parents-misled-cry-it-out-sleep-training-reports.

16. David Rettew, "Infant Sleep and the Crying-It-Out Debate," *Psychology Today,* July 20, 2014, https://www.psychologytoday.com/us/blog/abcs-child-psychiatry/201407/infant-sleep-and-the-crying-it-out-debate.

## Chapter 5: You Don't Have to Be Mary Poppins

1. National Institute of Child Health and Human Development, "The NICHD Study of Early Child Care and Youth Development," U.S. Department of Health and Human Services, January 2006, https://www.nichd.nih.gov/sites/default/files/publications/pubs/documents/seccyd_06.pdf.

2. Arjen Stolk, Sabine Hunnius, Harold Bekkering, and Ivan Toni, "Early Social Experience Predicts Referential Communicative Adjustments in Five-Year-Old Children," *PLOS One,* 8(8):e72667, August 29, 2013, https://journals.plos.org/plosone/article?id=10.1371/journal.pone.0072667.

3. National Institute of Child Health and Human Development, "The NICHD Study of Early Child Care and Youth Development."

4. Melinda Wenner Moyer, "The Day Care Dilemma," *Slate,* August 22, 2013, https://slate.com/human-interest/2013/08/day-care-in-the-united-states-is-it-good-or-bad-for-kids.html.

5. National Institute of Child Health and Human Development, "The NICHD Study of Early Child Care and Youth Development."

6. BabyCenter Staff, "How Much You'll Spend on Childcare," BabyCenter.com, June 30, 2017, https://www.babycenter.com/0_how-much-youll-spend-on-childcare_1199776.bc.

7. Sarah Jane Glynn, "Fact Sheet: Child Care," Center for American Progress, August 16, 2012, https://www.americanprogress.org/issues/economy/news/2012/08/16/11978/fact-sheet-child-care/.

8. Care.com Editorial Staff, "This Is How Much Childcare Costs in 2019," Care.com, July 15, 2019, https://www.care.com/c/stories/2423/how-much-does-child-care-cost/.

9. "The 2019 Nanny Survey Results Are In!," *Park Slope Parents,* 2019, https://www.parkslopeparents.com/Newsflash/2019-nannysurvey-results.html.

10. Saskia Hullegie, Patricia Bruijning-Verhagen, Cuno S. P. M. Uiterwaal, Cornelis K. van der Ent, Henriette A. Smit, and Marieke L. A. de Hoog, "First-year Daycare and Incidence of Acute Gastroenteritis," *Pediatrics,* vol. 137,

issue 5, May 2016, https://pediatrics.aappublications.org/content/137/5/e20
153356.

11. Ibid.

12. Tara Siegel Bernard, "Choosing Child Care When You Go Back to Work," *New York Times,* November 22, 2013, https://www.nytimes.com/2013/11/23 /your-money/choosing-child-care-when-you-go-back-to-work.html.

13. D'Vera Cohn and Andrea Caumont, "7 Key Findings About Stay-at-Home Moms," Pew Research Center, April 8, 2014, https://www.pewresearch.org /fact-tank/2014/04/08/7-key-findings-about-stay-at-home-moms/.

14. Edmund L. Andrews, "Eric Bettinger: Why Stay-at-Home Parents are Good for Older Children," Stanford Graduate School of Business, October 20, 2014, https://www.gsb.stanford.edu/insights/eric-bettinger-why-stay-home -parents-are-good-older-children.

15. Paul Cleary, "Norway Is Proof That You Can Have It All," *The Australian,* July 15, 2013, https://www.theaustralian.com.au/life/norway-is-proof-that -you-can-have-it-all/news-story/3d2895adbace87431410e7b033ec84bf.

16. Gretchen Livingston, "Growing Number of Dads Home with the Kids," Pew Research Center, June 5, 2014, https://www.pewsocialtrends.org/2014/06/05 /growing-number-of-dads-home-with-the-kids/.

17. Paul Taylor, Eileen Patten, Ana Gonzalez-Barrera, Margaret Usdansky, Suzanne Bianchi, Gretchen Livingston, Rick Fry, and Cary Funk, "Modern Parenthood," Pew Research Center, March 14, 2013, https://www.pew socialtrends.org/2013/03/14/modern-parenthood-roles-of-moms-and-dads -converge-as-they-balance-work-and-family/.

18. Sonya Michel, *Children's Interests/Mothers' Rights: The Shaping of America's Child Care Policy* (New Haven, CT: Yale University Press, 1999), 17.

19. "The Maven's Word of the Day," Random House via Wikipedia, October 24, 1996, https://en.wikipedia.org/wiki/Latchkey_kid.

20. Nancy L. Cohen, "Why America Never Had Universal Child Care," *New Republic,* April 23, 2013, https://newrepublic.com/article/113009/child-care -america-was-very-close-universal-day-care.

21. Mark DeWolf, "12 Stats about Working Women," U.S. Department of Labor (blog), March 1, 2017, https://blog.dol.gov/2017/03/01/12-stats-about-work ing-women.

22. Lynda Laughlin, "Who's Minding the Kids? Child Care Arrangements: Spring 2011," U.S. Census Bureau, April 2013, https://www.census.gov /prod/2013pubs/p70-135.pdf.

23. Sonya Michel, "The History of Child Care in the U.S.," VCU Libraries Social Welfare History Project, 2011, https://socialwelfare.library.vcu.edu/pro grams/child-care-the-american-history/.

24. Ashley J. Thomas, P. Kyle Stanford, and Barbara W. Sarnecka, "Correction: No Child Left Alone: Moral Judgments about Parents Affect Estimates of Risk to Children," *Collabra,* October 14, 2016, https://www.collabra.org/ar ticles/10.1525/collabra.58/.

25. Elaine A. Donoghue, "Quality Early Education and Child Care from Birth to Kindergarten," *Pediatrics,* vol. 140, issue 2, August 2017, American Acad-

emy of Pediatrics, https://pediatrics.aappublications.org/content/140/2/e20
171488.

## Chapter 6: Time Out!

1. Clorinda E. Vélez, Sharlene A. Wolchik, Jenn-Yun Tein, and Irwin Sandler, "Protecting Children from the Consequences of Divorce: A Longitudinal Study of the Effects of Parenting on Children's Coping Processes," *Child Development*, vol. 82, issue 1, January–February 2011, 244–257, https://www.ncbi.nlm.nih.gov/pmc/articles/PMC3057658/.

2. Bridget Murray Law, "Biting Questions: When a Toddler Bites, How Do You Handle the Biter, the Victim—and Both Sets of Parents?" American Psychological Association (blog), vol. 42, no. 2, February 2011, 50, https://www.apa.org/monitor/2011/02/biting.

3. "My Toddler Bit a Classmate: Should I Freak Out?" Yahoo! Parenting, March 16, 2015, https://www.yahoo.com/news/my-toddler bit-a-classmate-should-i-freak-out 112813783337.html.

4. Isabel Fattal, "Why Toddlers Deserve More Respect," *The Atlantic*, December 13, 2017, https://www.theatlantic.com/education/archive/2017/12/the-myth-of-the-terrible-twos/548282/.

5. Ibid.

6. Becky Batcha, "Why Time-Out Is Out," *Parents*, https://www.parents.com/toddlers-preschoolers/discipline/time-out/why-time-out-is-out/.

7. Lyz Lenz, "In Defense of Yelling," *Fast Company*, October 29, 2014, https://www.fastcompany.com/3037569/in-defense-of-yelling.

8. Ibid.

9. Laura Markham, "What's So Bad About Bribing Your Child?" *Psychology Today*, July 19, 2017, https://www.psychologytoday.com/us/blog/peaceful-parents-happy-kids/201707/whats-so-bad-about-bribing-your-child.

10. Ibid.

11. Christina Caron, "Spanking Is Ineffective and Harmful to Children, Pediatricians' Group Says," *New York Times*, November 5, 2018, https://www.nytimes.com/2018/11/05/health/spanking-harmful-study-pediatricians.html.

12. Jennifer O'Neill, "What Moms Really Think About Spanking, Judging Each Other, and Their Relationships," Yahoo! Parenting, October 5, 2015, https://www.yahoo.com/news/what-moms-really-think-about-spanking-judging-090037683.html.

13. Harry Enten, "Americans' Opinions on Spanking Vary by Party, Race, Region and Religion," FiveThirtyEight.com, September 15, 2014, https://fivethirtyeight.com/features/americans-opinions-on-spanking-vary-by-party-race-region-and-religion/.

14. Yilu Zhao, "Cultural Divide Over Parental Discipline," *New York Times*, May 29, 2002, https://www.nytimes.com/2002/05/29/nyregion/cultural-divide-over-parental-discipline.html.

15. Stacey Patton, "Some Black Parents See Physical Discipline as a Duty. The NAACP Shouldn't Agree," *Washington Post*, June 22, 2012, https://www

.washingtonpost.com/opinions/some-black-parents-see-physical-discipline
-as-a-duty-the-naacp-shouldn't-agree/2012/06/22/g.JQ Ayo5ovV_story.html.

16. Kelly Wallace, "The Cultural, Regional and Generational Roots of Spanking,"
CNN, February 7, 2017, https://www.cnn.com/2014/09/16/living/spanking
-cultural-roots-attitudes-parents/index.html.

17. Enten, "Americans' Opinions on Spanking Vary by Party, Race, Region and
Religion."

18. Melinda D. Anderson, "Where Teachers Are Still Allowed to Spank Students," *The Atlantic,* December 15, 2015, https://www.theatlantic.com
/education/archive/2015/12/corporal-punishment/420420/.

19. Valerie Strauss, "19 States Still Allow Corporal Punishment in School,"
*Washington Post,* September 18, 2014, https://www.washingtonpost.com
/news/answer-sheet/wp/2014/09/18/19-states-still-allow-corporal-punish
ment-in-school/.

20. Sarah Gonzalez, "Some Florida Students Make the Paddles Used to Discipline Classmates," *StateImpact,* a reporting project of NPR, March 15, 2012,
https://stateimpact.npr.org/florida/2012/03/15/some-florida-student-make
-the-paddles-used-to-discipline-classmates/.

21. Suzanne K. Steinmetz and Murray A. Straus, eds., *Violence in the Family*
(New York: Harper & Row, 1974), essay by R. Calvert, "Criminal and Civil
Liability in Husband-Wife Assaults," via Wikipedia.

22. Human Rights Committee, General Comment 20, Article 7 (Forty-Fourth
session, 1992), Compilation of General Comments and General Recommendations Adopted by Human Rights Treaty Bodies, U.N. Doc. HRI/GEN/1
/Rev.1 at 30, 1994, http://hrlibrary.umn.edu/gencomm/hrcom20.htm.

23. "Somalia and US Should Ratify UN Child Rights Treaty—Official," *UN News,*
October 13, 2010, https://news.un.org/en/story/2010/10/355732-somalia-and
-us-should-ratify-un-child-rights-treaty-official.

24. Brendan L. Smith, "The Case Against Spanking," American Psychological
Association, *Monitor on Psychology,*vol. 43, no. 4, 60, April 2012, https://
www.apa.org/monitor/2012/04/spanking.

25. Ibid.

26. Ibid.


## Chapter 7: Embrace Technology

1. Kayt Sukel, "The Truth About Research on Screen Time," Dana Foundation, November 6, 2017, http://www.dana.org/Briefing_Papers/The_Truth
_About_Research_on_Screen_Time/.

2. Nick Bilton, "Steve Jobs Was a Low-Tech Parent," *New York Times,* September 10, 2014, https://www.nytimes.com/2014/09/11/fashion/steve-jobs
-apple-was-a-low-tech-parent.html.

3. Isabel Fattal, "Why Toddlers Deserve More Respect," *The Atlantic,* December 13, 2017, https://www.theatlantic.com/education/archive/2017/12/the
-myth-of-the-terrible-twos/548282/.

# NOTES

4. "American Academy of Pediatrics Announces New Recommendations for Children's Media Use," American Academy of Pediatrics, October 21, 2016, https://www.aap.org/en-us/about-the-aap/aap-press-room/pages/american-academy-of-pediatrics-announces-new-recommendations-for-childrens-media-use.aspx.
5. "Global Mobile Consumer Survey: US Edition," Deloitte, 2018, https://www.2.deloitte.com/us/en/pages/technology-media-and-telecommunications/articles/global-mobile-consumer-survey-us-edition.html.
6. Sukel, "The Truth About Research on Screen Time."
7. "Behind the Common Sense Media Ratings System," https://www.commonsensemedia.org/about-us/our-mission/about-our-ratings.
8. Judith Newman, "To Siri, With Love," *New York Times*, October 17, 2014, https://www.nytimes.com/2014/10/19/fashion/how-apples-siri-became-one-autistic-boys-bff.html.
9. Deborah Roberts and Marjorie McAfee, "'Life, Animated' Parents Describe How Animated Characters Helped Son with Autism Connect," *Good Morning America*, June 29, 2016, https://www.yahoo.com/gma/life-animated-parents-describe-animated-characters-helped-son-00260 0808-abc-news-wellness.html.
10. Beth J. Harpaz, "How Disney Films Unlocked Autistic Boy's Emotions," Associated Press, March 26, 2014, https://news.yahoo.com/disney-films-unlocked-autistic-boys-emotions-151032350.html.
11. Mitchell K. Bartholomew, Sarah J. Schoppe-Sullivan, Michael Glassman, Claire M. Kamp Dush, and Jason M. Sullivan, "New Parents' Facebook Use at the Transition to Parenthood," *Family Relations: Interdisciplinary Journal of Applied Family Science*, vol. 61, issue 3, June 1, 2012, 455–469, https://www.ncbi.nlm.nih.gov/pmc/articles/PMC3650729/.
12. Clare Madge and Henrietta O'Connor, "Parenting Gone Wired: Empowerment of New Mothers on the Internet?" *Social & Cultural Geography*, vol. 7, issue 2, August 18, 2006, 199–220, https://www.tandfonline.com/doi/abs/10.1080/14649360600600528.

## Chapter 8: Technically, French Fries Are a Vegetable

1. Alison Fildes, Carla Lopes, Pedro Moreira, George Moschonis, et al., "An Exploratory Trial of Parental Advice for Increasing Vegetable Acceptance in Infancy," *British Journal of Nutrition*, vol. 114, issue 2, 1–9, June 2015, https://www.cambridge.org/core/journals/british-journal-of-nutrition/article/an-exploratory-trial-of-parental-advice-for-increasing-vegetable-acceptance-in-infancy/346443558B01D18C1C6CFD5B566CC474.
2. Kellogg's Pop-Tarts Frosted Strawberry toaster pastries, Nutrition Facts, https://www.kelloggsspecialtychannels.com/Home/ProductPrint/6839/.
3. "Steak-hmm," Philly.com, April 24, 2012, https://web.archive.org/web/2015 1228081430/http://articles.philly.com/2012-04-24/news/31393146_1_steak-rib-eye-tenderloin.

287

4. Ellyn Satter, "Raise a Healthy Child Who Is a Joy to Feed: Follow the Division of Responsibility in Feeding," The Ellyn Satter Institute, 2018, https://www.ellynsatterinstitute.org/how-to-feed/the-division-of-responsibility-in-feeding/.

5. "Americans Spend $30 Billion a Year Out-of-Pocket on Complementary Health Approaches," National Center for Complementary and Integrative Health, June 22, 2016, https://nccih.nih.gov/research/results/spotlight/americans-spend-billions.

6. "Organic Regulations," United States Department of Agriculture, https://www.ams.usda.gov/rules-regulations/organic.

7. Maria Carter, "5 Foods You Should Never Buy Organic," *Woman's Day*, May 9, 2017, https://www.womansday.com/food-recipes/g2994/foods-you-should-never-buy-organic/.

8. "How Much Water Should My Child Drink," CHOC Children's Hospital, 2015, https://www.choc.org/programs-services/urology/how-much-water-should-my-child-drink/.

9. Taylor Wolfram, MS, RDN, LDN, "Water: How Much Do Kids Need?" Eat Right Academy of Nutrition and Dietetics, August 10, 2018, https://www.eatright.org/fitness/sports-and-performance/hydrate-right/water-go-with-the-flow.

10. Aaron E. Carroll, "No, You Do Not Have to Drink 8 Glasses of Water a Day," *New York Times*, August 24, 2015, https://www.nytimes.com/2015/08/25/upshot/no-you-do-not-have-to-drink-8-glasses-of-water-a-day.html.

11. Betty Ruth Carruth, Paula J. Ziegler, Anne R. Gordon, and Susan I. Barr, "Prevalence of Picky Eaters Among Infants and Toddlers and Their Caregivers' Decisions About Offering a New Food," *Journal of the American Dietetic Association*, February 2004, vol. 104, suppl. 1, 57–64, https://jandonline.org/article/S0002-8223(03)01492-5/fulltext.

12. Roni Caryn Rabin, "Feed Your Kids Peanuts, Early and Often, New Guidelines Urge," *New York Times*, January 5, 2017, https://www.nytimes.com/2017/01/05/well/eat/feed-your-kids-peanuts-early-and-often-new-guidelines-urge.html.

13. Alkis Togias, Susan F. Cooper, Maria L. Acebal, et al., "Addendum Guidelines for the Prevention of Peanut Allergy in the United States: Report of the National Institute of Allergy and Infectious Diseases–Sponsored Expert Panel," *Annals of Allergy, Asthma and Immunology*, February 2017, vol. 118, issue 2, 166–173.e7, https://www.annallergy.org/article/S1081-1206(16)31164-4/fulltext.

14. Jessika Bohon, "I Grew Up on Food Stamps. I'll Never Forget the Sneering Looks," *The Guardian*, July 12, 2017, https://www.theguardian.com/commentisfree/2017/jul/12/food-stamps-poverty-america-shame.

15. "Characteristics of Supplemental Nutrition Assistance Program Households: Fiscal Year 2015 (Summary)," United States Department of Agriculture, November 2016, https://fns-prod.azureedge.net/sites/default/files/ops/Characteristics2015-Summary.pdf.

16. Josh Levin, "The Queen: Linda Taylor Committed Abhorrent Crimes. She

Became a Legend for the Least of Them," *Slate,* May 13, 2019, https://slate
.com/news-and-politics/2019/05/the-queen-linda-taylor-welfare-reagan-pod
cast.html.

17. Anahad O'Connor, "In the Shopping Cart of a Food Stamp Household:
Lots of Soda," *New York Times,* January 13, 2017, https://www.nytimes
.com/2017/01/13/well/eat/food-stamp-snap-soda.html.

18. Anne Fishel, "The Most Important Thing You Can Do with Your Kids? Eat
Dinner with Them," *Washington Post,* January 12, 2015, https://www.wash
ingtonpost.com/posteverything/wp/2015/01/12/the-most-important-thing
-you-can-do-with-your-kids-eat-dinner-with-them.

### Chapter 9: Busting the Myth of "Having It All"

1. Eric Barker, "How to Raise Happy Kids: 10 Steps Backed by Science," *Time,*
March 24, 2014, http://time.com/35496/how-to-raise-happy-kids-10-steps
-backed-by-science/.

2. Anne-Marie Slaughter, "Why Women Still Can't Have It All," *The Atlantic,*
July/August 2012, https://www.theatlantic.com/magazine/archive/2012/07
/why-women-still-cant-have-it-all/309020/.

3. Shane Shifflett, Emily Peck, and Alissa Scheller, "The States with the Most
Stay-at-Home Fathers," *Huffington Post,* May 13, 2015, https://www.huff
post.com/entry/stay-at-home-fathers_n_7261020.

4. Emily Peck, "Only 6 American Men Identified as Stay-at-Home Dads in the
1970s. Today, It's a Different Story," *Huffington Post,* May 8, 2015, https://
www.huffpost.com/entry/stay-at-home-dads_n_7234214.

5. Domingo Angeles, "Share of Women in Occupations with Many Projected
Openings, 2016–26," Bureau of Labor Statistics, March 2018, https://www
.bls.gov/careeroutlook/2018/data-on-display/dod-women-in-labor-force.htm.

6. Neil Irwin, "How Some Men Fake an 80-Hour Workweek, and Why It Matters," *New York Times,* May 4, 2015, https://www.nytimes.com/2015/05/05
/upshot/how-some-men-fake-an-80-hour-workweek-and-why-it-matters
.html.

7. Claire Cain Miller, "Mounting Evidence of Advantages for Children of
Working Mothers," *New York Times,* May 15, 2015, https://www.nytimes
.com/2015/05/17/upshot/mounting-evidence-of-some-advantages-for-chil
dren-of-working-mothers.html.

8. Jennifer Szalai, "The Complicated Origins of 'Having It All,'" *New York
Times,* January 3, 2015, https://www.nytimes.com/2015/01/04/magazine
/the-complicated-origins-of-having-it-all.html.

9. Leslie Loftis, "Irony, Thy Name Is Feminism," *The Federalist,* July 28, 2014,
https://thefederalist.com/2014/07/28/irony-thy-name-is-feminism/.

10. Szalai, "The Complicated Origins of 'Having It All.'"

11. Tiffany Dufu, "Tiffany's Epiphanies: Five Questions to Help You Drop
the Ball," *YouTube,* August 27, 2018, https://www.youtube.com/watch?
v=goheRvGY9G0.

12. Donna St. George, " 'Free Range' Parents Cleared in Second Neglect Case

After Kids Walked Alone," *Washington Post,* June 22, 2015, https://www
.washingtonpost.com/local/education/free-range-parents-cleared-in-second
-neglect-case-after-children-walked-alone/2015/06/22/82283c24-188c-11e5
-bd7f-4611a60dd8e5_story.html.

13. Steven Pinker, *The Better Angels of Our Nature: Why Violence Has Declined* (New York: Penguin Books, 2012).

14. Elizabeth Nolan Brown, "Enough Stranger Danger! Children Rarely Abducted by Those They Don't Know," *Reason*, March 31, 2017, https://reason
.com/2017/03/31/kidnapping-stats.

15. "And the Quality Most Parents Want to Teach Their Children Is . . ." *Time*,
September 18, 2014, http://time.com/3393652/pew-research-parenting-
american-trends/.

16. Leah Shafer, "Summertime, Playtime," Harvard Graduate School of Education, June 12, 2018, https://www.gse.harvard.edu/news/uk/18/06/summer
time-playtime.

17. Ibid.

18. Randi Zuckerberg, *Pick Three: You Can Have It All (Just Not Every Day)*
(New York: HarperCollins, 2018).

19. Julianne Holt-Lunstad, Timothy B. Smith, Mark Baker, Tyler Harris, David
Stephenson, "Loneliness and Social Isolation as Risk Factors for Mortality: A Meta-Analytic Review," *Perspectives on Psychological Science,*
vol. 10, issue 2, March 1, 2015, 227–237, https://journals.sagepub.com/doi
/pdf/10.1177/1745691614568352.

20. Ibid.

21. Emily Sohn, "More and More Research Shows Friends Are Good for Your
health," *Washington Post,* May 26, 2016, https://www.washingtonpost.com
/national/health-science/more-and-more-research-shows-friends-are-good
-for-your-health/2016/05/26/f249e754-204d-11e6-9e7f-57890b612299
_story.html.

22. Miller McPherson, Lynn Smith-Lovin, and Matthew Brashears, "Social Isolation in America: Changes in Core Discussion Networks over Two Decades,"
*American Sociological Review,* June 1, 2006, https://archive.org/stream
/SocialIsolationInAmericaChangesInCoreDiscussionNetworksOverTwo/So
cialIsolationInAmerica_djvu.txt.

23. Lisa Wade, "American Men's Hidden Crisis: They Need More Friends!"
*Salon,* December 8, 2013, https://www.salon.com/2013/12/08/american
_mens_hidden_crisis_they_need_more_friends/.

24. "Parents Now Spend Twice as Much Time with Their Children as 50 Years
Ago," *The Economist,* November 27, 2017, https://www.economist.com
/graphic-detail/2017/11/27/parents-now-spend-twice-as-much-time-with
-their-children-as-50-years-ago.

25. Brigid Schulte, "Making Time for Kids? Study Says Quality Trumps Quantity," *Washington Post,* March 28, 2015, https://www.washingtonpost.com
/local/making-time-for-kids-study-says-quality-trumps-quantity/2015/03/28
/10813192-d378-11e4-8fce-3941fc548f1c_story.html.

# NOTES

## Chapter 10: Get It On

. Amy Muise, Ulrich Schimmack, and Emily A. Impett, "Sexual Frequency Predicts Greater Well-Being, But More Is Not Always Better," *Social Psychological and Personality Science*, vol. 7, issue 4, November 18, 2015, 295–302, https://journals.sagepub.com/doi/full/10.1177/1948550615616462.
2. Eric W. Corty and Jenay M. Guardiani, "Canadian and American Sex Therapists' Perceptions of Normal and Abnormal Ejaculatory Latencies: How Long Should Intercourse Last?" *Journal of Sexual Medicine*, May 2008, vol. 5, issue 5, 1251–1256, https://www.jsm.jsexmed.org/article/S1743-6095(15)32017-8/abstract.
3. "Infant and Young Child Feeding: Model Chapter for Textbooks for Medical Students and Allied Health Professionals," World Health Organization, 2009, https://www.ncbi.nlm.nih.gov/books/NBK148970/.
4. Stephanie Pappas, "Low Sexual Desire Plagues Men, Too," *LiveScience*, November 7, 2013, https://www.livescience.com/41031-low-sexual-desire-men.html.
5. Maurand Cappelletti and Kim Wallen, "Increasing Women's Sexual Desire: The Comparative Effectiveness of Estrogens and Androgens," *Hormones and Behavior*, vol. 78, 178–193, February 2016, https://www.ncbi.nlm.nih.gov/pmc/articles/PMC4720522/.
6. Wednesday Martin, *Untrue: Why Nearly Everything We Believe About Women, Lust, and Infidelity Is Wrong and How the New Science Can Set Us Free* (New York: Little, Brown Spark, 2018), chapter 3.
7. "Inside the Secret Sex Lives of Millennial Moms," Peanut-app, August 2018, https://www.peanut-app.io/millennialmomsurvey.
8. HuffPost Live, "Sexless Marriages: Why Many Couples Go Years Without Sex After Having Children," *Huffington Post*, March 4, 2014, https://www.huffpost.com/entry/sexless-marriages_n_4896110.
9. Holly V. Kapherr, "Rekindling Your Sex Life After Baby," *Parenting*, https://www.parenting.com/article/sex-after-baby.
10. Ibid.
11. *Us Weekly* Staff, "Giuliana Rancic: 'We Put Our Marriage First and Our Child Second,'" *Us Weekly*, February 27, 2013, https://www.usmagazine.com/celebrity-moms/news/giuliana-rancic-we-put-our-marriage-first-and-our-child-second-2013272/.

## Chapter 11: There's No Such Thing as Normal

1. Brigid Schulte, "Unlike in the 1950s, There Is No 'Typical' U.S. Family Today," *Washington Post*, September 4, 2014, https://www.washingtonpost.com/news/local/wp/2014/09/04/for-the-first-time-since-the-1950s-there-is-no-typical-u-s-family/.
2. Philip Cohen, "Family Diversity Is the New Normal for America's Children," briefing paper prepared for the Council on Contemporary Families, Uni-

NOTES

versity of Maryland, September 4, 2014, https://familyinequality.files.word
press.com/2014/09/family-diversity-new-normal.pdf.

3. Gretchen Livingston, "The Changing Profile of Unmarried Parents," Pew
Research Center, April 25, 2018, https://www.pewsocialtrends.org/20108
/04/25/the-changing-profile-of-unmarried-parents/.

4. "Historical Marital Status Tables," United States Census Bureau, November
2018, https://www.census.gov/data/tables/time-series/demo/families/marital
.html.

5. Gretchen Livingston, "Births Outside of Marriage Decline for Immigrant
Women," Pew Research Center, October 26, 2016, https://www.pewsocial
trends.org/2016/10/26/births-outside-of-marriage-decline-for-immigrant
-women/.

6. Livingston, "The Changing Profile of Unmarried Parents."

7. "Attitudes on Same-Sex Marriage," Pew Research Center, May 14, 2019,
https://www.pewforum.org/fact-sheet/changing-attitudes-on-gay-marriage/.

8. Carrie Craft, "How Many Children Have Gay Parents in the US?" Child Welfare League of America via Live About, May 8, 2019, https://www.liveabout
.com/how-many-gay-parents-in-us-27175.

9. Isabel Fattal, "Why Toddlers Deserve More Respect," *The Atlantic,* December 13, 2017, https://www.theatlantic.com/education/archive/2017/12/the
-myth-of-the-terrible-twos/548282/.

10. Nanette Gartrell, Henny Bos, and Audrey Koh, "National Longitudinal Lesbian Family Study—Mental Health of Adult Offspring," *New England Journal of Medicine,* vol. 379, July 19, 2018, 297–299, https://www.nejm.org
/doi/full/10.1056/NEJMc1804810.

11. Wolters Kluwer Health, "Psychological Adjustment: No Difference in Outcomes for Children of Same-Sex versus Different-Sex Parents," *Science-
Daily,* June 28, 2018, https://www.sciencedaily.com/releases/2018/06/180
628120036.htm.

12. Beth Greenfield, "$70K and 8,000 Miles to Become a Father," Yahoo! Parent-
ing, October 22, 2014, https://www.yahoo.com/news/8-000-miles-and-70k
-to-become-a-father-99064287817.html.

13. Johnny Wood, "The United States Divorce Rate Is Dropping, Thanks to Millennials," World Economic Forum, October 5, 2018, https://www.weforum
.org/agenda/2018/10/divorce-united-states-dropping-because-millennials/.

14. Fattal, "Why Toddlers Deserve More Respect."

15. Nile Cappello, "Why I'm Happy My Parents Are Divorced," *Huffington
Post,* August 18, 2013, https://www.huffpost.com/entry/why-im-happy-my
-parents_n_3764552.

16. "Marriage & Divorce," American Psychological Association, 2019, https://
www.apa.org/topics/divorce/.

17. Lisa Herrick, Robin S. Haight, Ron Palomares, and Lynn Bufka, "Healthy
Divorce: How to Make Your Split as Smooth as Possible," American Psychological Association, 2019, https://www.apa.org/helpcenter/healthy-divorce.

18. Dave Quinn, "Josh Lucas and His Ex-Wife Are 'Bird-Nest' Co-Parenting

292

Their Son After Divorce: 'He Loves It,'" *People,* March 2, 2018, https://www.yahoo.com/entertainment/josh-lucas-ex-wife-apos-154049827.html.

19. Deborah Carr, Vicki A. Freedman, Jennifer C. Cornman, and Norbert Schwarz, "Happy Marriage, Happy Life? Marital Quality and Subjective Well-Being in Later Life," *Journal of Marriage and Family,* vol. 76, issue 5, October 1, 2014, 930–948, https://www.ncbi.nlm.nih.gov/pmc/articles/PMC4158846/; Kathleen Elkins, "Here's How Much More Money Married Men in America Are Making Than Everyone Else," CNBC, September 24, 2018, https://www.cnbc.com/2018/09/21/married-men-are-earning-much-more-money-than-everyone-else-in-america.html.

20. Laura Vanderkam, "Revisiting 'The Second Shift' 27 Years Later," *Fast Company,* January 14, 2016, https://www.fastcompany.com/3055391/revisiting-the-second-shift-27-years-later.

21. "A Portrait of Stepfamilies," Pew Research Center, January 13, 2011, https://www.pewsocialtrends.org/2011/01/13/a-portrait-of-stepfamilies/.

22. "Trends in U.S. Adoptions: 2008–2012," Child Welfare Information Gateway, U.S. Department of Health and Human Services, January 2016, https://www.childwelfare.gov/pubPDFs/adopted0812.pdf.

23. *Edie's Clothes: Raising a Beautiful, Compassionate, Powerful Girl,* 2019, https://ediesclothes.com/.

24. Fattal, "Why Toddlers Deserve More Respect."

# INDEX

# INDEX

Berman, Laura, 243
Berman Women's Wellness Center, 243
Bertsche, Rachel, 223–27
*Better Angels of Our Nature, The: Why Violence Has Declined* (Pinker), 213
*Beyond the Sling: A Real-Life Guide to Raising Confident, Loving Children the Attachment Parenting Way* (Bialik), 90
Bialik, Mayim, 90
biological clock, 23
birdnesting, 6, 255–56
birth, *see* childbirth
birth weight, 14–15, 19, 21
biting, 125–26
blame, *see* shame, blame, and criticism
blood pressure, 22, 41, 55
*Bloomberg View*, 65
*Born in the Wild*, 54
Boston University, 205
bottle feeding, *see* formula feeding
boundaries and limits, 122, 129, 133
Bowman, Alisa, 243
*Brain, Child*, 88
*Breakup Bible, The* (Sussman), 255
breastfeeding, 1–2, 5, 6, 41, 56, 59–78
  asthma and allergy risk and, 47, 61, 62
  benefits of, 62–64, 73–75
  combining formula feeding with, 68–69
  C-section and, 45, 47
  extended, 77
  historical attitudes toward, 69–70
  hormones and, 234
  household power shift and, 66–67
  La Leche League and, 3–4, 71–72, 87
  studies on, 62–64
  and working outside the home, 61, 64, 73, 74
  *see also* formula feeding

breast milk, 6, 45, 59, 61
  pumping, 66–68
  bribing, 137–38
Brigham Young University, 219–20
Brown, Helen Gurley, 207, 208
Bucknam, Robert, 81
Bündchen, Gisele, 61
*Business of Being Born, The*, 49

## C

caffeine, 12, 16–17
Cahill, Mary Ann, 71
carbohydrates, 180
Care.com, 106
career, *see* job and career
Carroll, Aaron E., 186
Carter, Christine, 199
catechin, 16
Caughey, Aaron, 5
CDC (Centers for Disease Control and Prevention), 37, 39, 54, 63, 184, 248
Ceauçescu, Nicolae, 92
cell phones, 145–47, 153–58
cheese, 17–18
Chen, David, 139
child abduction, 213
childbirth, 31–57
  birth weight, 14–15, 19, 21
  business of, 37–40
  by C-section, *see* C-section
  due date, 19–20
  epidurals in, 33–36, 39–43, 57
  free birthing, 54
  at home, 32–34, 37–39, 48–55
  infant mortality rates and, 37, 52
  instruments in, 41
  maternal mortality rates and, 37, 39–40, 43, 52
  "natural," 40
  plans for, 31–34
  premature, 14, 19, 21
  sex after, 231, 232, 234, 239–40
  stillbirth, 12, 27, 54

# ABOUT THE AUTHOR

Lindsay Powers has worked as a journalist at media and technology companies for more than fifteen years. As the editor in chief of Yahoo! Parenting, she founded the #NoShameParenting movement, which has reached more than 170 million people across social media and trended on Twitter. Her work has also appeared in the *Washington Post*, the *New York Post*, *Cosmopolitan*, *Us Weekly*, the *Hollywood Reporter*, AP, Reuters, CNN, and many other nationwide outlets. She regularly travels for speaking engagements at universities and corporations. Powers lives in Brooklyn with her husband and two sons.